The Abingdon Guide to Funding Ministry

An Innovative Sourcebook for Church Leaders
An Almanac for Good Stewards

Volume 2

EDITORS

Donald W. Joiner
Norma Wimberly

ABINGDON PRESS
NASHVILLE

THE ABINGDON GUIDE TO FUNDING MINISTRY:
AN INNOVATIVE SOURCEBOOK FOR CHURCH LEADERS
VOLUME 2

Copyright © 1996 by Abingdon Press

ISBN 0-687-01989-3
ISSN 1081-4957

For permission to reproduce the following items, please contact the copyright owners indicated:

Church of God
1303 E. 5th St.
Anderson IN 46012
 "The Grace of Giving"
 "A Tithing Testimony"
 "Guiding Young Stewards"

Presbyterian Church (USA)
100 Witherspoon St.
Louisville KY 40202-1396
 "Worship Resources"
 "Signposts of a Financially Healthy Congregation"
 "15 Stewardship Activities for Children and Youth"
 "Worship Time with Children"

Ministry of Money
2 Professional Dr., Ste. 220
Gaithersburg MS 20879
 "Write Your Will and Live to Enjoy It"

United Church of Christ
Stewardship Council
700 Prospect Ave.
Cleveland OH 44115
 "Calls to Worship/Prayers"
 "Good Communication"
 "Building a Budget"
 "The Financial Potential"
 "Suggestions for Preparing a Narrative Budget"

Ecumenical Center for Stewardship Studies
1100 W. 42nd St., Ste. 225
Indianapolis IN 46208
 "13 Stewardship Ideas for Children and Youth"
 "Children and Offerings"

The cartoons on pages 55 and 137 are by Joseph A. Brown, 1220 Nassau St., Kalamazoo, Michigan.

This book is printed on recycled, acid-free paper.

96 97 98 99 00 01 02 03 04 05—10 9 8 7 6 5 4 3 2 1

Book Review

 Budget Tool

 Bulletin

 Calendar

 Checklist

 Commitment Campaign

 Devotional

 Drama

 Handout

 Meditation

 Money Talk

 Newsletter

 Planned Giving

 Planning Tool

 Sermon Help

 Small Group Study

 Tax Clinic

 Teaching Help

 Legal Clinic

CONTENTS

INTRODUCTION

You have opened this second volume of *The Abingdon Guide to Funding Ministry* because you are looking for ways to increase the revenue in your congregation. You want to pay for the ministries that God has called into your midst. This volume will offer you hundreds of ideas for securing the future of your ministries. Many of these ideas will require you to teach and learn about generosity.

This issue of *The Abingdon Guide to Funding Ministry* has as its focus, "Teaching the Joy of Generosity." Such simple, almost ordinary words—words we hear and use on a regular basis in the church. However, we invite you to reflect on some of the definitions of those words and view them with new eyes, listen to the possible meaning of the theme with new ears, and enter the teaching and learning dynamic with a new and open heart. Funding ministry is exciting territory in which to be a teacher and challenging in which to be a learner.

To *educate* is to impart knowledge and skill. *Teaching* is a process, an act, an art, and also a principle to be practiced. To participate in the teaching experience, in whatever capacity, one needs to be teachable, capable of being educated—willing.

Joy is a condition of supreme well-being, a feeling of extreme gratification, happiness, delight, great pleasure—-usually marked by celebration.

Generosity is the state of being generous. It is characterized by abundance, a willingness to give of oneself and one's possessions. One who is in a state of generosity is usually thought of as happy, greathearted, unselfish, open-handed, magnanimous.

As the church, we are called to transmit the faith. We, as stewards, are called to teach the possibility of a state of being—-the joy of generosity! Should one generation of the Christian community forget what the prior generation knew, or fail to pass on its heritage, Christian communities will disappear from the earth, and the gospel as we know it will die because we were selfish with its benefits.

Recently, I observed an energetic music leader with a group of grade-school children during an after-school program in a small church. Everyone was restless, chattering about a variety of things, looking around, familiar with, yet uncomfortable with the noise. The music leader called out, "Class! Focus!" As he said the word *focus,* he held his arms straight out in front, forefingers extended, and brought those fingers together, side by side. The class focused. They were brought to attentiveness. The words were learned, the song was sung. (The leader, of course, was called upon to repeat, "Class! Focus!" several times.)

Perhaps the church is called upon to "Focus!" in teaching the joy of generosity. Perhaps we have been restless too long, chattering about a variety of interesting topics, looking around at others, accustomed to, but uncomfortable with, where we find ourselves.

Pastors, denominational leaders, lay people, youth, and children have the opportunity and the authority to focus, and to help others focus, on giving. In the past, it appears that the task of defining the terms, carrying the message, naming the ministry, and proscribing the shape of mission has been lodged with those we presumed to have authority.

In some instances, that authority has made assumptions about terms, message, ministry, and mission that are lost on current generations. We don't know the words to the song, nor how to sing it! False assumptions passed on as tradition radically change the nature of a community or group.

Have we forgotten the joy to be found in giving? Were we ever taught that joy was possible? Were we ever witness to that joy in others? For many of us, these questions are like the dissonance of a choir unfocused, unrehearsed, with no leader. For others, the questions ring with pain—we missed the rehearsal! We have

> "The heart that gives gathers."

been robbed of an important part of our faith tradition, a vital hymn indeed.

When approaching financial giving from another perspective, if we have been taught "principles," what notes have we been taught? Perhaps we learned that churches spend too much time worrying about their own organizations and money. Perhaps we have learned that stewardship is synonymous with begging. Perhaps we learned that mission means "taking care of our own." Perhaps we have learned distrust of any institution! Perhaps we have learned that authority and leadership in churches is equated with being exempt from accountability. Perhaps we have learned to distrust joy, to distrust the state of being generous, to look askance at willingness to give of oneself and one's possessions.

Sometimes we look in unlikely places for tools for teaching, descriptions of joy, and analogies for generosity. Terry, the music leader, was focused, and he offers us an analogy for shifting our attention to what is important right now. Jim, a layperson in another church, teaches the joy of generosity with his very inability to give voice to what he knows and what he feels. Jim wasn't taught the joy of generosity, but he is coming to know that his need to give is greater than the church's need to receive.

Jim's friend tells the story this way: Jim was excited about attending Sunday morning worship after so many years away from the church. As we sat in my living room drinking coffee, he shared the tale of attending church as a youth, but never feeling that he belonged. He served as the church janitor when he was a teenager:

"I used to walk into the sanctuary on Saturday mornings to clean it. I hated going in there. I felt like God could see me cleaning, but I couldn't see God. I just didn't belong there."

In middle age, Jim's spiritual journey has brought him to the church where I am a member. A frequent visitor there, he told me how surprised he was to feel at home:

"You know, I've really thought about talking to the pastor about joining. But, to be honest, since my work takes me out of town so much, I don't feel I could be a part of the church committees, and so forth. I just don't see how I'd have the time."

He leaned back in the chair with a troubled look:

> "When it comes to giving, some stop at nothing."

"I don't want to be a member unless I'm able to give something to God in return. Some Sundays I sit in the pew enjoying the service, then start feeling guilty."

Suddenly, his face brightened, and he leaned forward intently, cupping his hands as if he were holding a newfound and precious gift: "You know what it's like? It's like drinking a tall, delicious milk shake I haven't paid for."

Jim is teachable. He already knows the feeling of joy, and he has a deep need to be generous. Jim is a learner, and he is a teacher. He gives me hope that I can learn to focus on learning the joy of generosity and become more willing to teach. Jim offers the truth that, at all times, each of us is both a learner and a teacher, that every experience of our lives is an opportunity to do and be both.

Terry and Jim are symbols for me, symbols of the way we learn, the way we teach. Their stories also provide examples of who we are and who we can be. We learn by focusing. We learn by experience. We teach by inviting focus and sharing experiences. Many of us are restless, chattering, distracted. We can settle down and concentrate on what is necessary to impart the faith. Some of us feel as if we don't belong here in the realm of funding ministry. But now we can reach out for that tall, delicious drink of the Spirit and know that we have something to offer in return.

Teaching the joy of generosity is simple. It can be fun. It can happen in a variety of ways, in a variety of settings. We want to learn and teach with you.

A Vision

Our vision of funding ministry is like a painting that appears blurry from a distance, but assumes clarity as we approach it step by step. Our vision is that pastors and church leaders will begin, or continue to develop, a perspective on giving, that they will teach giving consistently and effectively, and will proclaim the joy of giving.

To achieve that vision, to step ever closer to the picture, we present this "almanac for good stewards," with stories of giving and suggestions, sermons, tips, tools, worksheets, and much more for developing generous disciples. The aim in this volume of *The Abingdon Guide for Funding Ministry* is to provide a resource to encourage pastors and leaders to examine and continue to develop their skills for teaching giving.

This publication on finance is informational and motivational. We want it to help leaders look not only at themselves, but beyond current programs, for tangible results.

We assume a diverse readership, and we know that reliable and faithful Christians disagree about money as often as they do about doctrine. Some of you have significant experience in financial stewardship and are hungry for new ideas. Others have little or no history of exploration in this discipline, and we hope to delight you with usable tools and practical suggestions. As we assemble the parts of this "almanac," we imagine a diversity of age, denomination, theology, geography, church size, and "comfort zone" with the topic.

We believe that growth in giving is an ongoing, life-long process. The *Guide* is compiled to suggest, as well as to direct each of us to the next steps of the journey. The next step may be clear for some of you. For others, it may include a question, a doubt, more searching. In some instances, the next step may offer a choice. What is God leading you to do?

How This Guide Will Help You

1. It will reveal ways to motivate people to give more generously.
2. It will offer tips for eliminating waste.
3. It will broaden your perspective on fund development possibilities.
4. It will provide the latest information on legal challenges.
5. It will suggest ways to attain better accountability. And much more . . .

In Volume 3, we will concentrate on "proclaiming the joy of giving." (Volume 1 focused on developing a perspective on giving).

A COVENANT WITH THE READERS

We hope to help people look at the critical issues of their relationship with God, their relationship with money, and find faithful ways to practice generosity and healthy church finance. We believe that developing Christian givers is a process, rather than a quick-fix program, that it takes daily practice and is a journey, rather than a destination.

Donald W. Joiner is a director of local church funding for the General Board of Discipleship of The United Methodist Church. He also directs the Planned Giving Resource Center for that agency. He is an ordained clergyman from the Detroit Conference of The United Methodist Church.

Norma Wimberly is Executive Director of the Nashville Area United Methodist Foundation (Memphis and Tennessee Conferences). She was formerly a director of Stewardship Education and Resource Development for the General Board of Discipleship of The United Methodist Church.

The Abingdon Guide to Funding Ministry is committed to:

1. Open dialogue with you. Each of us is a learner and a teacher. We will listen. We will impart. We desire to be co-searchers.

    What are some of your questions, concerns, insights?

    What topics would you like to have addressed?

    What experience, strength, and hope can we share?

2. Providing a leading edge of direction and information on church finance in North America.
3. Being inclusive—theologically and denominationally.
4. Being accessible. We want to hear from you.

Norma Wimberly
Donald W. Joiner
Abingdon Guide to Funding Ministry
c/o Abingdon Press
P.O. Box 801
201 Eighth Avenue South
Nashville TN 37202-0801

PART ONE

HELPING CHURCH LEADERS TEACH THE JOY OF GIVING

Introduction

NORMA WIMBERLY

Teaching is a ministry, a gift, a special calling. For Christians, Jesus is the master teacher. He taught more than he preached. He took his teaching to the people. He spoke to their situations, reaching them at the pressure points of their lives—money, sex, and power.

In the first article of this section, Dr. Hilbert Berger urges us to look at the economic facts that influence giving, just as Jesus faced the economy of his time. We are then faced with answering the questions "Why?" "When?" and "What?" Glenna and Roy Kruger continue the teaching traditions of Jesus and Paul by using contemporary business trends to offer organizational tools to assure that the church is a teaching and learning organization.

Jim Cook reminds us that Bible study is crucial as we explore teaching giving. He combines scripture, historical traditions, theological experience, and contemporary reasoning to align stewardship with teaching and faithful discipleship.

Father Ed Hays turns teaching and giving on their heads in "Beggars." He contends that to pray well and to give well, we must be beggars with a passion!

Robin Wood and Noah Reid complete this section by offering suggestions for telling stories and for more traditional learning situations.

Jesus' teaching made a difference in people's lives. Attitudes and behavior changed. We may not be able to really teach anybody anything, but like Jesus, we can create a spiritual climate, an opportune time to live the joy of giving.

 MONEY TALK

Teaching Christians to Give

HILBERT J. BERGER

Our people do not know what they have not been taught. A most neglected area in our Christian teaching is in the area of giving. This may be due to the fact that, as leaders, we were not taught. We have been admonished—that is, it has been suggested that we tithe or give sacrificially, or give some percent, or at least give more, and there have been times that we have been coerced (we have you down for ?$), but we have not been taught to give or how to decide the amount to give.

It is my experience that most people who give through the church do not feel good about what they give. This conclusion is the same for both the $10 and the $100 per-week giver. This is true because their giving is not based on any rational perspectives, but on what the budget is, or on an immediate need, or on their feelings of guilt at the moment. The church has not taught us how to decide how much or how to give, or, in emotional terms, how to feel good about our giving. To put it in "church jargon," Christians must be taught how to be blessed through their giving.

The Facts

First, we live in a different economic world from the one many of us grew up in. Self-sufficiency and affluence surround us. Eastablished American Protestants are seldom listed among the very poor. We have much to give, but generous giving always requires careful planning. The number of dollars our parents earned do not equal the number of dollars that we should give today!

Change in the money world has been just as dramatic as change in all other areas of our lives. I can remember the "barter world" of an agrarian culture. When I took a basket of eggs to the grocer for my grandmother, I received in return the items on her grocery list. No real money changed hands. We are now on the threshold of "guaranteed annual incomes." This has been a fact for those receiving payments from Social Security or pensions since World War II. Yet our congregations have changed their economic lifestyle very little in the last hundred years. Our funding procedures have changed very little.

There is little doubt about what will happen to our economic base if we fail to grapple with these new economic lifestyles. For instance, we are living in a cashless society; the only people who carry money are those who are denied credit. The affluent members of our churches carry debit and credit cards. In a matter of five years, most of us will manage our money with PCs and PDAs. But in the congregation, we still depend largely on cash gifts and the offering plate, to remind us of the barter economy that defined an agrarian era.

It is a new-money world, and I am concerned that churches and well-educated pastors are the last to know or care about it. Four new economic facts have altered the economic horizons of the church in America:

1. Vastly increased personal income and net worth.
2. Near limitless credit.
3. Baby boomer extravagance.
4. The world's first prosperous retired generation.

Our economic growth in personal income and net worth is so startling, and its effect so profound, that it amounts to nothing short of a revolution. Most of the people who relate to our churches now can afford some of the luxuries in America. Ordinary people with regular employment now have money for things they do not need. That fact is revolutionary in the church, and we have not been trained to deal with it.

Millions of church members now have the privilege of making decisions about much of their spending. Former generations did not have that privilege. Two-thirds of the people in our world do not have it today. Even though many in this country do not have this luxury, most church members do!

The revolution is that most of the people who attend our churches are rich. A person is rich when there is money working for him. A person is rich when she has things to throw away. People are rich when they have adequate housing, transportation, more than one pair of shoes, a change of clothing, employment, or a pension. I am rich, you are rich. We do not come to this conclusion by comparing ourselves to the hungry of this world, but by looking at our discretionary wealth.

The second economic fact that we all know about is the limitless credit offered to the vast majority of our people. The church has real trouble with this, because though we live by credit, we want the church to operate on a cash basis.

The third economic fact that has caused revolution is the extravagance of the baby boomers. There are now about 76 million people who fall into this group. An Omaha newspaper recently stated that more than half of these people will divorce. They will make radical changes, and most of them will experience more severe financial problems than their parents did. They are viewed as a disillusioned group. Their main goal is success, meaning economic success, at any cost. Baby Boomers work longer hours than did their parents. Most of them live in two-income families.

The fourth economic fact is that we now have the world's first prosperous retired generation—the first retired generation in all history that is not dependent upon its families. "On the average," said Otis Bowen, "the over-sixty-five population has the largest net worth of any group in the American society." This

> "Thoughtful giving begins with thoughts on giving."
> —ARTHUR C. FRANTZREB

generation stands in our churches as a totally untapped resource. We must see these senior citizens as the new energizers we have been waiting for. Most of them want to be generous, but they need guidelines, special training, and motivation to give those larger gifts. Most of them have not been involved in a seminar on Long-Range Planned Giving. Fifty percent of them do not have legally drawn wills. Seniors have choices that previous retired generations did not have.

Yet, in spite of these facts, many of our churches cannot make it financially. Church closings far outnumber the establishment of *new* churches. New strategies for multiparishes, shared clergy, and yoke relationships have allowed us to maintain many smaller churches in our cities and rural areas. Economically depressed areas have found help in these ways.

Often, however, members of these smaller churches have quite adequate resources for funding significant ministries, but no one has helped them understand the principles of Christian giving. No one has helped them to decide when, with what, and how to be a Christian giver!

Why?

Aristotle said that "all learning and action must begin with the question why?"

Why should we teach Christians to give? What right do we have to expect Christians to give? Whenever I get into a serious discussion with a layperson about generous giving, they always want to know, "Why?"

Pastors usually respond by illustrating that needs are increasing and inflation is rampant. Our costs are going up.

But rather than beginning with our own needs, we must begin our answer to this "why" question by affirming clearly that our Christian faith puts giving at the central point in our relations with God. The biblical story is about giving, receiving, using, and giving back, and the indisputable giver is always God.

God gives. God's followers give. Stewardship is not an elective; giving is not an option such as the disposal of discretionary assets. All Christians are givers, or they cannot wear the label: "GOD GIVES SO YOU CAN!"

We give because we have been graced. God has given each of us time, potential, and opportunities so that our lives can fulfill a purpose, and at the same time, strengthen the work of Christ. God's giving is not determined by our giving. God is the continual giver who waits for our responses to those gifts.

We frustrate the people who worship with us when we fail to teach them the principles of Christian giving. The televised images of want, added to the mail's saturation with children, pain, and hunger, puts pressure on our people. Their lack of knowledge produces guilt. Guilt paralyzes! Selfishness is a neurosis that we have tolerated too long.

When?

Giving, as a principle of our faith, should be taught and retaught at every age. Giving is both a very difficult act for a child, and a very easy act for a child. The same might be assumed for persons at other levels of maturity. Sometimes giving is easy, sometimes very difficult.

Few churches solicit or expect financial commitments from children, and offering envelopes are considered too expensive! We also tend to believe that many parents would not understand such an effort, in order to ask for their children's money. Or we place education about giving in the summer handout, when most children are on vacation with their parents.

Few youth are expected to give. They are seldom asked to make financial commitments. Few receive offering envelopes. We don't expect them to give. Our neglect forces our youth to remain takers, and we do little to dissuade them. Most youth projects expect adults to be the source of funding!

> "To be without some of the things you want is an indispensable part of happiness."
> —BERTRAND RUSSELL

17

Giving is extremely painful to newlyweds, while giving opportunities are sought by senior citizens. Yet the economic fact is that couples often have their highest income in those first years of marriage, while seniors often have a vastly reduced income.

When Should We Teach?

1. Stewardship education should be a requirement for all who seek membership, either at the confirmation level or at the adult membership level. We must give special attention to those who are transferring membership to our church.
2. There should be a strong stewardship education program prior to and throughout every finance campaign or funding program.
3. Sermons can highlight giving as the basic Christian lifestyle. This kind of emphasis will become more and more important, as worship attendance for many congregations continues to outstrip growth in membership. Millions of baby boomers are not joiners, but are willing to give if informed during worship about giving as a primary definition of Christian behavior.
4. We can teach during regular hours of worship. We foolishly miss our greatest opportunity to teach prior to the offering. This is the time to answer their question "Why?" Have we seen that the offering and the sacrament of Holy Communion stand in mutual relationship? In the offering, *we* give.
5. We can teach stewardship through our end-of-the-month report to givers.
6. We can teach stewardship through our parish newspapers.
7. We can teach stewardship as we report to our church's board.
8. We can teach stewardship during pastoral visits.
9. When questions are asked, we can see those questions as opportunities for teaching the principles of Christian giving.
10. When there is an economic crisis in a family or community, we can teach the helpful concepts of family financial planning.

What and How?

What is the method and content of our teaching about Christian stewardship? We must be careful and intentional:

1. We must stress the need for Christians to respond to grace, God's initiative.
2. We must stress the need for commitment to giving.

   (The role of a pastor is to force decisions. God can work with a yes or a no from God's people, but not even God can do much with a maybe!)
3. We must stress giving as a Christian witness.

   (Not to God, but to ourselves. By our gift, *we* see how much we care.)
4. We must stress the legitimacy of different levels of giving.
5. We must stress the different ways of giving—the different things to give.
6. We must stress giving as a relational experience.
7. We must stress growth in giving as a normal expectancy.
8. We must stress regular weekly giving.
9. We must stress giving beyond the local church.
10. We must stress giving as a *lifestyle*.
11. We must stress giving as being very personal.
12. We must stress giving as a personal response to God's gifts to us.
13. We must stress the need for at least an annual review of family giving (a new commitment each year).
14. We must stress giving as a declaration of one's humanity.
15. We must teach the nature of money—what it is, what it can and cannot do.
16. We must stress the need to get information before we give.

    ("Don't give another dime until you know where the money will go!")
17. We must teach that all giving is not a good investment. We must help people make good investments through their giving.
18. We must teach people to exercise faith in their giving (wills, insurance, trusts, etc.).
19. We must teach accountability, response, gratitude, First Fruits, the tithe, and generous giving.
20. We must be prepared to answer all questions about giving and tithing, to local and community needs.
21. We must be prepared to answer questions about how much of our giving should go the local church. We must help people in their deciding.

22. We must help people see excitement in all giving, especially in the offerings during the hour of worship.

23. We must be prepared to answer all questions about "how much?"

    (Offer no rigid standard, no amount, no legalism, no average. Offer only to accept their starting point. Giving must be a *personal response* (see No. 7). People give according to their spiritual development more often than according to their net worth.

24. Finally, we must teach by personal example and by corporate example.

A national survey to discover why people give indicated that their initial response in giving is usually dependent upon:

1. Whether they came from a giving family.
2. What their previous church taught or did not teach.
3. Their present set of values.
4. Their spiritual maturity.
5. Their present economic status.
6. Feelings at the moment about the church, which imply: "Start where you are!"

Grimm's Three Commands for Stewardship Ministries
1. Keep it positive.
2. Keep it biblical.
3. Stress the mission.

 PLANNING TOOL

The Church As a Learning Organization

GLENNA AND ROY KRUGER

Have you watched children learn? They explore. They reach out for experience. They ask questions. Children are natural, fearless learners. As we get older, we become comfortable, afraid of risk-taking, embarrassed by failure. Organizations can choose to be "childlike," learning new skills, taking risks, and reaching for new experiences. The other option is to become atrophied, doing things the way they always have been done.

Successful churches have a strong commitment to constant improvement in all they do. They anticipate and respond to changes in their community, become more efficient and productive with their limited resources, and assist parishioners in discovering and enhancing their individual God-given talents and abilities. Successful churches continue to learn, no matter how "old" they become.

We believe the learning organization model artic-ulated by Peter Senge in *The Fifth Discipline: The Art and Practice of a Learning Organization* has great applicability to the church. Becoming a learning organization helps us ensure that we make the best use of all our resources, achieve results, and keep the delivery of the Word fresh and alive in our communities.

Becoming a Learning Organization

What can your church do to become a learning organization? Three key steps can be taken to begin:
1. define your unique mission;
2. examine your leadership style;
3. implement a program of continuous improvement.

The following is a guide to help you with each of these steps.

Define Your Unique Mission

All Christian churches share the ultimate mission to "go into all the world and preach the good news." Your church exists in a particular place and time that defines special opportunities for ministry. During the life of any congregation, these particular emphases may alter as the demographics of your congregation shift, or as the environment surrounding your church changes.

Exploring your unique mission is a wonderful exercise to engage lay leaders, and the congregation as a whole, in valuable discussion. Here are some examples of unique ministries. See which ones might fit your congregation:

_____homeless
_____inadequately housed
_____university students
_____international students
_____elderly
_____suburban families
_____singles
_____single-parent families
_____ethnic minorities
_____street kids
_____non-English speakers
_____persons needing counseling
_____new residents in the community
_____teenagers

You may add to the list as you discuss your community and the impact your church makes upon it.

Having a challenging vision is critical to engaging parishioners in the life of the church. Have you ever wondered why employees of secular organizations are willing to sacrifice time and energy for their company? It's not just the paycheck—it's belonging to an exciting group with a clear sense of purpose (mission). Many nonprofit organizations operate with little or no paid staff. Volunteers give hours of their time, resources, and talent. Why? Because they understand and believe in the mission of the organization. The mission is expressed in concrete terms, enabling the volunteers to relate to those served.

Write a mission statement that captures the particular purpose of your congregation. You may want to appoint a special task force, or have a subgroup of your board draft the statement. Here are some examples to help you start:

"Northside Community Church exists primarily to serve the needs of the low-income families that surround us in our community. We will demonstrate the love of God as we develop and deliver programs designed to hold families together, heal broken relationships, and develop skills for improving their economic situation."

"Westside church exists to meet the needs of those individuals alienated from, or unacquainted with the traditional church. We will offer worship, counseling, and introduction to the Christian faith at times which meet the needs of our community."

"Downtown Church will focus its ministry on the needs of those residing in the core city center: the homeless, elderly, and university students. We will offer services in God's name to all those who seek to fill the special needs of these communities."

Examine Your Leadership Style

Leadership in a learning organization differs from a traditional hierarchical structure, where all decisions are made at the top. Senge describes several characteristics required of a leader in a learning organization:

1. Leaders in learning organizations express the vision in concrete terms and inspire the people to action. One leader with a clear vision of the church as the catalyst for community rebirth has helped his people create a miracle in the midst of despair. His congregation, located in the heart of an integrated, working-class neighborhood, bought a run-down grocery store, with an equally run-down bowling alley next door. Today, the Word is preached in the space previously occupied by canned peaches and boxes of cereal. A community center with basketball courts, after-school care for children, and classes in parenting have taken over from the pinball machines.

2. Leaders in learning organizations allow people to learn through challenging assignments, and by setting high standards for performance. We saw a great example recently in the youth room of a growing suburban church. The walls of the room were covered with posters—not of teen idols or even admonitions to behave in proscribed ways—but rather with the mission statement of each teen committee, along with the names and telephone numbers of each committee member. The goals were specific and measurable, such as, "Greet each visitor within one

minute of their entering the room," and "Deliver a 2.5-minute devotional at each meeting." Accountability and involvement were insured with the public display of the lists of names.

Leaders in learning organizations not only set high standards, but act as teachers and mentors to those around them. Think back to some individual early in your life who made a difference. Like Paul with the young Timothy, the leader as teacher or mentor coaches privately and praises publicly.

3. Leaders in learning organizations are stewards. The steward keeps reminding the workers of their high calling and purpose. This is what energizes people to go beyond the ordinary. The steward has a great sense of responsibility toward the highly committed volunteers and staff working in the church. This may mean the need for short-term commitments, or a "project approach" to work. Volunteers are more likely to be enthusiastic about making a commitment to a project with an ending. It is also important to match the appropriate talent to each project. Talented professionals and knowledgeable workers will expect to use their knowledge at church as well. Give them every opportunity.

4. Leaders in learning organizations challenge the status quo. They experiment with new methods, risking that not every idea will succeed. When new methods fail, they assess what worked and didn't, learn from the experience, and apply their learning to the next challenge. No effort is made to place blame for the failure. In fact, it is not labeled as failure, but rather as the foundation for the next experiment.

5. Leaders in learning organizations facilitate dialogue. Decisions are reached through talking out the pros and cons of ideas, freely criticizing, and evaluating. There is no attempt for consensus. Too often, consensus simply means that everyone has given up something, and no one is happy. Learning organizations talk about issues and exchange ideas until generally the "best" solution is identified. The pastor's role is to facilitate this dialogue, ensuring that all viewpoints are heard and respected. When a decision is made, it is in harmony with the mission statement and core values of the church.

6. Leaders in learning organizations are constantly learning. Leading a learning organization is a great challenge. You no longer will be "in control," but watching as others lead. It means constantly reexamining the way you make decisions, communicate to others, and plan your work.

Implement a Program of Continuous Improvement

Learning organizations are marked by continuous improvement. This drive to improve is clearly different from the old adage, "If it ain't broke, don't fix it." Learning organizations know that there is always a better way, a more productive method, a more cost-effective program. We will discuss four methods which you can use to help your church: benchmarking, process and project evaluations, planning, and staff development.

Benchmarking

Benchmarking is a way to learn from other organizations by understanding the elements of a particular successful program or system. You may compare your program or practice with one at another church, or seek out a unique program that does not currently exist in your church. Here's how to make benchmarking work for you.

1. Select a single program you want to improve or create. For example, you may want to improve your Sunday school program to attract young families.

2. Identify a church that is known to have an outstanding program. You can contact pastors in your area for recommendations, use your denominational office for referrals, or send a committee out to review several programs.

3. Once you have identified your "benchmark" program, gather information. This will probably include an on-site visit, interviews with pastors and lay leaders, and perhaps the obtaining of planning documents or communication pieces. Develop a set of questions before you go. You are looking for key elements of the program: organizational structure, objectives, roles and responsibilities, methods, measurements. A sample interview format is located at the end of this article.

4. Once the information has been gathered, analyze the results, looking for the practices and methods that made the program successful.

5. Discuss how the practices can be adapted by your church. The idea is not to copy, but to use what has been learned from your research. Perhaps you will adjust your current program, within the context of your own environment and mission. You may find some ideas that lead you into a whole new area of ministry not previously considered.

6. Implementing the changes will require careful planning to involve all the necessary volunteers and staff, as well as communication to the congregation about the objective and changes.

7. Evaluate. Build into your planning an opportunity for those involved to evaluate the changes, adjust as needed, and learn from the changes.

Process and Project Evaluation

This is another method for continuous improvement, unlike benchmarking, in which you are looking externally for improvement ideas. In this case, you are reviewing internally to improve activities or programs. Here are some ways to do it:

1. *Conduct project reviews.* This works best for reviewing short-term projects or programs that have a defined ending date. For example, you planned a church work day to fix up the building. Afterward, the building committee, along with the staff in charge of this area, gather to assess what worked well and what part of the process needed improvement. Put your discussion notes in a file for the next project team that conducts the same event. The idea is to learn from both the mistakes and the successes.

2. *Showcase successful programs.* Ask lay leaders of programs to present to the whole congregation the mission of their program, how they get their work done, and why they feel good about their work. Eyewitness accounts are powerful testimonies of how God works through the people. Other groups in the church can learn from their successes, as well as feeling inspired by and becoming more knowledgeable about the work of the total church. Depending upon the style and structure of your congregation, these presentations could occur as part of the worship service, during congregational business meetings, or at other regularly scheduled events.

3. *Assess new technology tools.* You may consider yourself a technology illiterate, but chances are that someone in your congregation is knowledgeable about the latest tools. Harness technology to increase the productivity of your staff and yourself. Numerous software programs exist to aid in publication, church finances, word processing, and even theological scholarship.

Planning

Learning organizations use planning as a way to improve. This means planning clear objectives with measurable results. Examples of organizational objectives might be:

• grow in membership by 10 percent within the next 12 months;
• develop the spiritual life of members by offering a new series of evening discussion groups;
• plan and implement an after-school program for youth by September 1;
• facilitate attendance by the elderly and disabled by reserving special parking places.

Perhaps from your benchmarking research, you have identified the need to restructure your Sunday school program. What is the outcome you want to achieve? What steps are involved to get there? Who will be responsible for each step? What are the due dates for each piece? How will the program changes be evaluated?

As you plan, use your mission statement as a guide to ensure that the programs you plan and budget for will fit within the framework of the vision you feel your church is called to follow.

Developing Staff and Volunteers

In a learning organization, people feel responsible to learn how to do things better. They become proactive about improvement. Learning plans might include formal education, attendance at seminars, responsibility for a project such as planning a conference, chairing a task force on a church issue, writing a new policy, or representing the church at a community meeting. Staff members or volunteers can become very creative in defining stretch assignments that will benefit the church and help them exercise their talents.

Please don't forget your pastors. If you have a multi-staff church, you may have inexperienced clergy, for whom a development plan will be critical to their future ministry. This may include additional formal training, but also opportunity for experience in administration, teaching, preaching, program planning, and staff to lay committees. Also consider designating a mentor for inexperienced pastors. This might be a retired minister or a layperson whose experience and wisdom can help guide through the learning experiences.

Conclusion

We hope the possibility of making your church a learning organization inspires you to explore these ideas with your lay leadership. Do you have a clearly defined and unique mission? Are you ready to lead a learning organization? Are you committed to continuous improvement in all aspects of the ministry? Becoming a learning organization will provide a positive environment for individual growth and expanded opportunities for ministry in an ever-changing world.

SAMPLE BENCHMARK QUESTIONNAIRE

1. What were the needs behind the development of your program?
2. Where does the program fit organizationally? (What particular committee or staff person?)
3. How is the program staffed?
4. Do you have job descriptions for the persons involved?
5. How often are results evaluated?
6. What measures are you using for your evaluation?
7. What have been the biggest challenges?
8. What would you do differently after your experience?
9. What has worked especially well, and why?
10. How was the program introduced to the congregation or community?

 MONEY TALK

Christian Giving

JAMES I. COOK

(Before reading this article, read II Corinthians, chapters 8 and 9.)

All discoveries of value are meant to be shared. The wonderful discovery I want to share is that every important thing the New Testament has to say about the place of giving in the Christian life is represented in chapters 8 and 9 of Paul's second letter to the church at Corinth. Indeed, so focused are these chapters on the single subject of giving, that some scholars have argued that they originally formed a separate letter, given over exclusively to that topic.

What prompted the content of these chapters, however, is the fact that at least once in his ministry, the Apostle became passionately involved in a major fund-raising effort. Its object was to offer concrete aid to "the poor among the saints at Jerusalem" (see Rom. 15:25-28). We encounter reference to that same benevolent project at the end of First Corinthians, when after his classic witness to the Resurrection (and without missing a beat), Paul specifies that the way for this congregation to excel in the work of the Lord is to put aside "on the first day of every week" money for their gift to Jerusalem (see I Cor. 16:1-4)! It was only when the Corinthians failed to follow this instruction that Paul was forced to revisit, in great detail, the critical importance of Christian generosity. His words, then, were called out by a specific crisis in the life of one first-century Christian congregation, but in the providence of God, they continue to speak powerfully and helpfully to Christian congregations of every time and place. Practical limitations preclude touching on everything Paul has to say, but here are five fundamentals.

Christian giving has to do with grace.

It was the grace of God granted to the churches of Macedonia that enabled them—during a severe ordeal of affliction and in extreme poverty—to overflow in a wealth of generosity, and it was this same grace alone that would enable the church at Corinth to excel also in this generous undertaking. Now at first glance, it may seem the height of folly to begin an appeal for money by talking about the grace of God.

23

But Paul knew exactly what he was doing. If he was not fully aware that any invitation to give, like any call to sacrifice, runs absolutely counter to every natural human instinct, his experience with the Corinthians surely made it clear. The Apostle's initial appeal had been greeted with a burst of enthusiasm. Now a year had passed, and their desire and eagerness to do something had not been matched by their action. Paul was fearful that when the time to present their gift arrived, both he and they would be humiliated by their lack of response.

> ## "The love you give away is the only love you can keep and carry in your heart."
> —ROBERT SCHULLER

It is only when Christians of any age come to confess, with Frederick Buechner, that "life is grace . . . the givenness of it, the fathomlessness of it, the endless possibilities of its becoming transparent to something extraordinary beyond itself," that they will be able to respond graciously, with gifts from open heart and hand. As Paul says, there is ultimately only one place to behold grace in all its splendor and experience it in all its power: "For you know the grace of our Lord Jesus Christ, that though he was rich, yet for your sakes he became poor, so that you through his poverty might become rich" (II Cor. 8:9 NIV)! Only after being overwhelmed by that great given can Christians begin to understand that giving is not primarily about money, but about grace.

Christian giving has to do with attitude.

Everyone knows that people may make gifts from a variety of motivations. They may do it out of a sense of duty, out of a desire for self-satisfaction, or out of a hunger for prestige. Such motivations are not completely bad, because at least, in each case, the gift is given. Far worse are gifts made against the giver's will, for involuntary giving is a contradiction in terms. The Apostle would have nothing to do with that contradiction.

Although Paul obviously had a strong desire that the Corinthians should give—and to give generously—his emphasis on grace guarded against any hint of compulsion. His fervent hope that they would be moved both by the grace of God granted to the Macedonians, and by the grace revealed in the Lord Jesus Christ, was genuine. He therefore stated candidly that his appeal to them to excel in this generous undertaking, as in everything else, was not a command, but an offering of advice. As earnestly and eagerly as Paul sought their contribution, he wanted it to be prepared and presented as a voluntary gift, and not as an extortion. Clearly, this emphasis on attitude stemmed not from diplomacy but from theology: "Each of you must give as you have made up your mind [literally, "as you have decided *in your heart*"], not reluctantly or under compulsion, for God loves a cheerful giver" (II Cor. 9:7).

Because "cheerful" translates the same Greek word that has given us "hilarity," someone has suggested that the phrase be translated, "for God loves a *hilarious* giver"! In any case, we may be confident that Paul's extensive training in both Hebrew and rabbinical studies would have taught him the vital connection between generosity and cheerfulness. "Give liberally and be ungrudging when you do so," says Deuteronomy 15:10*a*, and "When a man gives alms he should do it with a joyful heart," said the rabbis. Little wonder, then, that Paul underlined the importance of the giver's attitude, not only here to the Corinthians, but also to the Christians at Rome, urging the compassionate to exercise their gift "in cheerfulness" (Rom. 12:8).

> "Give generously to him and do so without a grudging heart; then because of this the LORD God will bless you in all your work and in everything you put your hand to."
> DEUTERONOMY 15:10 NIV

Christian giving has to do with trust.

Security is a natural, universal human priority. In most cultures, both ancient and modern, the degree of security experienced is in direct proportion to the amount of money in hand. Our own money may proclaim, "In God we trust," but a more honest motto probably would read, "In money we trust." Therefore, any call to give money away, rather than save it or invest it, collides head-on with what a church fund raiser once labeled PBP, "pocketbook protection," or what I might call SLOT, "severe lack of trust"!

The Apostle initially addressed this distrust by an appeal to human prudence:

> I do not mean that there should be relief for others and pressure on you, but it is a question of a fair balance between your present abundance and their need, so that their abundance may be for your need, in order that there may be a fair balance.
>
> (II COR. 8:13-14)

That is, if the Corinthians met the needs of the Jerusalem saints in the present, the Jerusalem saints would meet the Corinthians' need in the future.

Paul countered this problem of distrust decisively with a bold proclamation of divine promise. He summoned his readers to trust in the goodness and providence of God! Again he invoked the theology of Deuteronomy 15:10: "Give liberally and be ungrudging when you do so, *for on this account the Lord your God will bless you in all your work and all that you undertake*" (emphasis added). In re-aiming this ancient promise of God to the Corinthians, Paul combined allusions to Proverbs, Deuteronomy, Exodus, I Chronicles, Psalms, Malachi, Genesis, Isaiah, and Hosea, with words of his own:

> And God is able to provide you with every blessing in abundance, so that by always having enough of everything, you may share abundantly in every good work. As it is written,
> "He scatters abroad, he gives to the poor;
>   his righteousness endures forever."
> He who supplies seed to the sower and bread for food will supply and multiply your seed for sowing and increase the harvest of your righteousness. You will be enriched in every way for your great generosity.
>
> (II COR. 9:8-11a)

Paul certainly thought so. Early in chapter 8, he told the Corinthians that his desire that they excel in this generous undertaking was his way of "testing the genuineness of your love against the earnestness of others" (v. 8). It then turned out that the "others" they were being measured against was primarily the Lord Jesus Christ, whose generous act of giving himself for them, they well knew! At the end of the chapter,

> "We can only learn to love by loving."
> —IRIS MURDOCH

after alerting them to the impending visit of a Titus-led delegation to receive their generous gift, he concluded: "Therefore openly before the churches, show them the proof of your love and of our reason for boasting about you" (v. 24).

Christians who know anything about the gospel at all will recognize the organic connection between love and giving.

The heart of John 3:16, the classic golden text of all Christians—"For God so loved the world that he gave his only Son, so that everyone who believes in him may not perish but may have eternal life"—can be summarized in six words: "God so *loved* that God *gave!*" In First John 3:17-18, we encounter the opposite side of the coin—namely, that the absence of giving can be explained only by the absence of love: "How does God's love abide in anyone who has the world's goods and sees a brother or sister in need and yet refuses help? Little children, let us love, not in word or speech, but in truth and action."

And the same connection between love and giving runs like a golden thread through the great central section of the letter to the Romans, Paul's masterwork! At 5:8—"But God proves his love for us in that while we still were sinners Christ died for us"—the act of giving is implicit. But at 8:32, it becomes explicit: "He who did not withhold his own Son, but gave him up for all of us, will he not with him also give us everything else?" That incomparable gift was the bedrock of Paul's unshakable conviction that nothing in all creation will ever be able to separate Christians from the love of God in Christ Jesus, their Lord!

Paul Scherer, one of the great preachers of his generation, was quite right when he said, "Love is a spendthrift, leaves its arithmetic at home, is always 'in the red.' And God is love (Rom. 8:32)."

Finally, Christian giving has to do with thanksgiving.

This is not thanksgiving sung by a single voice; this is

thanksgiving performed by full chorus and orchestra! This is not thanksgiving for solo flute; this is thanksgiving expressed by cathedral organ, with all stops pulled, for this thanksgiving involves God, the givers, and the recipients. Great generosity produces, or creates, "thanksgiving to God through us," Paul concluded, "for the rendering of this ministry not only supplies the needs of the saints but also overflows with many thanksgivings to God" (II Cor. 9:11*b*-12). What Paul envisioned here was a kind of theological chain reaction: Christians exhibit great generosity; recipients offer thanksgiving to God; and God is glorified!

This would all be wonderful enough, simply on a mundane, practical level. But there are further profound spiritual results from Christian giving. The recipients of the gifts would also recognize that there was more going on than the meeting of their concrete needs, important as that was. They would perceive that the Corinthians' response belonged to their confession of trust in the gospel; it was a vivid demonstra-

"Gratitude is the memory of the heart."

tion that this confession went beyond words, to a genuine act of obedience to that gospel. The recipients, therefore, would long for, and pray for the givers—not only out of gratitude for the gifts, but also because of the surpassing grace of God that had been given to their benefactors.

To read and reflect on Second Corinthians 8 and 9 inevitably leads to the conclusion that Christian giving was a most needful and fitting subject for Paul's inspired eloquence. Much of the Apostle's theological insight, much of his clear grasp of the multiple blessings of Christian giving, were captured in the words placed on the lips of Jesus by James Russell Lowell in *The Vision of Sir Launfal:*

> Not what we give, but what we share,
> For the gift without the giver is bare;
> Who gives himself with his alms feeds three,
> Himself, his hungering neighbor, and Me.

The ultimate goal of all Christian giving is that the grace of God be acknowledged by all people. Thus, Paul ended as he began: "Thanks be to God for his indescribable gift!" (II Cor. 9:15).

SERMON HELP

The Grace of Giving

ROBIN WOOD

I'll never forget "Ole John." I was just beginning my ministry as an associate pastor. I was nineteen. John was over sixty and a new convert.

Since he hadn't been in church all of his life, he knew little about the routine events in worship. Pastor Ken Mishler and his wife Judy befriended John, so every Sunday he would sit by Judy. When he didn't understand something, he would lean over and ask Judy for help—usually in a loud voice.

One of my favorite memories of John was his Sunday morning routine during the offering. Pastor Ken would say, "Now it's time to honor the Lord with our tithes and offerings," and start to pray. The church would be quiet, and right on schedule, John would shout out his weekly question to Judy, "How much should I give?"

Most Sundays Judy would pat John on the shoulder and say quietly, "Just give what you can." Judy had a great sense of humor, however, and one Sunday when John shouted, "How much should I give?" Judy shouted back, "Give it all!"

The entire congregation erupted in laughter, but Ole John didn't hear a thing, because he was serious about his question. Later, Judy told us that John had emptied his wallet that morning, with a big smile on his face. He did indeed give it all!

After twenty years of ministry, I have never forgotten "Ole John." He was asking one of the most relevant questions any Christian can ask: "How much should I give?"

What does the Bible say about giving? Is the tithe or percentage giving a New Testament or an Old Testament concept? Why is it so important? What should we practice and teach?

Since 1987, I have served as Senior Pastor of a new church in Phoenix, Arizona. Our Mountain Park Community Church has developed primarily by conversion growth.

As a result, we've had a number of people like "Ole John." We also have attracted many "mature" Christians who continue to struggle with the principles and practice of their stewardship.

I believe the Apostle Paul gives us some great insight into this sometimes difficult area. Two principles from Second Corinthians, chapter eight, have changed our hearts and attitudes toward tithing and percentage giving here at Mountain Park.

First, in II Corinthians 8:1, Paul says, "And now, brothers, we want you to know about the grace that God has given the Macedonian churches" (NIV). That phrase leaps right off the page at me.

What is this grace that Paul is referring to? As I studied this chapter, I realized that the word *grace* was being used in the context of stewardship. Throughout the New Testament, however, the word *grace* is usually tied to the message of salvation.

We're all familiar with Ephesians 2:8-9: "For it is by grace you have been saved, through faith—and this not from yourselves, it is the gift of God—not by works, so that no one can boast" (NIV). In Galatians, Paul is calling the church back to the message of grace, and again, the context is salvation.

Simply defined, grace means, "God's unmerited favor." But since "unmerited favor" seems a little stiff to me, I've come up with the following definition of grace: "God did something for you and me that we couldn't do for ourselves."

We couldn't save ourselves. We couldn't earn God's forgiveness, so God sent Jesus to provide for our salvation by grace. Jesus died on the cross for our sins. It was a once-and-for-all free sacrifice. Now that's grace!

If you're still with me, I hope you're beginning to ask yourself, "What does grace have to do with stewardship and tithing?" Let me see if I can answer.

Over the years, I've asked many people the following question: "When it comes to giving, what does God have to do for us that we cannot do for ourselves?" In other words, what is the hardest thing for us to do with our money and resources?

The answer is clear. The hardest, most unnatural thing to do with material wealth, is to give it away and let it go.

What is tithing all about? Tithing is letting go of 10 percent and giving it away.

The second insight from this passage deals with the issue of trust. Trust is our response to God's grace.

If we truly believe that God's grace penetrates our lives in every way, we will be able to trust God with every aspect of our lives—including our giving. For Paul, tithing is a test of our love and discipline, through which we prove to ourselves and to others that we really trust God for our provision.

I'm not the only one who has tried to divert attention from deficient giving by elevating my discipline in Bible study, or prayer life, or witness. But Paul doesn't give us that option. Paul ranks our giving right up there with all the other Christian disciplines.

"But just as you excel in everything—in faith, in speech, in knowledge, in complete earnestness and in your love for us—see that you also excel in this grace of giving.

"I am not commanding you, but I want to *test the sincerity of your love* by comparing it with the earnestness of others" (II Cor. 8:7-8 NIV, emphasis added).

Paul wanted us to excel in the grace of giving. For him, it's obvious that giving is not a secondary spiritual issue.

In addition to all this, something very unusual was happening in the Macedonian churches. They were in great poverty, yet they released their resources, far beyond what anyone expected. They were experiencing God's grace in giving.

"For I testify that they gave as they were able, and even beyond their ability" (II Cor. 8:3 NIV). Even in the words of economic times, God's grace was helping that group of new Christians do something they could never do in their own power. They were giving their resources away.

When we are prospering financially, it is still difficult to let go of our resources. But the text says that God's grace was active, even in a time of poverty.

I am so thankful that God used a church in poverty to teach us about trust and grace. You and I both know that if these churches were being blessed financially, we might be saying, "I would tithe and give generously, if I were blessed as they were." But God teaches us the truth through a group of churches that were experiencing oppression and financial distress.

Finally, Paul says, "They urgently pleaded with us for the privilege of sharing in this service to the saints. And they did not do as we expected, but they gave themselves first to the Lord and then to us in keeping with God's will" (II Cor. 8:4-5 NIV).

In a culture consumed with issues of power and control, trusting anyone with our resources can be difficult. If we hope to experience the joy and freedom God intends, however, we must grow in the grace of giving.

> "Giving is the highest expression of potency. In the very act of giving, I experience my strength, my wealth, my power. This experience of heightened vitality and potency fills me with joy. I experience myself as overflowing, spending, alive, hence as joyous. Giving is more joyous than receiving, not because it is a deprivation, but because in the act of giving lies the expression of aliveness."
>
> *ERICH FROMM*

One particular problem related to a lack of trust in this area is the increasing tendency to designate our giving. Designated giving takes place when a person or church gives money or resources, but it also dictates where and how the money can be spent.

I am not entirely opposed to designated giving, however, I do want to raise this concern: If we designate all our giving to the church, or to our national agencies, or to a specific mission, I am convinced that we have not learned the "grace of giving." The grace of giving involves our letting go, and the freedom that accompanies it.

I am learning that control and power are at the center of all sin. In fact, I always spell sin like this: sIn. Why? Because the sin of Adam and Eve had to do with believing the lie.

What was the lie? That you can become like God. That you can control your own life. That you can be God.

I don't know about you, but to me, designated giving looks a lot like control—sin. I'm in control. I decide where my money will go and how it will be spent. The secret of tithing is letting go and trusting other members placed in the Body of Christ to also know and accomplish God's will.

The fourth chapter of the book of Acts records giving in the early church this way; they brought their offering and "laid it at the apostles' feet." They refused personal control and submitted to a plurality of leadership. And what happened? They experienced the grace of giving, and every need was met.

It is my passion to call the church-at-large to the grace of giving. It starts with rejecting the power and control that this world so often encourages. It starts with tithing and percentage giving.

Certainly there is a need for designated giving, but it takes place long after we have learned to reject our personal control over our tithes and offerings in the church.

Once we have learned to give ourselves first to the Lord and then to the Body of Christ, we will be free, especially in an affluent culture, to designate even more of our resources to other Kingdom causes.

At Mountain Park, we are learning the grace of giving. A tithe is important to us because it becomes the very foundation of our rejecting power and control and placing our trust in God.

In the end, New Testament teaching takes us beyond the tithe to extravagant and generous giving. But the key is God's grace.

God is doing for us what we could never do for ourselves. God is helping us to do the most unnatural thing with our money and resources—give it away.

 MONEY TALK

A Tithing Testimony

NOAH REID

Christian stewardship started for me at the age of fourteen. My parents instructed me to tithe out of my weekly $12 "income." I learned early that God wants us to be just as responsible for what Scripture says about giving as about sharing the good news of salvation.

I do not tithe because I fear I will go to hell if I don't. I do not do it out of a burdensome sense of duty, although I do feel I have a responsibility that compels me to give out of the love Christ has placed in my heart.

Leviticus 27:30 states what God's minimum share should be: "All the tithe of the land, whether of the seed of the land, or of the fruit of the tree, is the LORD's: it is holy unto the Lord" (KJV). The passage continues: "Concerning the tithe of the herd, or of the flock, even of whatsoever passeth under the rod, the tenth shall be holy unto the LORD" (v. 32 KJV).

The prophet Malachi is even plainer in stating what belongs to God. He does not stop with the tithe. Malachi 3:8 reads, "Will a man rob God? Yet ye have robbed me. But ye say, Wherein have we robbed thee? In tithes and offerings" (KJV). In other words, anyone blessed with an abundance is to give God offerings, *over and above the tithe.*

I offer my tithe to God, through the church, to acknowledge divine ownership over all that I am and have. I believe with the psalmist that "The earth is the LORD's, and the fulness thereof; the world, and they that dwell therein" (Ps. 24:1 KJV). The Lord is my Creator and Sustainer, and he has a right to receive an increase from that which really belongs to him.

I offer my tithe to God, through the church, because it helps me be more Christlike. The law of the earth is selfishness. We are taught to grab all we can. It is easy to believe that our lives consist of the abundance of the things we possess. We are encouraged to measure success in terms of what we get. God, however, measures us in terms of what we give, and the manner in which we serve.

I offer my tithe to God, through the church, because it is the best possible investment I can make. Some people invest in stocks and bonds. Others invest in lands, businesses, and homes. But the greatest investments we make are the gifts we offer to the Lord. They yield present and future dividends that cannot be surpassed or equaled.

I offer my tithes and offerings, through the church, to demonstrate my love and gratitude to God. My giving is an expression of my love to the God who proved his love for me, in that he gave his Son to die for me. You and I can prove our love by giving out of the resources with which we have been blessed. As we yield the very substance of our lives to the Lord—our tithes, time, talents, and energy—it is like holding a mirror up to our hearts.

As a pastor, I have never known anyone who experienced serious financial difficulty for lack of the money they gave to the Lord. On the contrary, I have heard many testimonies given by individuals who indicated that it was, in fact, easier to meet their financial obligations after they became faithful tithers. I can testify to that experience myself.

When we decide to become joyful, regular givers to the work of God, it does something to our spirit. It deepens our love. It increases our enthusiasm. It multiplies our joy. It makes our worship more vital. I commend tithing to you, for the blessing it will bring to your own heart and life.

 DEVOTIONAL

Beggars

EDWARD HAYS

Beggars: they seem to be everywhere today! They hassle you on the street, panhandling for money, or they stand at stoplights with crudely lettered signs, begging for a job. They come in so many forms that even in the privacy of your own home, you are not free of them. They call on the telephone, begging you to buy some product or service. When you open your mail, they invariably appear, pestering you for money in a continuous flow of pictures of starving children or disaster victims. No sanctuary exists to protect you from their cries for help—not even the church sanctuary! From their pulpits, pastors beg you for money to address this or that need, and visiting missionaries add their voices to the chorus of pleas.

So many causes and organizations beg for money and volunteers that we seem to be continually caught between guilt and compassion. The old and frail, women and children beggars, are especially difficult to pass by without guilt tap dancing on the roof of our hearts. Survival in the midst of so many beggars has caused ugly mutations to evolve in us, producing stony hearts, ears selectively deaf, and eyes blinded to those with outstretched palms.

Bombarded by beggars, we are forever gliding back

and forth on an emotional swing, and we realize that each of us began life as a beggar! As infants, we begged, crying for food or attention and care. As small children, we continued to plead for attention and affection. As we grow older, we learn the art of camouflage and engage in clever forms of manipulation to get what we require. We beg both openly and in hidden ways, for the compliments and affirmation we so need. We learn to employ the silent treatment, becoming sullen or pouting to gain leverage for our pleas. Perhaps we so dislike pushy people and street beggars because we see in them an enlarged image of ourselves. And we find that image distasteful.

Of the great variety of beggars, the ones I personally find most distasteful are those who panhandle for affection. "Don't I get a hug?" "Give me a hug," begs a casual acquaintance, or even a complete stranger at some gathering. We all have a legitimate need for affection, but the heart-pockets of these emotional beggars apparently are so empty of a sense of being loved that they must beg for a hug!

I came from a loving Irish-American family, where affection was openly expressed to everyone in the family, including aunts, uncles, and cousins. I am not against public signs of affection. And I realize that in certain social and religious circles, affectionate hugs are as common as handshakes. However, to hug everybody—even strangers—seems to cheapen and devalue the affection I show to those I truly love. On one level, expressions of affection are ritual gestures, whose value is built upon honesty and integrity. Yet while my heart is not often in it, whenever I am confronted by these hug beggars, Old Guilt pushes me forward to hug them. It impels me, despite the fact that part of me feels it's better to die than to have to beg someone for a hug!

The wisdom of the First Testament reflects my feeling. The book of Sirach expresses the ancient view toward all begging: "It is better to die than to beg"; and "A beggar's life is not a life." While Sirach expresses my sense of sadness and pity for those who must beg for affection, it does not answer a haunting voice of my soul. Since hug beggars are like street beggars, as a pilgrim on the Spiritual Path, I cannot go blindly past anyone in need without making some response of compassion!

Furthermore, a good, healthy spirituality which includes all of life should cultivate a sound attitude toward begging. I have turned to the Jewish-Christian Scriptures to begin to create for myself such a reli-gious response. I found to my surprise that beggars are rare in the early part of the First Testament, yet they abound in the Second or New Testament! When Israel was a wandering desert tribe, it was a close-knit community, in which all members were cared for as mutual goods were shared. A beggar, then, among the Israelite community in its desert days, would have been as rare as a beggar among the Native American Sioux.

While beggars must have existed in the early stages of Jewish city life, they began to appear in great numbers as King David and King Solomon established their royal houses. The rise of the monarchy changed tribal social status by creating a few very wealthy people, and a majority of the very poor.

> "There was a notoriously stingy old man who would never give anything to anyone. In fact, he was so stingy that he would not even help his own relatives. One night this stingy old man was walking home. He was confronted by two muggers. They said, 'Old man, give us your money.' The man was actually a black belt in karate. He was not about to surrender his money. He attacked his muggers. He knocked the guns from their hands. He kicked both of them. He was beating them when one of them got loose and found a large 2×4 nearby. He whacked the man over the head and knocked him unconscious. Quickly, they searched his pockets. Guess how much money he had in his pockets? Just 78 cents! As the two robbers walked away, wiping blood from their faces, one said to the other, 'We are lucky. We should count ourselves fortunate. If that fellow had had $1.00, he would have killed both of us!'"
>
> —JOE HARDING

In the Gospels, it is commonplace to find blind, lame, and poor beggars outside the temple and city gates. Begging was often the response to some physical affliction that prevented a person from working. The poor were impoverished by heavy taxes and tolls levied by both the king and the temple. Add crop failures and personal misfortune, and the very poor were left with few options. If you were in debt, you could steal, sell yourself and your family into slavery, or become a beggar.

> "One can pay back the loan of gold, but one is forever in debt to those who are kind."
>
> —*MALAYAN PROVERB*

As in today's economics, whenever a great division exists between the "haves" and the "have-nots," thieves and beggars abound. Then as now, it is likely that there were professional beggars who chose a handout lifestyle instead of hard work. Whenever we, like beggars, are overwhelmed, we tend to respond, "There ought to be a law!" And for beggars, there is. It's called vagrancy, and it's a crime!

Today, vagrancy is a misdemeanor punishable by a small fine, or a jail sentence of a few weeks or months. By definition, vagrancy means living in idleness without a visible means of support. It's a catchall which can include beggars, derelicts, and loiterers. In the 1930s, the law was used to arrest union strikers, who were "idle" from their work, "beggars" pleading for decent wages and safe working conditions.

Vagrancy as a crime was established by a Christian society. Good, sober, Bible-loving, hard-working Christians have, over the centuries, looked with disdain upon beggars and anyone who isn't working. In previous centuries, it was no minor misdemeanor. Vagrants and beggars were punished with everything from branding, whipping, being condemned to slavery or the workhouse, or sentenced to the stocks for three days with only bread and water. The law provides a harsh, non-Christlike response to the problem.

The ancient Greek and Roman world showed little kindness toward the poor. While some cultures maintained that it was "decent" to look kindly on beggars and the poor, a more common attitude was resentment. Resentment or compassion: the problem of how to respond to beggars today is not very different from the one that Jesus or his disciples faced. He gave them and us a clear commandment and a difficult challenge: "Give to one who begs from you!"

The challenge is so difficult because if you were to give something—your money, time, or talent—to everyone who begs from you, you would be broke and a beggar yourself by the end of the week! Yet the spirituality of Jesus promised that those who follow it will be rich, laying aside a treasure beyond the reach of thieves. To live out his challenge of giving to the needy, as well as investing in that secret bank account in heaven, requires good eyes! Jesus said, "Remember, where your treasure is there your heart is also. The eye is the body's lamp. If your eyes are good, your body will be filled with light." As a shrewd investment advisor, Jesus encouraged us to make long-term investments, out of the reach of the IRS or corporate raiders.

A good personal spirituality is always catholic. It is global, containing echoes from the other great religious traditions—since God isn't partial when it comes to sharing Truth. And when it comes to a holy attitude about beggars, God's message to us is catholic—for those with ears to hear.

The words of Jesus about what to do with whatever wealth you have are the same as those of the Chinese holy man Lao-tzu. Five hundred years before Christ, he said, "The wise do not lay up treasures! The more they give to others, the more they have for themselves!"

According to the Jewish wisdom of the Talmud, "The one who gives to the poor in secret is greater than Moses!" The Koran teaches that giving gifts to the poor and beggars is an obligation in Islam! The prophet Muhammad declared that it is one's duty to share one's wealth with the poor, the needy, those in debt, prisoners, wayfarers—all those less fortunate than oneself. In Islam, among the ninety-nine names of God, one of the greatest is "Allah the Generous."

From India, the Rig-Veda instructs those seeking perfection: "Say not, 'This poor man's hunger is a heaven-sent doom.'. . . The liberal person is the one who gives to the beggar who wanders in search of food, lean and forlorn. . . . The powerful (rich) person should give to the one who is in need; let that person consider the road that lies ahead."

When I reflect on these traditions of joyous generosity, I am brought face to face with my own negative feelings whenever affection-beggars come pleading for a hug. I realize that I am rich, a millionaire when it comes to the love that people give and have given me. My heart-account is overflowing, so why should I not be generous with my love? Jesus promised that whatever we do to the least of his brothers and sisters, we do to

> "Riches are not from an abundance of worldly goods, but from a contented mind."
>
> —*MUHAMMAD*

him. If this is true, should I not respond to requests for affection with joyful generosity? I realize that any affection given in the name of Christ does not devalue my signs of affection to those I love; it only heightens them, because it increases my capacity to love.

These reminders also ignite in me a desire to use the numerous occasions to share my time, talents, and money as opportunities for joy, rather than as demands of duty. It is not duty, but delight that is the motivater! This insight dances in my heart as luminous as a flame-lit candle. Yet, like other spiritual insights, it can be overshadowed by the hassles of daily existence. For the light of the Inner Lamp to shine continuously, a visible symbol is helpful: A possible useful reminder might be a tin cup! It could be a contemporary version of the beggar's bowl. Purchase a tin cup and place this Beggar's Cup in your prayer corner.

Begin your prayers with your Beggar's Cup held upward in your hand. See yourself sitting like a beggar at heaven's gates. See your prayers as daily begging God for your needs, the needs of those you love, and the needs of the world. To beg is to plead for something that is not rightfully ours. We realize that we really do not have a rightful claim to good health, happiness, success, or even peace, and so we must beg for these things for those we love.

To pray well is to plead with tireless passion. Jesus told us to pray like beggars. When you pray, he said, do so like the man who came to his neighbor's door in the middle of night and kept begging for bread till he got it. Pray like the poor widow who ceaselessly begged the crooked judge for justice till he gave in to her. Moreover, if you daily prayed like a beggar, would not your prayer open your eyes, to see all those who beg in a different light? Your prayer Beggar's Cup would also remind you to beg daily, that in the various encounters of your day, God might give you a heart that finds its joy in giving.

The scripture scholar John Crossan says that the words of Jesus, "I am the way, the truth and the life," could better be put, "I am the authentic (truth) vision (way) of existence (life)." As we give ourselves, our time, and even our patience, to those with whom we work and live, may we always find joy in our giving. In our daily joy-filled generosity to life's known and unknown beggars, may Christ, the Authentic Vision of Existence, grant us eyes to see all of existence with that authentic and sacred vision.

PART TWO

FOR PASTORS AND WORSHIP TEAMS

Introduction

DONALD W. JOINER

A principle of financial stewardship that is high on my list is this: "If people are to learn about giving as a response to what God has done in Jesus Christ, the pastor needs to teach it!" If a pastor fails to teach giving, it probably will not be done.

A pastor is a leader in teaching the spiritual gift of giving. Lay leadership can model that gift as they organize and lead the church. A pastor preaches stewardship sermons; lay leadership witnesses to the joy of giving in their life. A pastor can provide "teaching moments" in meetings, in small group study, and by providing an opportunity for leaders to be invited into the "giving journey." Lay leadership can support and encourage the pastor.

Jerry Jackson begins this part of the *Guide* by describing the specific role of the pastor in teaching stewardship. Wayne Barrett shows how worship itself can be a "teachable moment." As the pastor and the worship team plan worship, they finds aids, helps, and resources in this section.

For many churches, the offering has become an apologetic intermission to the rest of worship. Yet, this time can be full of celebration for who we are, whose we are, and where God is leading us. The article by Don Joiner and Norma Wimberly, "The Offering: A Story and Symbol of Life," provides a model to transform the offering into a "teachable moment" and a time of exciting celebration.

For the pastor considering a stewardship sermon, or a lay person seeking a stewardship devotional, Betsy Schwarzentraub has a wealth of ideas. Ben Alford provides three sermons as part of the annual finance campaign.

Are there times when you wished for a short quote or paragraph for a bulletin or newsletter that would focus on giving? Using the common lectionary, Sharon Hueckel provides thoughts and ideas for church bulletins, newsletters, and devotional ideas to begin a meeting.

Teaching stewardship, awakening the giver to the joy and excitement of giving, is a wonderful and inviting time for all who lead the church.

 PLANNING TOOL

The Pastor's Role in Fund Development

JERALD JACKSON

The connection between the ministry of the church and the funds required for that ministry is a clear but subtle one. It is obvious that almost all the ministries of the church depend upon the availability of funds. Yet many otherwise dedicated persons do not make the connection between their giving patterns and the church's ministry.

I have heard many times that if the church provided the services, there would be no financial problems. People would give readily and without prompting. I did not find that true in my circumstances, nor did it seem to be true for my colleagues in churches that seemed to be doing everything "right."

I often find myself pondering the anomalies of the church. In the midst of several years of struggling to "make a budget" a church can suddenly launch and complete a highly successful Capital Funds Campaign, or can quite unexpectedly be confronted with a special need and oversubscribe the amount requested.

I recall one instance in my most recent appointment. Right before Christmas, the congregation had become restive over the issue of fund-raising. "This church asks for money too much," was a typical complaint. In this atmosphere, we received a letter from a member who had recently taken a mission post in another state. A member of the staff came to me and asked if there wasn't something we could do.

I said, "You know the mood of the church, but if you are willing to stand up and ask for it, I'll support you." In a matter of weeks, more than $10,000 had been given and a semitrailer load of goods donated. There was not a word of complaint. There was joy in giving.

> "I would suggest that you commit yourselves not to tithing but to proportionate giving, with tithing as an economic floor beneath which you will not go unless there are some compelling reasons."
> —REINHOLD NIEBUHR

I believe there are four areas in which the pastor must exercise leadership in fund development:

Preaching and Teaching

Christian preaching cannot avoid the implications of the faith for the pocketbook. Basic to fund development in the church is a vision of the significant mission to which the church has been called. That should be a part of every sermon, even as it shaped the entire ministry of Christ.

Luke tells us that Jesus began his ministry in Nazareth, articulating just such a vision:

> The Spirit of the Lord is upon me,
> because he has anointed me to preach good news to the poor.
> He has sent me to proclaim release to the captives
> and recovering of sight to the blind,
> to set at liberty those who are oppressed,
> to proclaim the acceptable year of the Lord.
> (Luke 4:18-19 RSV)

"When I started out to make my own living, my first year's salary was $410. I gave a tenth of that to the Lord. I have done it every year since. I do not care to argue with anybody about it, I just want to testify that it pays. It pays in peace of mind and conscience, and it pays financially. I have never known a person to tithe who did not feel it was a great blessing to his own life."

—CHARLES L. ALLEN

Through preaching, teaching, and other forms of communication, people need to be made aware of the concept of tithing and proportionate giving. It has been my experience that those who are not tithers are defeated by the message that we ought to tithe. One relatively successful stewardship campaign owed its measure of success by challenging individuals to grow toward tithing by increasing their giving by one percent of their annual income for the coming year.

Pastoral Administration

The pastor usually provides leadership in the administration of the church. In many cases, the pastor directly carries out that administration. Either directly or indirectly, that leadership should emphasize the importance of planning, process, and accountability.

Whether we like it or not (and my feelings admittedly are mixed), the modern church tries to emulate a democratic process in making decisions. The church must devise a realistic process in which all aspects of the mission and ministry of the church are considered. Part of the accountability lies in regular and accurate reporting to the congregation. It is only reasonable that once a church has made a decision concerning ministry goals, it should celebrate when those goals are reached.

The *New York Times* carried a story concerning developments at Riverside Church in New York. The gist of the story was that Riverside was in deep financial trouble. Not only was congregational giving low, the church had seen its once large endowment sliced in half by the stock market drop and spending beyond the reasonable limits of the investment.

William Sloane Coffin, pastor at Riverside for ten years, was quoted as saying, "The responsibility for the finances fell to the trustees and the business manager. None of us went to seminary to be a financier." Truer words were never spoken. But a seminary education does not preclude the ability to see when a church is spending itself out of business, or the responsibility to take decisive action when the problem is revealed.

"Pastoral Example—In congregations with effective stewardship, the pastors give leadership to the stewardship ministry in at least four ways:
1. The pastor's life sets an example.
2. The pastor's words set an example.
3. The pastor's stewardship education sets an example.
4. The pastor's biblical teachings on percentage giving and tithing set an example."

—EUGENE GRIMM
GENEROUS PEOPLE

Pastoral Care

If we believe that giving has something to do with spiritual well-being, then it is an appropriate matter for a pastor to consider.

Shortly after beginning my present appointment as director of a Conference Foundation, a colleague phoned, inviting me to visit an elderly widow with him. He had grown concerned that since the death of her husband, this parishioner might need some advice in financial planning.

Through the pastoral relationship of trust that this minister had developed, I was able to establish a basis for conversation. The result was a new investment approach that brought a higher current income for her and gave her a renewed confidence in her ability to "take care of things," now that her husband was gone.

As her sense of confidence returned, she discovered that she was able to make a significant gift to the church in memory of her husband. Both the new assurance and the joy in making the gift were fruits of good pastoral care and the willingness of the pastor to turn to others for assistance.

Pastoral Fund Leadership

The pastor's involvement in direct solicitation for funds is a difficult issue. Whether the church is seeking to raise funds for yearly operations, for a special mission project, or a Capital Funds Campaign, one cannot avoid the crucial decision about who does the asking.

The pastor has an important role to play in this aspect, which is a truth that I learned very late in life. The need of the individual to give and the need of the church to be funded come together at this point. If we believe enough in the ministry and mission of the church, we must be ready to admit that the pastor is directly involved in funding the church.

PLANNING TOOL

Using the Worship Service for Stewardship Education

W A Y N E   B A R R E T T

The weekly worship service offers an unusual opportunity for stewardship education. The worship experience is the largest single "energy event" in the congregation's life. More that its mere size, however, the worship hour offers education within the *context* of the faith. When properly presented, stewardship education takes on new vitality, credibility, and efficacy within the worship experience.

Teachable Moments in the Regular Worship Service

The Worship Bulletin: For mere regularity of opportunity, few media offer as many possibilities as the bulletin. Whether within the bulletin itself or through inserts, you will be able to communicate with your prime target audience—those about to make an offering.

Litanies/Calls to Worship/Prayers: When words such as "stewardship," "giftedness," and "commitment" are heard with regularity in the worship experience, they no longer are perceived as code words, meant to manipulate increased giving. They gain increased validity when used with theological and liturgical integrity.

Announcements/Testimonies/Thank Yous: Strive for regular "feedback" showing the connection between what is given and what occurs as a result.

Scripture Reading: The Bible contains a wealth of stewardship themes. Both Old and New Testament readings can be used to create a context for stewardship awareness.

Hymns/Anthems: In addition to offertory hymns and hymns of commitment, never underestimate the power of music to undergird the atmosphere of the worship experience.

Preaching: Beyond the pure proclamation, the homiletical event is a splendid opportunity for regular stewardship education. One is struck by how much of Jesus' preaching and teaching focused upon money and possessions. Surely, our preaching warrants similar focus.

Illustrations: Perhaps more important than a complete sermon on a stewardship text, regular use of stewardship illustrative material can add spice and validity to the regular diet of sermonic material. The hearers often get the point of stewardship messages when their "guard is down," a time when there is no obvious relationship between the message and the commitment campaign. Strive toward at least one stewardship illustration in a sermon each month. The daily newspaper is a wealth of material regarding corporate, environmental, and financial stewardship themes.

Sermon: Before attempting to preach a stewardship sermon, pause and reflect on at least two issues: (1) What do we *believe* about stewardship in this commu-

> ## "Donors don't give to institutions. They invest in ideas and people in whom they believe."
> *—G. T. SMITH*

nity?; and (2) How can we proclaim a "gospel of good giving"?

As we evaluate the many failed attempts at stewardship preaching, we are struck by how many of those failures can be attributed to these two issues. Preachers who are unsure of what they really believe about any subject can scarcely be expected to proclaim it with much power or persuasiveness. Similarly, the scolding stewardship message which comes across as judgmental will lack the power to motivate.

Build your preaching around integrity of belief and uplifting invitation, and you will be ready to deliver powerful stewardship messages.

The Offering: As the offering is received, check to be certain that you have introduced it as an "offering," rather than a "collection"—not as an interruption of the service, but as a significant moment in the act of worship.

Prayer of Dedication: Any offering worth receiving is also worth dedicating to God. Whether the prayer is spoken by the pastor, the liturgist, or the congregation, make certain that these words enhance the stewardship experience. Hilbert Berger tells how a prayer can, all by itself, deliver a powerful stewardship message. Berger tells of a pastor who prayed, "In spite of what we say and do, this is what we think of you. Amen."

Benediction: As the congregation is sent out into the world, why not a parting word to encourage stewardship throughout the week?

Using Special Occasions

Special occasions are splendid times to underscore the importance of stewardship. What you do (or don't do) can make a powerful statement. Look for ways to incorporate stewardship themes on special days, such as:

- Commitment Sunday
- Memorial Day/All Saints
- Thanksgiving
- Christmas
- Any special offerings

The worship hour is a splendid time for stewardship education. It is targeted at the ideal audience—your most faithful members. Moreover, its immediacy makes it, in marketing terms, the equivalent of a "point of purchase" display. Use the teachable moments of your worship service with creativity and theological integrity, and you will begin to see results almost immediately.

"A collection plate bears a certain resemblance to the outstretched hand of Christ. The prohibition of taking 'the name of the Lord thy God in vain' also has a fascinating history. There is reason to suppose that originally it meant, 'Thou shalt not call on the Lord when thou art empty-handed'; or, as we would say, there should be no church service without the taking of a collection."

—*GEORGE HEDLEY*

 BULLETIN

Worship Resources

Season After Pentecost

Gen. 18:1-15 (21:7); Ps. 116:1-2, 12-19; Rom. 5:1-8; Matt. 9:35–10:8 (9-23)

CALL TO WORSHIP

Leader: Praise God who hears your prayer and your supplications.

People: God has richly blessed me.

Leader: What shall I return to the Lord for all his bounty to me?

People: I will pay my vow to the Lord in the presence of all God's people.

Leader: I will lift up the cup of salvation.

People: I will call on the name of the Lord.

All: Let us worship God.

PRAYER OF CONFESSION

God of Abraham and Sarah, you call us to your ministry of reconciliation and renewal. We confess that we often seek to enlist you in our causes, rather than submit to yours. You direct us to minister without consideration of reward, yet we give measured portions; we try to determine how our "investments" in your work will create "returns" for us. Forgive our selfishness. Teach us that the act of freely giving is itself a proclamation of the good news of your kingdom. Amen.

PRAYER OF INTERCESSION

God of our salvation and hope, we thank you for the peace you bestow through our Lord Jesus Christ. You have poured your power into our hearts through your gift of the Holy Spirit, bringing confidence to every corner of our lives.

Teach us to proclaim the wonder and power of these gifts. When we encounter those who are sick or in pain, may we boldly touch their wounds with the compassion you provide. Fine-tune our perception, that we might recognize prejudice and oppression, and proclaim your justice with boldness. When the stench of devastation and destruction rises up, make us your voice of reconciliation and rebuilding.

Enable us to see the hurts of our neighbors, but also the hurts and pain of the world. Challenge us to recognize that some of the abundance you have given us can and should be shared with the rest of your people. In so doing, help us to bring honor to your name. Amen.

PRAYER OF DEDICATION

Almighty God, you call us into service and equip us with strength and talent equal to our tasks. We bring to you now the results of our labors. Use these funds and our pledges of time and talent to continue your ministry in this world. Amen.

BENEDICTION

Keep alert, stand firm in your faith, be courageous, be strong. Let all that you do be done in love. Amen. (I Cor. 16:13-14)

SUGGESTED HYMNS

O Thou, My Soul, Return in Peace
We Give Thee But Thine Own
When We Are Living

> ## "If we do not do the work we were meant to do, it will forever remain undone."
> *—ANNA LINDSAY*

Third Sunday of Easter

Acts 2:14*a*, 36-41; Ps. 116:1-4, 12-19; I Peter 1:17-32;
Luke 24:13-35

CALL TO WORSHIP

Leader: We are here because we have heard the call to be God's people.

People: We are here seeking guidance about how to be God's stewards.

Leader: We come seeking to be challenged by the Holy Spirit.

People: We come celebrating Christ's presence in our midst.

Leader: Let us come with open hearts, promising to follow Christ.

People: Let us worship God.

PRAYER OF CONFESSION

Gracious God, you continue to pour out the Holy Spirit upon all humanity, but too often, we hold back the Spirit with our sinful ways. We are a selfish and self-indulgent people. You call us to minister to the needs of our brothers and sisters, yet we point our fingers at one another and gossip. We are timid disciples who walk past your children, blinding ourselves to hunger and homelessness. O God, although we are unworthy of your love and care, guide us in the acceptance of opportunities for joyful service. Amen.

PRAYER OF THANKSGIVING

God of salvation and love, we thank you for the gift of your son, Jesus Christ. Through Christ, you pour blessings into our lives, and through Christ, you grant us a glimpse of your eternal kingdom.

We thank you that we are among your children who have been called to walk in your light. All that we have is from you. All of our potential is born of your love. All of our achievements are credits to your graciousness.

We thank you for the joy of participation in your service. Your concern for all people teaches us much about our neighbors and ourselves. Use our hands, we pray, to reach out to your children in our community and in all the world.

We are grateful, Lord, for the counsel of your Holy Spirit. Open our eyes to the hurts of the world and direct our hands to touch those wounds with compassion. Open our ears to hear the cries of the oppressed, and empower us to give them justice and freedom. Lift our voices to proclaim your love and your will.

Teach us, O God, to share our stories as we travel your pathway. Although discipleship can be risky and obedience costly, in your strength we shall prevail. May we look to your Spirit's guidance as we continue our journey, singing songs of alleluias, remaining steadfast in your love, and proclaiming the vision of the day when Christ shall return again. Amen.

PRAYER OF DEDICATION

Eternal God, in the rich diversity of our many voices, we praise you. With the full diversity of our talents, we serve you. Take our differing gifts and mold them into a vessel to carry your love into all the world. May our service advance your ministry as we proclaim your truth, which sets men and women free. Amen.

BENEDICTION

May the God of hope fill you with all joy and peace in believing, so that you may abound in hope by the power of the Holy Spirit. Amen. (Rom. 15:13)

SUGGESTED HYMNS

Come, Ye Thankful People, Come
We Are Your People
What Shall I Render to the Lord?

 BULLETIN

Calls to Worship/Prayers

Leader: And God created the heavens and the earth.

People: And gave them to us to use and enjoy.

Leader: And God breathed life into each of us, and set us upon the earth.

People: And God sent Jesus Christ to save us from the pull of death.

Leader: Everything that fills our souls with gladness and light is a gift from the loving Creator.

People: We have been entrusted with unfathomable riches.

All: For all of this, God is to be praised.

ADAPTED FROM PSALM 146:

Leader: Praise God!

People: Praise God, O my soul!

Leader: Put not your trust in princes, in whom there is no help.

People: Happy are those whose help is the God of Jacob and Rebekah,

Leader: Whose hope is in God who made heaven and earth.

People: Who keeps faith forever;

Leader: Who executes justice for the oppressed;

People: Who gives food to the hungry.

Leader: The Lord will reign for ever.

People: Praise God!

ADAPTED FROM PSALM 41:

Leader: Blessed are those who consider the poor!

People: The Lord delivers them in the day of trouble.

Leader: The Lord sustains them on their sickbed.

People: They are called blessed in the Lord.

ADAPTED FROM PSALM 49:

Leader: Hear this, all peoples!

People: Give ear, all inhabitants of the world!

Leader: Why should we fear in times of trouble?

People: Not one of us can ransom our life,

Leader: Yet God will pay the price for us.

People: God will ransom our soul from the power of darkness.

ADAPTED FROM PSALM 95:

Leader: Let us come into God's presence with thanksgiving.

People: Let us make a joyful noise with songs of praise.

Leader: For our God is a great God,

People: In whose hands are the depths of the earth and the heights of the mountains.

Leader: O come, let us worship and bow down,

People: Let us kneel before our Maker.

CONFESSIONS

O most gracious God, we confess that we spend much of our lives on that which does not satisfy. We do not always count our time and resources as precious gifts, but squander them in meaningless activities and seemingly urgent needs. Look kindly upon us, for the temptation to waste is overwhelming in our world. Enable us to understand what is important, and to use the gifts of life responsibly, for we want to be your people in word and in deed. Amen.

Eternal God, creator of the whole human family, you set us in a world richly endowed with material and spiritual wealth. Forgive us for wasting your treasures and always wanting more than we have. Have mercy upon us, who never share as fully as you give. Heal our deafness to your call in our neighbors' cry for help. By a clear vision of the community you intend for humankind, stir up in us the will to use money and skill for the advance of your realm of mercy, love, and peace, through Jesus Christ we pray. Amen.

OFFERTORY PRAYERS

Pastor: The Creator of all life and love has endowed our earth with bountiful blessings.

People: God has created humanity to share in the wonder and joy of these blessings.

Pastor: All thanks be to God, giver and receiver of all that is good.

People: We return to God portions of what God has given us: our time, the fruits of our labors, our commitment.

Pastor: May the giving from the fullness of our lives be acceptable in God's sight.

People: May the gifts we bring prove that God's rule is at hand—both now and to come.

Pastor: God calls us to participate in the construction of a new reality. We now dedicate these, our offerings, toward the enrichment of our life as a covenant community, and toward the ministry God has given us.

People: We dedicate our labors, our time and our commitment to God, who calls us into discipleship, who surrounds us and sustains us with everlasting love.

All: Praise God, from whom all blessings flow.

* * * *

O Giver of life, behind this offering lies the busy world of our labor: the office, the production line, the home, the classroom, the laboratory. Save us from creating a world where wealth accumulates and people decay. Accept this offering and our lives, limited as they may be, as willing instruments for good in your world. Amen.

* * * *

We give in response to love, and gifts, and blessings given. May our offerings today reflect God's generosity. Amen.

* * * *

OFFERTORY HUMOR

"I would like to remind you that what you are about to give is deductible, cannot be taken with you, and is considered by some to be the root of all evil."

* * * *

As Christ has transformed our lives, may these gifts be transformed into the hands, mind, heart, and will of God in our midst. We pray in the spirit of Jesus Christ. Amen.

* * * *

Dear God, you have taught us the miracle of paradox—
    that in dying, we live,
    that in despairing, we hope,
    and that in giving, we receive.
    Bless these offerings that give us so much.
    In Jesus' name, we pray. Amen.

INVOCATIONS

Adapted from Psalm 146:2
Praise the Lord, O my soul!
We will praise God as long as we live;
We will sing praises to God while we have being. Amen.

We give thanks for your steadfast love, O God.
For your wonderful works, we offer thanksgiving.
We call upon the Lord—our hope in times of trouble,
our delight in all our days. Amen.

A Call to Worship

L. G. D. WERTZ

I call you now to look above,
To Him who shows such gracious love.
It is our God who reigns on high,
Who clears our minds, relieves the sigh.
I call you now to look within,
Where life is often filled with sin
Of lust, and jealousy, and greed.
There's something greater that we need.
I call you now to look around
At all the beauty on the ground—
There's human life and harvest grain.
Still, some will starve while others gain.
I call you now to worship God,
And give Him thanks upon this sod,
And praise Him for his gifts so rare,
As gratefully, with Him we share.

A Congregational Prayer

BETSY SCHWARZENTRAUB

Our God and Father, we thank you that we have been daily recipients of your great bounty. We do not ask you to increase our blessings, but to make us worthy of the least of your gifts. Enable us to rejoice in the privilege of honoring you with our substance and the first fruits of all our increase. Keep us from wasting your blessings in the pursuit of worldly pleasures. Give us wisdom to heed your injunction not to lay up treasure on earth, but to set aside a heavenly price that nothing can destroy.

Help us make our financial resources serve the causes of Christ, so that the mission and ministry of his glorious Church can be strengthened and fulfilled through our giving.

41

Offertory Prayers

MARK L. SCHUTT

How do you know we love you, Lord? Perhaps you hear us say it. Perhaps you surmise it through our occasional acts of kindness. How do you know we love you? You know when we give ourselves to you—our gifts, our talents, our minds, our hearts. To you, we give ourselves this morning. Amen.

＊＊＊＊

Dear Lord, you created us in your image, forming us in love. When our love fails, you remain steadfast. With gratitude for your enduring love and grace, we offer our gifts to you. We give ourselves and our love to you. Through Christ we pray. Amen.

＊＊＊＊

We do not know what real sacrifice is, dear Lord. Yet you invite us to be sacrificial givers. Teach us what it means to trust you with what we have, as well as with who we are. Freely open our hearts, to give more freely to you. In Jesus' name we pray. Amen.

＊＊＊＊

Lord of forgiveness and mercy, please accept the gifts we bring this morning. What we bring is yours, a thankful response for all you have given us. Please share our gifts and use them to bring all your children back home. Encourage us to continue to share cheerfully and generously. Amen.

 PLANNING TOOL

The Offering: A Story and Symbol of Life

DONALD W. JOINER AND NORMA WIMBERLY

The offering, in the context of the worshiping community, is the bridge between Word and Table, a response to God's Word. It is a symbol of the relationships of our lives—with God, with others, and with ourselves. The offertory experience can provide a powerful way to integrate the whole life of the community. How do our offerings reflect our lives? Is it possible that the offertory can serve as a time for rediscovering a personal relationship with God?

Begin to think about some of the recent worship services in which you have participated. Describe the offertory time in what you consider a typical service. Include everything you can remember in the description: the invitation, ushers, music, gathering, presentation, scripture, prayer—even the way the offertory is announced in the service bulletin. What messages are conveyed? Is the offertory symbolic of our lives and relationships, or is it an apologetic intermission?

Our offering is a response. Abraham, because of the nature of his relationship to God, obeyed the call to consider Isaac as a sacrifice (Gen. 22:1-18). A brief perusal of the scriptures reveals a rich and fulfilling variety of faithful responses:

Deuteronomy 26:8-11 defines offering as first fruits.
First Chronicles 29:10-20 recounts David's prayer for the offerings of the people for building the Temple.

Psalm 116:12-19 urges us to ask, "What shall I offer the LORD?"
Romans 12:1-2 reminds us of the transformation of living sacrifice.
Romans 15:1-2 urges sharing among the total community of faith.

The nature and substance of our response leads us to prayerfully examine our attitudes of offering. From Amos to Mark to Paul, we are reminded that love of God, love of ourselves and our neighbors, and a desire for justice and righteousness must be reflected in our lives.

How can we celebrate the offertory? What changes would be called for to make "a joyful noise" a reality in our congregations? Accept the invitation to plan and participate in the offering, which is the story and symbol of our lives as faithful stewards, beloved children of God!

The offering is a worship experience by itself! It is an opportunity for God's people to respond to their understanding of what God has done for them in Jesus Christ, and in every day of life.

An Outline

● The Introduction
A statement by the pastor or worship leader to signal the congregation

Scripture passage(s) as a call to celebrate the offering

- The Story

How funds given are touching the lives of individuals and churches in the name of Jesus Christ (This may be a brief personal witness by a member, a guest, a missionary, or the pastor. What happens when people give?)

- The Invitation

A prayer may be used.

- The Gathering

The response of God's people to the Word (of God), and the word (of the people) when the offering is taken

- The Blessing

Include a doxology, a prayer of dedication, a hymn, or a shared litany.

An Offertory Design

THE INTRODUCTION

A part of our preparation for worship is our preparedness for giving. Listen to these words: "All shall give as they are able, according to the blessing of the LORD your God that he has given you" (Deut. 16:17).

"I appeal to you therefore, brothers and sisters, by the mercies of God, to present your bodies as a living sacrifice, holy and acceptable to God, which is your spiritual worship" (Rom. 12:1).

The Story

Mary Susan is struggling with a call to ministry. If she determines that God is calling her into ordained ministry, she will start the route of a candidate. Her church and her district committee will meet with her. They will prayerfully determine whether she has the gifts and graces for ministry. Next year, she might qualify for one of the scholarships for pretheology studies. A part of our offering provides the funds for these scholarships. As you give today, remember that a portion of these funds will help Mary Susan and others as they prepare for ministry in our churches.

The Invitation

Dear Lord, it is a mystery that you have decided to work through persons like us. But we believe that you do and that you empower us to be helpers. May every act of generosity in this offering be blessed by your strong, guiding Spirit. Amen.

THE GATHERING
THE BLESSING
DOXOLOGY

An Offertory Prayer (optional):

O God, you loved the world so much that you gave your only begotten Son, that whoever believes in him will not perish but have everlasting life. Receive and bless our offerings, and let them be an appropriate celebration of your great gifts to us. Amen.

SUGGESTED OFFERTORY SCRIPTURES

For the Church: I Peter 4:10-11
Romans 12:4-8
I Corinthians 12:12-28
Ephesians 4:4-6

For the Gifts of Empowerment:
Isaiah 11:2
Galatians 5:22-23
I Corinthians 12:1-13
Ephesians 4:11-16
II Timothy 1:3-14
I Corinthians 1:1-9
Romans 12:6-8
I Corinthians 13:1-13

For the Ministry of the Church:
I Corinthians 3:21-22; 4:1-2
I Peter 1:1-10
I Peter 2:1-10
Romans 12:1-5; II Corinthians 6:3-10
II Corinthians 5:16-19

Our Offering

L. G. D. WERTZ

Accept today the gifts we bring
To honor You, O King of kings,
And as they come from earthly store,
May they reach out to do still more.
In showing love, your gift divine,
Make us aware that we are thine.

So as we share from bounties' store,
May life be more that passing lore.
You are the Lord of all of life
'mid joys supreme and changing strife.
With thanks to You, our gifts we bring,
With love, and joy, and thanks we sing.
Amen.

 SERMON HELP

Worship Time with Children

EUGENIA B. GAMBLE

Time with Children

As the children gather, greet them and hold up an apple. Ask them what it is, where it comes from, and what we do with it. Let them respond. They probably will focus on ways to eat it. One may come up with planting the seeds to grow more apples. If not, suggest that possibility. Say that apples are a lot like money. We don't make pies from money, but if we eat all the apples and don't plant any seeds, we will soon run out of apples.

If we spend all our money on things we want for ourselves and don't invest in things we care about, we will soon be out of money, and the things we care about will be neglected. Ask the children what things, other than things for themselves, would they like to invest their money in? Let them answer. If no one suggests it, talk about feeding hungry people, supporting the church and its mission. Tell the story of the widow and how she invested in what was important to her.

Children's Prayer:

Dear God, help us to invest in what is important to you. Amen.

Time with Children

Provide a large jar filled with cooking oil and water. Be sure the lid is tightly closed. As the children gather, show them the jar and ask if they know what is in the jar. Tell them the jar is filled with oil and water and let them watch what happens when you shake the jar. It all goes together, doesn't it? But look at it again after just a few seconds, and the oil and water are sep-arate again. Why is that? We know that some things in this world just don't mix. Oil and water will never go together. Truth and lies will never go together. And selfishness and the reign of God will never go together.

Tell the story of Jesus and the young man who could not give up his possessions to be with Jesus. We can be grateful for this story, because it teaches us that we can make a choice that is different from the one the young man made. Give each child a coin and ask them, sometime during the next week, to give it to someone or something they believe needs it.

Children's Prayer:

Dear God, help us to follow you. Amen.

Time with Children

Fill a large fruit jar with small change. Ask the children to look at the jar and think of all the things they might buy with that money. Invite a child to reach into the jar and grab as much money as possible. (Since the size of children's hands vary, prior to worship, you will need to enlist the help of a particular child, so that you can practice.)

When the child grabs the money, the hand will get stuck in the jar. The children will see immediately that the only way to get the hand out of the jar is to let go of the money. The only way to get the money out of the jar is to pour it out. Talk with them about what it means to let go and pour out.

Children's Prayer:

Dear God, help me to give all for you. Amen.

 SERMON HELP

Stewardship Sermon Starters

BETTY SCHWARZENTRAUB

Stewardship themes sparkle like gems throughout the scriptures. If you follow the common lectionary texts, you'll find many opportunities to preach from a stewardship perspective. Here are some textual treasures to mine each quarter of the year:

FIRST QUARTER

March—Third Sunday in Lent   Exodus 17:1-7

Journeying by Stages

The early Hebrews "moved by stages" as they traveled together through the wilderness. What they experienced physically on the arid terrain, we also know psychologically in the local church. For the whole congregation to move together, often the progress is slow, as we change our attitudes and actions one step at a time.

Inevitably, there is rebellion. "We're thirsty," the Israelites cried, as they accused Moses of bringing them out of Egypt only to die. So too, in the local church. Members who think they know exactly where God wants the church to be are annoyed by having to wait for others to catch up. Other members, who are slow to move, aren't sure why they left Egypt in the first place, and imagine ever-sweeter moments in the "good old days" that never were.

Effective church leaders are good stewards of relationships within the community of faith. They listen to the people as Moses did, and bring those complaints and conflicts fully to God. They listen for God's response, and then risk acting upon it, even when their behavior seems crazy to people around them.

Moses took some of the leaders with him to witness as he struck the desert rock and the water gushed forth. As effective stewards of relationships within the church, we work with the "elders"—teams of church leaders—to bring the people out, moving by stages toward the new land on our horizon.

SECOND QUARTER

April—Fifth Sunday in Lent   John 11:1-45

A Community of Stewards

When Jesus came to Lazarus' home, Lazarus had been dead for four days. The entire community had gathered around his tearful sisters, Mary and Martha, to share their grief.

But Jesus came to raise Lazarus from the dead, not to mourn him. Thanks to this astonishing act of resurrection, Christ has destroyed the finality of death over any human being.

Yet Jesus chose to involve the community in bringing Lazarus to new life. He called upon Lazarus' neighbors to risk rolling away the stone from his tomb, expecting new life, despite the rank reality of the grave. When Lazarus emerged like the walking dead, wrapped in bandages from head to toe, Jesus told this same community of mourners, "Unbind him and let him go!"

We know from our own experience that God gives us a literal new life through Christ. But it is up to the community of faith to roll away the stone that would seal us off from abundant living and keep us in our old, deathly ways. And it is this same community that Christ calls to unwrap our bandages—all the hindrances of our old ways of loving—so that we are free to begin anew, one day, one moment at a time.

Members of the local church are called to be a community of stewards. Stewards are those entrusted to carry out the work of the One who is truly in charge. There is no greater work for a community of faith than to unwrap the bandages, so that people can walk in the new life that Christ offers them.

THIRD QUARTER

August—Ninth Sunday   Matthew 14:13-21
After Pentecost

Living Out of Abundance

Do we respond primarily out of a sense of scarcity, or of abundance? People who lived through the 1930s Depression remember what it was like to have next to nothing, and they may have a hard time recognizing the material resources they have now. Yet other people

45

live in an economic "underclass" that is all too current today.

The attitude of many of us can determine far more than we think. Facing thousands of people at the close of day, Jesus' disciples asked him to send them away, fearing they would turn into a hungry, blaming mob. Jesus' perspective was different. He turned back to the disciples and asked, "What do you have to work with?"

Five little barley loaves and two fish! That's often how it feels when we look among our own church leadership and face the seemingly infinite needs of the people we seek to serve in our congregation and community.

Yet the key is not what we have, but what we do with what we have—and that's stewardship. We may not have millionaires ready to give all to God through the church. But we might be rich in resourceful people with needed abilities and perspectives, a passion for certain issues, or community contacts that can help make good things happen.

Jesus didn't feed the crowd directly. He chose to work through his leadership, as a good steward of personal resources. We can do the same, beginning with the abundance we have, and letting Christ bless and break it open to satisfy all.

FOURTH QUARTER

December—First Sunday   Isaiah 63:16–64:8
in Advent

The Potter? or the Pot?

If it weren't for God's grace, we would have plenty of cause for despair. In this text, the prophet puts words to the people's desperation. They realize that they've been completely off track and haven't listened for divine guidance. In their agony, they blame God for their own hardened hearts, even asserting that God should have coerced them into being faithful!

Yet in the midst of this gut-level honesty, Isaiah affirms, "We are the clay, and you are our potter; we are all the work of your hand"!

Jeremiah 18:11-11 also uses this image to assert God's rights as Artist and our need for total reformation. Paul adds humor to the same metaphor in Romans 9:20-21, when he imagines us like a pot that accuses the potter of not making it the right shape!

This image of our relationship with God is a stewardship issue, for at least three reasons:

- First, it forces us to answer the question, "As between God and ourselves, which is the Potter, and which is the pot?" Stewardship is knowing that we are not the Creator, and then deciding to live on behalf of the One who is.

- Second, a potter is absolutely free to decide how to design the various pots for different uses. Likewise, God has fashioned a personal call to ministry for each of us. As stewards, we are to live according to this design.

- Third, like pliable clay, we are continually being reshaped by God. God continually offers to forgive and recreate us according to God's purposes, in the changing circumstances brought about by humanity's free will.

- Fourth, God has shaped us to hold the treasure of the gospel and pour it out by the way we live. Whether we see ourselves as fancy vases or earthenware jars, God has entrusted each of us with the authentic Good News of God's love, to receive and to share by God's sheer grace.

> "Halford Luccock recalls an outline of a sermon by Dr. A. H. Boyd of England. The speaker spoke of the rich fool and his three mistakes: He mistook his body for his soul; he mistook man for God; and he mistook time for eternity."
>
> *THE CHRISTIAN ADVOCATE*

A Call to Prayer and Spiritual Growth

BEN R. ALFORD

Scripture: Philippians 3:8-14

Note: In preparation for the fall financial campaign, members of the Steering Committee, First United Methodist Church, Hendersonville, Tennessee, decided to use the approach of emphasizing stewardship, instead of concentrating solely on pledges, dollars, and percentages. They discussed the meaning of Christian stewardship and asked the pastor to devote three sermons to the theme. Bookmarks bearing selected scripture texts were printed in the Sunday worship bulletins and distributed to each worshiper.

Do you know what you want? I mean, do you know what you want most of all? Think about it. Is there something you'd really sacrifice for? I ask this because until we know what we want most of all, it is very hard to get our lives together, hard to get any kind of plan. Life goes in circles, instead of progressing toward a goal. Most of us want many things, but what is it we want most of all?

We are very fortunate in the West. We have unlimited possibilities. We even call our country the "land of opportunity." "What do you want to be when you grow up?" we ask our children, hoping they will aim high. If one of them says, "I want to be President of the United States," we smile and respond, "Fine! It's good to have ambition. *It's nice work if you can get it, and you can get it if you try.*"

Almost anything is possible in this cornucopia of opportunity—especially for those in the majority, those who have their health and are fortunate enough to live in this place at this time. In fact, there are so many opportunities available today that the very act of choosing is getting to be a problem. I read that young adults don't know which thing from life's menu to choose. As our culture has progressively embraced individualism and secularism, young people find it harder and harder to make choices. Oh, the little ones aren't much of a problem, but the big ones have a way of following us to bed at night. Making decisions—choosing between available options—isn't easy when human lives are going to be affected by the choice!

Recently when two couples arrived at their vacation beach resort, one of the foursome said, "O.K., I'm on vacation as of this moment. I do not plan to make a single decision this entire week. It seems that is all I do at home. So whatever the three of you decide is fine with me. I am in a seven-day neutral zone."

We have developed a multiple-choice society, and many are suffering from choice burnout. Our own freedom has a way of trapping us. We don't like to choose, because we are fearful of the very thing we thought we wanted: lots of choices. Several things have contributed to our dilemma.

One is that we've made the mistake of thinking that all options are equally important. It's hard to choose when everything is of the same value. It's downright paralyzing.

Another reason we can't choose well is that we haven't taken the pains to remember who we are and where we come from. In our rush to follow the latest fad, to seek out the manifest destiny of modernity and embrace the future, we have cut ourselves off from our history and our heritage. Sensing that loss, many people are showing interest these days in discovering their roots.

As they make attempts to dig into genealogy, they are often frustrated by a lack of information about those within the first generations of their immigrant ancestors. Many of those immigrants, tired and suspicious of hereditary social structures, held contempt for such connections. They oriented themselves toward the future with reckless abandon, resulting in a subsequent loss of something valuable. When we lose contact with our past, we lose the traditions and value systems accumulated over thousands of years which serve to sustain people and help them make decisions.

The most significant reason so many people have difficulty making good and wise choices is that they have outgrown God. They don't believe that God is "dead," as one theologian announced a few years ago. Not many people would go quite that far. It is more as if God has been retired. God grew old and tired and wasn't really needed in the functions our parents and grandparents were used to, so, like all aging executives, God was put on a pension and given an honorary but harmless title. "Heavenly Father" connotes a comfortable distance. "The Man Upstairs" doesn't convey much of a personal relationship either—something like "God Emeritus." God just isn't needed very much any more. Most of God's work has been assigned to someone else: doctors and nurses, preachers and counselors and therapists. We do get a good feeling when we drive by one of the branch offices and think that God might be there, or at the heavenly house or somewhere. But God isn't consulted personally on many decisions these days. God has been outgrown.

> "Churches cannot wait until people grow spiritually so they will give; some people cannot grow spiritually until they decide to give. And asking people to improve their treasure management is asking them to grow spiritually—the two matters cannot be separated. When we look at principles for vital stewardship, we are looking at principles that can help people grow spiritually."
>
> EUGENE GRIMM
> *GENEROUS PEOPLE*

Of course, along with the "decline of God" comes a growing conviction that human sinfulness is some kind of ancient, outmoded, simplistic myth. Despite abundant evidence to the contrary, more and more people have come to believe that our flaws are only temporary shortcomings, and our downfalls are still salvageable through the use of bootstraps or a simple attitude adjustment.

Remember the attitude of the small boy who said to his father, "Hey Dad, watch!" as he threw a ball into the air? He swung his bat fiercely, and missed.

"Wait, Dad," he said, "Watch this one!" And for the second time, he swung and missed.

"Here's the one, Dad!" he shouted, but the third result was the same.

Then he yelled, "Three strikes and out. Gee, Dad, aren't I a great pitcher?" (*Homiletics,* Oct.–Dec. 1992, p. 13)

The old shell game is a parable for our day. Put a spin on the facts. Cloak the truth. There's nothing seriously wrong here. Give us a little time, some more self-help courses, and we'll have it made. Instead of a cross, give us a sweet-smelling, colognelike religion to mask the scent of our dead spirits, so that no trace of odor or decay can be detected.

The New Age proponents tell us that all we need to do is believe in ourselves. In other words, you don't have a god *in* you, you *are* one. Of course, that leads to another conclusion. If there is no place for the Old God, the God of Abraham, Isaac, and Jacob; if the God of Amos, Isaiah, and Jeremiah has been retired; if there is no need for the God of Luther, Calvin, and Wesley, then there is no need for salvation. Consequently, Jesus *did* die in vain. Maybe we ought to replace all these old-fashioned crosses in our churches with something more modern, like the peace sign of the 1960s, or a "smiley face."

Of course, a great number of us have faced the dark consequences of our sin, have seen the sickening outcome of systemic evil, and have looked long enough in the face of death that we can no longer trivialize any of those results. The four horsemen of the Apocalypse have thundered past our house. We, who would like perfume and a smiley-face religion, know that it just won't do. We know that nothing on this earth is powerful enough to break our chains. Only a power outside ourselves has the strength to bind the evil one, only a force that comes from beyond.

That is what the Apostle Paul discovered. He had first sensed an unusual strength in people like Stephen and other martyrs he had helped to kill—a force that made people bold and forgiving, even in the face of death. He knew he had been in the presence of a superhuman power. Then, on the road to Damascus, he was struck down in very mysterious circumstances and blinded by a searing white-hot light. He heard a strange but familiar voice calling his name. The old Paul died that day, and a new one was born. He found within himself a new life that was not his own. He discovered new convictions, a new purpose and direction, all centered in Jesus Christ. He became convinced that Jesus really had risen from the dead and was gloriously alive again. From that day onward, Paul walked in newness of life. He even changed his name from Saul to Paul.

It was the new Paul who wrote the words of our text to the Philippian congregation he had founded on his first trip into Europe:

> Indeed I count everything as loss because of the surpassing worth of knowing Christ Jesus my Lord. For his sake I have suffered the loss of all things, and count them as refuse, in order that I may gain Christ and be found in him . . . that I may know him and the power of his resurrection . . . . Not that I have already obtained this or am already perfect; but I press on to make it my own, because Christ Jesus has made me his own. . . . But one thing I do, forgetting what lies behind and straining forward to what lies ahead, I press on toward the goal for the prize of the upward call of God in Christ Jesus.
>
> Philippians 3:8-9*a,* 10*a,* 12, 13*b*-14 RSV

In the Bible, a steward was one who controlled and directed the affairs of a household or establishment. The steward had the responsibility for supervising others, controlling finances, making necessary decisions, and reporting regularly to the owner or lord. It was an important and responsible position. In the New Testament, bishops are expected to be stewards of the things of God (Titus 1:7). Every Christian believer is understood to be a

> "No one has ever risen to the real stature of spiritual maturity until they have found it finer to serve someone else than to serve themselves."

steward "of the mysteries of God" (I Cor. 4:1 RSV).

In the Bible, it is clear that stewardship is not limited merely to money or material goods. It involves everything God provides: ability, talent, time, emotions, even life itself. The Bible tells us that the earth is the Lord's, that God has placed you and me on the earth as stewards, to "till it and keep it" (Genesis 2:15 RSV). This means that our job is not only broad in scope, it is global. We are the guardians and custodians of the earth, and we will have to give an accounting of our stewardship.

Consider today your relationship to the Lord. How is it with you and God? Is your spiritual pilgrimage satisfying and meaningful? Are you growing spiritually? If not, what is the problem? Is there a roadblock that needs to be cleared away so your journey with God can continue? Do you need help? Have you sought help? Are you on speaking terms with God? Have you set a regular time for prayer? Do you keep it? And study? How often do you read your Bible? If it's hard for you to study the Bible alone, there are many aids. Enroll in one of our Bible courses—we have several.

Our stewardship committee believes that when we get our relationship with God in tip-top shape, financial campaigns will become as extinct as the dinosaur. They will cease to exist because we won't need them anymore. Ask yourself, "What do I really want?" Is it time you had a little "newness" in your life?

Paul had a checkered past. He had vigorously persecuted members of the new church of Jesus. He was prejudiced, closed-minded, and had even given his consent to murder. He could easily have been enslaved by guilt. But he turned his past over to the only One who could fix it—God. No doubt he also was paralyzed by fear of the future and didn't know which way to turn. So he let go of the future and gave it to God. He found that Christ had forgiven him and was giving him a new power with which to live in the present and the future. Only God can do that.

Then we can be like Paul. We have the three essentials of a happy life: we can *forget*; we can *reach forth*; and we can *press on*. Can you do that? Can you forget? Is there some hurt or wrong that you cannot let go? Is something holding you in place and controlling you? Can you reach forth? Or are you a grasper? Reaching forth involves reaching out as well. Can you do that? Can you press on? Can you move ahead and embrace the new? Are you willing to risk because of the confidence you have in the One who holds you

and holds the future?

In short, do you trust God? Staying spiritually fit will help you to live one day at a time. Keeping in touch with God today puts us in touch with the realities of tomorrow, because both are cut from the same piece of reality. God is Lord of both.

What priority have you focused on today? Paul talked to the Philippians about priorities. He was a man of many talents. He wrote, he traveled, he preached, he taught, he found time for friends, he made tents for a living. What did he mean when he said, "This one thing I do?" Well, I think he meant that the "upward call of God in Christ Jesus" would order and guide everything else. That priority was the focus of all his activities and interests. The upward call of God in Christ Jesus.

No matter what else he did, Paul never forgot that day when he lay in the dust of the Damascus road, broken and defeated. The grace of the living God passed through his shattered self that day and made him well and whole. He was given a new life.

God wants to do that for every one of God's children. You are God's child. You are wanted, you are loved, and you are special to God. But God's children must acknowledge their need for God and open their lives to receive the power and blessing that is theirs by grace.

Take a step toward home. Give your spiritual life priority. The best way to take that step is to pray. Turn to God and acknowledge God's Lordship. Confess your need and request God's help. Prayer is powerful, but you must do more than believe in it. You must do it. Prayer is far more than simply using words. The real power of prayer begins when we learn that it is a way of living. A starting place is saying the Lord's Prayer, but the goal is *being* the Lord's Prayer. That's when the power really flows. When what we say and what we do proclaim, "Our Father, may your name be hallowed"—that's real stewardship! When your life is so related to God that there is no need for periodic reporting. Communication occurs all the time when life is prayer.

Remember what I asked you to do earlier? Think about what you really want. Now let's read this passage together:

One thing I do, forgetting what lies behind and straining forward to see what lies ahead, I press on toward the goal for the prize of the upward call of God in Christ Jesus.

Stewardship of Presence, Time, and Talent

BEN R. ALFORD

Text: II Corinthians 9:1-6

In the first of a three-part series, I asked you to think about stewardship in terms of spiritual growth and prayer. Second, I want to help you to consider stewardship of **presence, time**, and **talent.** Two verses in II Corinithians 9 are the basis for consideration of these three matters. The first is verse one: *Now it is not necessary for me to write you about the ministry to the saints.*

Paul founded the church at Corinth and loved it very much, although at times the relationship between him and the congregation was strained. In his first letter to the Corinthians, he had asked the new church to set aside some money on the first day of every month, as an offering for the relief of impoverished Christians in the mother church at Jesusalem. This project was dear to his heart, so in his second letter to Corinth, he brings the subject up again: I know it isn't necessary for me to write you about our ministry to the saints, he writes, *"for I know your eagerness, which is the subject of my boasting about you to the people in Macedonia" (9:2).*

Paul is being very diplomatic. He says he doesn't need to bring the matter up, and then proceeds to do just that! There is a little uneasiness in his mind, I think. And there is more than that at stake. I believe he is very concerned that the Corinthians learn something about the importance of sharing—about stewardship, if you will. A few verses earlier, he says, *"I do not mean that others should be eased and you burdened, but that as a matter of equality your abundance at the present time should supply their want, so that their abundance may supply your want, that there may be equality"* (8:13-14 RSV).

No more powerful statement could be made in behalf of the benefits of generosity. When you and I shift over into the economy of the Kingdom of God and share our goods with those in need, a mysterious reciprocity occurs. In ways we never expect, the poor bless the rich. The recipient blesses the donor.

"Living is the art of loving. Loving is the art of caring. Caring is the art of sharing. Sharing is the art of living."

Paul knew this, and he didn't want the Corinthians to miss out on one of the great serendipitous experience of following Jesus.

There isn't time to discuss the rationale of Paul's collection for the poverty-stricken Christians at Jerusalem—"the saints"—but verse one in our text is very timely and opens the way for a few remarks about what you and I are facing today and tomorrow—Halloween and All Saints Day.

In our church and in many others, there is a tradition that on the Sunday nearest November 1, the names of church members who have died in the past year be read and remembered in thanksgiving. All Saints Day, in Reformation faith, blends All Saints and All Souls days into a celebration of the new life in Christ. It is a time when members of the Church Militant honor and remember those who are now members of the Church Triumphant. In these moments, we may be tempted to feel a sense of loss and diminished strength. But the faith of the Bible teaches that the church's numbers and the church's strength are actually swelling and growing! As each name is called, the "cloud of witnesses" grows more substantial.

Paul never uses the term *saint* to allude to the dead. When he speaks of saints, he is talking about those who are a part of the Body of Christ—those who are set apart by baptism for God's possession, use, and service. In this case, it is those who had been impoverished in Jerusalem because of their faith. Who should know better than Paul about the persecution they had endured? Paul himself had engaged in such tactics before his experience with the Risen Christ on the road to Damascus.

The saints on earth and the saints in heaven are united because they are all "in the Lord Jesus Christ." They are connected. We are not like those who have no hope. There is more, infinitely more, than can readily be seen by the eye. For centuries, Jesus' disciples have been saying the very words we affirmed together this morning: *I believe in the Holy Spirit, the holy catholic church, the communion of saints, the forgiveness of sins, the resurrection of the body, and the life everlasting.*

We believe in the communion of saints. There is a

50

mysterious connection by which all of God's people are united and able to help one another. Our faith validates the faith of those who have died and carries their commitment forward. That is why it is so thrilling when the confirmation class stands before the church to affirm the faith into which they have been baptized. Their faith helps validate our own. Of course, the labors and sacrifices of the saints of the past affect us in profound and innumerable ways. In God's kingdom, there is a reciprocity and a connectedness that surprises and blesses. The light that shines from All Saints Day utterly triumphs over All Hallow's Eve.

Currently, there is a rather intense effort being waged in many circles against Halloween. Some Christians believe that Halloween embodies all that is wrong with our culture, our schools, our children, even ourselves. Genuinely frightened parents actually are pulling their children out of public schools, with Halloween as their prime reason. To them, Christianity is being excluded, and a form of Satanism is being unwittingly welcomed.

There are some excesses in the observance of Halloween. There have been since I was a child. There is—God forgive us—great violence in our society. There is widespread unbelief, secularism, humanism, and even the worship of Satan in our time. But I do not think Halloween is the cause. Indeed, it may be a victim.

The truth is that Christianity itself took over Halloween—a pagan festival called by another name—from the Druids centuries ago. Missionaries quickly baptized the pagan celebration into Christian usage and transformed it into a day to commemorate the lives of the saints of the Church. But it is hard to keep paganism down! Mardi Gras and Fat Tuesday have pushed themselves ahead of Ash Wednesday and Lent on every calendar page. The human fascination with death, with fear, and with evil itself plays right into the devil's hands.

Banning Halloween would abolish neither fear nor death. Even if it were banned, each of us has to deal individually with the cultural influences which demean our faith and

> "Don't let your life be sterile. Be useful. Blaze a trail. Shine forth with the light of your faith and of your love."
>
> —*JOSE MARIA ESCRIVA*

oppose the Kingdom. We face it all the time, especially at Christmas and Easter. The Easter bunny trivializes the central doctrine of Christianity—the resurrection. For many the crass materialism at Christmas has obscured the profound theological claim about the self-emptying, incarnate love of God.

The followers of Jesus can face evil, fear, death, and anything else symbolized by Halloween with the knowledge that these things are not supreme. Just as the power of death, so clearly seen on Good Friday, was beaten down by the good news of Easter, Halloween has a macabre hold upon many because they don't know or can't trust the good news of Jesus Christ. Death doesn't plunge Jesus' people into separation and darkness. It ushers them into an even greater communion—the Church Eternal.

In the face of the fearsome specters conjured up by the practitioners of Halloween, Christians should smile and move on, to find creative new ways of proclaiming and expressing what they believe. Some years ago, our church began to downplay the observance of Halloween. Instead of using scare tactics about suffering in hell, we held an All Saints carnival, with appropriate scenes, sets, props, and persons depicting some of the great saints of the faith. Those who came were informed, enlightened, cheered, and encouraged by the memories of lovely, living, and courageous persons from the past.

What is it about these heroes and heroines of yesterday that thrills us? What is it we remember? It is more than their mere physical existence. It is more than the date of their birth on the calendar. It is their personhood we remember. Their essence. Their character. What they stood for and against. The sacrifices they made. Their depth of commitment. That is true as well for our personal loved ones. As I recall my grandparents, it is not their physical existence that controls my memory. I remember attitudes and characteristics. One of the great legacies they gave me was the ardor of faith.

What will you and I bequeath to those who come after? To what have we committed ourselves? What is our legacy? What is your testament? Consider these words: *"The point is this: the one who sows sparingly will also reap sparingly, and the one who sows bountifully will also reap bountifully"* (II Cor. 9:6).

If you think of stewardship in terms of time, talent, and resources—as any understanding of the subject requires—then stewardship is not such bad news after all, is it? Not if what Paul says is true. The rabbis of his day said it a little differently: *"The man who gives freely grows all the richer—another who withholds what he should give, only suffers want."*

Consider stewardship of **time.** Most people can prioritize their use of money. What they have trouble putting to good use is their time. The Bible tells us **again and again** about time. It teaches that there are two things that enhance the value of time in this life: its brevity and its uncertainty. Remember the phrases, "swift as a weaver's shuttle"; "grass which grows up in the morning and is cut down in the evening"? Jesus said, "Night comes when no man can work." He never wasted time. "I must be about my Father's business." Stewardship of time is more than just a prioritization of physical activity. It involves setting apart some time just to be with the ones you love most. Those of us whose professional lives are highly demanding would do well to heed Jesus' consistent attention to his filial responsibilities.

Where have you placed God in the list of those you love? Have you designated time to spend with the One who gave it in the first place? God deserves our respect and desires our company. Why? Because God loves us.

We all know the parable of the talents. Look again at the talents and skills you have been given. Who benefits from them? Are they used primarily for personal gain? One of the central teachings of Jesus is that those who sow bountifully will also reap bountifully. God's kingdom needs your skills and abilities. The church needs your time.

Will you be loyal to the church and uphold it by your prayers, your gifts, your service, and your **presence?** Never underestimate the importance of presence! When you are in your place in this place, you are ministering in several ways: **First,** you have voted—by your presence—for the most important thing in the world. **Second,** you have—**by your presence**—influenced everyone with whom you come in contact. **Third—by your presence**—you have made a witness. You have said, "This is important to me." **Fourth—by your presence**—you have enabled God to use you, in innumerable ways, to accomplish the divine will. **Fifth,** you have—**by your presence**—placed yourself in the company of other pilgrims who, like you, are on the journey of life, and by being present to one another, will have the opportunity for enrichment and encouragement. **Sixth—by your presence**—you place yourself in the center of God's people, where the acts of God are remembered and treasured, and where the Spirit of God is both welcomed and affirmed. It is there, waiting upon God—like the Apostles in the upper room—that wonderful things occur and power is discovered. **Finally, by your presence here,** you are involved in the greatest force for good in the entire world. The sun never sets on the army of which you are a part. The work of God's people is really what makes the difference in this world.

Stewardship of time, talent, and presence: our greatest responsibility and our highest privilege. In recognition of that, let us now read together this message:

The one who sows sparingly will also reap sparingly, and the one who sows bountifully will also reap bountifully.

Stewardship of Resources

BEN R. ALFORD

Text: II Corinthians 9:7-15

Today is Commitment Sunday. At the request of our leadership team, I have devoted three sermons to the subject of stewardship. First, I talked about stewardship in terms of prayer and spiritual growth. Second, it was stewardship of time, presence, and talents. We come now to a third component of Christian stewardship—stewardship of our resources. Today we talk about money. The text for my remarks is a portion of Paul's second letter to the Corinthian church, chapter 9. There are three verses to remember. The first is verse 8: *"And God is able to provide you with every blessing in abundance, so that you may always have enough of everything, and may provide in abundance for every good work"* (RSV).

Who can argue with that? God is gracious and good. God gives us life and abundant blessings. The Bible says that God has even given the earth into our keeping—yours and mine (Gen. 1:27-28, 31):

So God created man in his own image, in the image of God he created him; male and female he created them. And God blessed them, and God said to them, "Be fruitful and multiply, and fill the earth and subdue it; and have dominion over the fish of the sea and over the birds of the air and over every living thing that moves upon the earth. . . . And God saw everything that he had made, and behold, it was very good.

That's the Bible's first statement. Creation is God's; God made everything good, and human life—God's best creation—has both privilege and responsibility. The gift of life is beyond value, isn't it? But God wasn't content to wind up the clock and saunter off to let it run down all by itself. God intended, from the beginning, to engage in a loving relationship with creation. The Bible is the story of the divine/human encounter. As the story unfolds from Genesis to Revelation, we learn more and more about our marvelous God. In Jesus, we see more clearly the full extent of God's benevolence.

Once I heard a story about a missionary. An African boy in her class listened carefully as she explained why Christians give gifts to each other on Christmas day. "The gift is an expression of our joy over the birth of Jesus," she said, "and because of him we are not enemies, but friends who love each other." When Christmas came, the boy brought the teacher a sea shell of lustrous beauty. "Wherever did you find such a beautiful shell?" she asked in wonder. The boy said that there was only one spot where such shells could be found—in a certain bay, several miles distant. "Why, it is gorgeous," she said. "But you shouldn't have gone all that way to get it for me." The boy's eyes brightened, and he replied as best he could in the teacher's language, "Long walk part of gift."[1]

The long walk of God with you and me and the human family is part of the gift. *God is able to provide you with every blessing in abundance, so that you may always have enough of everything."* Isn't that the way it is? God may not always have provided me with everything I wanted, but God has always given me everything I needed, and more.

I like Ralph Seager's words about God's extravagance:

More sky than mortals can see, more seas than they can sail,
More sun than they can bear to watch, more stars than can be scaled.
More breath than we can breathe, more yield than we can sow,
More grace than we can comprehend, more love than we can know.[2]

Now comes the second verse to remember—verse 11: *"You will be enriched in every way for great generosity."* Paul had the rank courage to tell the Corinthians the greatest truth of life. It was central in the teaching and the work of Jesus, who said, "A new commandment I give to you, that you love one another; even as I have loved you, that you also love one another" (John 13:34 RSV). When one loves, one is generous. When one is generous, one begins to understand blessedness. Truly, we are enriched in every way when we are generous.

Thomas Carlyle said that when he was a boy, a beggar once came to the door of their house. His parents were away, and he was alone in the house. On a boyish impulse, he ran into his bedroom, broke open his savings bank, and gave the beggar all that was in it. Years later, as a grown man, he said that never before or since had he known such sheer happiness as came to him in that moment.[3] You are enriched in every way when you are generous.

Being generous is the opposite of being possessive. It is at the top end of the scale of generosity. Someone has said that there are seven levels of giving:
- Giving to the needy, but giving reluctantly.
- Giving with a good attitude, but not enough.
- Giving enough, but only after being asked.
- Giving without being asked.
- Giving without the beneficiary knowing who is giving.
- Giving one's life to eliminate the causes of need.

The old adage, "We make a living by what we get out of life, but we make a life by what we give," is on target with Paul's advice to the Corinthians. You are enriched in every way for generosity. You can trust that word from the Bible. My experience is that those who argue that giving hasn't enriched them need to take a look at where they are on the scale of giving.

Now we come to the third verse, verse 7. This is really the verse our leadership team wanted to focus on: *"Each one must do as he has made up his mind, not reluctantly or under compulsion, for God loves a cheerful giver"* (RSV).

Isn't that the way it has to be?

Every member of the church has received a copy of our church's proposed budget. It includes not only the amount of every line item, but an explanation of what the money in that line item will do. When all the requests from the five major areas came in, the amount needed totaled $_____. That's the largest budget our church has ever had—17 percent higher than last year. We are attempting to do more than we have ever done before!

The planning and visioning for next year is complete. Now it is up to each of us. If every person will prayerfully consider how he or she needs to respond as a steward of God's gifts, we will be well on our way. That is the first step. Remember that we are stewards. Good stewards are always accountable for that which is entrusted to them.

The second step is to make a conscious effort to move up on the scale of giving. We can never out-give God. If you are a $5 per week steward, why not move up to $10? If your giving is currently at 5 percent of your income, take a percentage step up to 6 percent. If you do that deliberately, intentionally, and conscientiously each year, one day you'll have the satisfaction of knowing that you are practicing the biblical standard of giving—the tithe—giving 10 percent of your income. Maybe you haven't yet come to the point of regular and systematic giving. I can't think of a better time to commit to that than now.

So much depends on how we respond today! It really doesn't matter what the budget document's bottom line is. What really matters is what you and I do in response to God. As your pastor, I am telling you that we are going to do exactly what you tell us to do. If you say "do less," we have no choice but to heed you. But I believe in my heart that you want us to continue to move forward. You want this church to continue to grow and increase its outreach in the name of Jesus Christ. Because you do, you'll each do your part.

There are commitment forms in each pew. There is a place for you to indicate your commitment of time, talent, and resources. I hope each of you has already given this matter serious and prayerful consideration. If not, I hope you are doing so now.

In a few minutes you'll be given the opportunity to bring your commitment sheet to the chancel as an act of dedication. Before we do that, and before we come to the covenant meal of our Lord, I want you to remember Paul's word to the Corinthians: *Each of you must give as you have made up your mind, not reluctantly or under compulsion, for God loves a cheerful giver.*

Our leadership team really believes that. This is the way it must be. I want you to remember that verse as we move to the act of commitment. Some of you have already turned in your commitment sheets. Others, who are still considering the matter, will do so later. I want you to feel perfectly free today to bring your commitment to the chancel or not. This is a time when we are not focused on what others are doing. Let us consider only how *we* shall respond to God's gifts in our lives. One final story is in order.

As some of you know, the Koh-i-noor diamond is among the most spectacular in the world. James S.

Hewett tells the story of how Queen Victoria received the beautiful gem as a gift from a maharajah when he was just a boy in India. Later, as a grown man, the maharajah visited the Queen in London. He requested that the stone be brought from the Tower of London to Buckingham Palace. He took the diamond and knelt before the Queen.

He handed her the precious stone and said, "Your majesty, I gave this jewel to you when I was a child,

Christ Can Satisfy
L . G . D . W E R T Z

We give because God gives to us
His life of peace and love.
Implants within an impetus
To share with Him above.
In lowly manger Jesus came,
A blessing to all men;
an angel chorus did proclaim
To us His love again.
He calls for tithes of what we earn,
Our God to glorify,
And help that all the world can learn
That Christ can satisfy.

too young to know what I was doing. I want to give it to you again in the fullness of my strength, with all my heart, affection, and gratitude, now and forever, fully realizing all that I do."[4]

As followers of Jesus Christ, we need to reiterate those words today, offering again our lives to the One who gave his life for us. "I want to give you back my life, Lord Jesus, that I gave you several years ago. I want to give it again to you with gratitude, fully cognizant of what I am doing." There is no finer stewardship than that. That is the top rung on the ladder of giving. Now, read with me this message:

Each of you must give as you have made up your mind, not reluctantly or under compulsion, for God loves a cheerful giver.

Christ our Lord invites to his table all who love him, who earnestly repent of their sin and seek to live in peace with one another. As you prepare to take your place at the Lord's table this morning, make your confession to God in silent prayer. Those of you who are prepared to do so may bring your commitment sheet and place it in the container as you come for Holy Communion.

Notes

1. *Illustrations Unlimited,* ed. Jame S. Hewett (Wheaton, Ill., Tyndale House, 1988), p. 233.
2. Ibid, p. 241.
3. Ibid, p. 240.
4. Ibid.

A Sermon Illustration

MARK L. SCHUTT

A young preacher finished his first stewardship sermon by suggesting that everyone go home and think seriously about what it means to be thankful for God's gifts. The suggestion was good, but the way the young preacher got there had put most folks to sleep.

After the service, someone mumbled, "Too many big seminary words that don't mean a hoot around here."

Encouraged by his friends to speak to the young preacher, the chairman of the Administrative Board went up and offered a few words of advice: "You did a good job, preacher. But we need you to talk to us and not to your seminary professors."

"What do you mean?" said the young preacher.

"Well," said the chairman, "if you want us to say thanks for God's gifts, tell it to us straight. Around here, we need to be reminded we came into the world bare-bottomed and bawl'n. Everything, from then on out, is a gift."

"So then I said to the IRS agent, 'Receipts? What do you mean I need receipts for my charitable gifts?'"

 BULLETIN

Stewardship by the Book

SHARON HUECKEL

Bulletin bits based on the Sunday Gospel readings, Year A

Stewardship is a spiritual attitude that begins with the understanding that all we are and all we own are gifts, freely given by our loving God. And when that fact—that everything is unmerited gift—seeps deeply into consciousness, there are at least two outcomes: (1) a deep yearning to somehow "give back" in thanksgiving some share of all that has been given; and (2) a dawning understanding of the need to use those gifts wisely and responsibly. One definition of stewardship, then, is "an attitude of responsive and responsible gratitude." Our stewardship becomes, in some sense, the *measure* of our discipleship—the way we live out the call to follow Jesus.

Just defining stewardship, however broadly, is not enough. Our challenge is to teach it, to get the message out and reinforce it, encouraging believers to translate their discipleship into lives of faithful stewardship. Theorists of learning suggest that we assimilate new information best when we already have a familiar "hook to hang it on," and when we hear the same message repeated many times in many ways.

The underlying premise of "Stewardship by the Book" is that the stewardship message be more clearly heard if it consistently echoes the Scriptures that are read and preached. Whether a pastor is preparing to launch a stewardship "program," nurturing an earlier stewardship effort, trying to increase the congregation's understanding of the link between discipleship and stewardship, or just trying to keep the parish afloat financially, dropping these stewardship "echoes" of the Sunday readings into the bulletin each week is one fairly painless way to work at stewardship education.

1st Sunday of Advent—Matt. 24:36-44

The Son of Man is coming at an unexpected hour, says today's Gospel. Good stewards know that they are accountable to God for all they have and are, and they strive to live in readiness for His coming.

2nd Sunday of Advent—Matt. 3:1-12

We must be good stewards of God's gifts to us, receiving them gratefully and cultivating them with care, lest we be the ones about whom John the Baptist speaks today. "Every tree therefore that does not bear good fruit is cut down and thrown into the fire."

3rd Sunday of Advent—Matt. 11:2-11

Each of us has our own role to play in the coming of the kingdom of God. John the Baptist was called to be the herald of the Messiah, preparing the way of the Lord. To what is the Lord calling me?

4th Sunday of Advent—Matt. 1:18-25

When he discovered that Mary was with child, Joseph resolved to end their engagement as kindly and with as little disgrace as possible. But obedient to the voice of God, he changed those plans and became instead the protector of the child Jesus and his mother Mary. God grant that I may be as open to the leading of the Holy Spirit!

Christmas Day

For unto us is born this day a Savior! In response to so great a love, only the gift of my whole self will do. You have given us yourself, dear Lord; in love and thanksgiving, I commit myself afresh to you.

1st Sunday After Christmas—Matt. 2:13-23

Joseph's obedience to God was not a one-time thing. His attention to the warnings of the angel kept Jesus from being murdered by Herod and led to the fulfillment of the prophecy that the Messiah would be a Nazarene. Fidelity to God's will assures the best use of our talents, too.

New Year's Day—Matt. 25:31-46

Today's Gospel is a blueprint for good stewardship. Only if we are willing to share our blessings—of time and skills and financial resources—with those who are less fortunate, will the Day of Judgment find us among the blessed at the right hand of God.

1st Sunday After Epiphany—Matt. 3:13-17

Sometimes we are tempted to think that our small offerings of time and talent contribute very little to the coming of the Kingdom. Perhaps John the Baptist felt that way when Jesus came to him to be baptized. But Jesus knew it was important for John to play his part. And he knows and values *our* service to the Kingdom, too.

2nd Sunday After Epiphany—John 1:29-42

Today's Gospel recounts the calling of the first disciples. They hear the testimony of John the Baptist, hurry to follow Jesus, then go out to bring others to him. Evangelism is *still* the first task of those who have heard the call to follow Jesus!

3rd Sunday After Epiphany—Matt. 4:12-23

The watchword today is "immediately." Peter and Andrew, James and John, all respond to the call of Christ. May we be as open to God's call, and as ready to use our talents in his service as were those first disciples!

4th Sunday After Epiphany—Matt. 5:1-12

Blessed are they who are what they are and do what they do *for the sake of the kingdom!* The reading today is an assurance to good stewards that their suffering and service on behalf of the Kingdom *will* be rewarded!

5th Sunday After Ephiphany—Matt. 5:13-20

The Gospel today reminds us that our lives and our deeds must serve as examples to others, pointing the way to the Father. Not for our own benefit do we labor, but so that others may see our good works and give glory to our Father in heaven.

6th Sunday After Epiphany—Matt. 5:21-37

Stewardship involves more than just the gift we bring to the altar. Today's reading says clearly that it is fidelity to God's law that makes our offering acceptable.

Transfiguration Sunday—Matt. 17:1-9

Peter, James, and John wanted to build a dwelling for Jesus and stay on the mountain where his transfig-uration took place. But Jesus knew that he had to keep moving toward his Crucifixion. We, too, must rise from worship and do what we can to hasten the coming of the Kingdom.

Ash Wednesday—Matt. 6:1-6, 16-21

Today's Gospel reminds us that all our giving—whether of alms or of service—must always be done for love of God alone, not for the applause of our brothers and sisters.

1st Sunday of Lent—Matt. 4:1-11

Before he began his public ministry, Jesus faced and overcame temptation in the desert. Let us resolve to seek his help and guidance when the enticements of the world threaten to de-rail our discipleship.

2nd Sunday of Lent—John 3:1-17

John 3:16 is sometimes called "the Gospel in miniature" because it so succinctly sums up the Gospel message. In even more condensed form, "God loved . . . God gave . . ." is the model for steward-ship—we give because we love.

3rd Sunday of Lent—John 4:5-42

When Jesus asked the Samaritan woman for a drink of water, he opened the door for a life-changing relationship with the Master. Scripture says that her testimony drew many others to him as well. We too must be ready to respond whenever and wherever the Lord speaks to us, and be prepared for that relationship to change our lives!

4th Sunday of Lent—John 9:1-41

The blind man was willing to let Jesus minister to him and willingly did all that Jesus asked of him. The Pharisees were more resistant to his message, spending their time and energy in an attempt to disprove the miracle. Am I more like the man born blind, or the Pharisee?

5th Sunday of Lent—John 11:1-45

When Jesus heard about the illness of his friend Lazarus, he responded, "This illness does not lead to death; rather it is for God's glory, so that the Son of God may be glorified through it." Every aspect of our lives—our gifts as well as our sufferings—can, if surrendered to Christ, lead to blessings for ourselves and others.

Palm Sunday—Matt. 21:1-11

"Blessed is the one who comes in the name of the Lord!" shouted the crowds in today's Gospel. May *we* be always ready to share our blessings when *we* are sent in his name!

Easter—John 20:1-18 or Matt. 28:1-10

Very early in the morning after the Sabbath, Mary Magdalene went to the tomb to anoint Jesus' body with precious oils. The reward for this good and conscientious steward was to be among the first to know that Jesus had been raised from the dead! Alleluia!

2nd Sunday of Easter—John 20:19-31

Jesus meets the need of each disciple. To the fearful in the upper room, he speaks words of peace. To doubting Thomas, he provides the tangible proof of his resurrection. What do I need to become his disciple? What can I share that might meet someone else's need?

3rd Sunday of Easter—Luke 24:13-35

The disciples on the road to Emmaus walked and talked with Jesus all day long, but it was not until they offered him hospitality and he blessed and broke the bread that they recognized him. Simple acts of lovingkindness *still* reveal the presence of God in our midst.

4th Sunday of Easter—John 10:1-10

Jesus says, "I came that they may have life, and have it abundantly." Good stewards are grateful for the gift of life and joyfully share their abundance with others.

5th Sunday of Easter—John 14:1-14

"The one who believes in me will also do the works that I do, and in fact, will do greater works than these." Quite an assignment for the Christian steward!

6th Sunday of Easter—John 14:15-21

"They who have my commandments and keep them are those who love me," Jesus says. Does my stewardship reveal my love for Jesus?

7th Sunday of Easter—John 17:1-11

In today's Gospel, Jesus says, "I glorified you on earth by finishing the work that you gave me to do." Good stewards follow his example by using their time and talents for the glory of God.

Pentecost—John 20:19-23

"As the Father has sent me, so I send you," Jesus told his disciples. We too are sent. To whom, or to what service, is the Lord sending me today?

Trinity Sunday—Matt. 28:16-20

"Go therefore and make disciples," Jesus tells his disciples *and* us. But we need not fear the assignment, for he has promised to be with us always!

2nd Sunday After Pentecost—Matt. 9:9-13, 18-26

Jesus shared himself with all who needed him in today's Gospel—a tax collector, a chronically ill woman, and the daughter of a local church leader. As good stewards, we too must share our gifts with anyone who needs them.

3rd Sunday After Pentecost—Matt. 9:35–10:8

The end of today's reading is a clear call to stewardship: "You received without payment; give without payment."

4th Sunday After Pentecost—Matt. 10:24-39

"Nothing is covered up that will not be uncovered," Jesus tells us in the Gospel today, "and nothing secret that will not become known." May our stewardship of God's gifts be such that we would not be ashamed if it were seen in the clear light of day.

5th Sunday After Pentecost—Matt. 10:40-42

The Gospel speaks of hospitality and welcome. The ushers, our ministers of hospitality, are a most visible example of using our time and talents to welcome the people of God. But the Gospel assures us that all who give even just "a cup of cold water" to one of his little ones will be rewarded.

6th Sunday After Pentecost—Matt. 11:16-19, 25-30

In today's Gospel, Jesus invites the weary to lay their burdens down, and face those obstacles yoked with him instead. "Learn from me," he says. Help me to follow you, Lord, by showing me where I can lighten another's burden by sharing the load.

7th Sunday After Pentecost—Matt. 13:1-9, 18-23

May our stewardship of time, talent, and treasure show us to be among those who have heard the message of Christ and taken it in, yielding a hundred- or sixty- or thirty-fold!

8th Sunday After Pentecost—Matt. 13:24-30, 36-43

Today's parable assures us that we must continue to be good stewards of our God-given gifts and talents, even when it seems that selfishness is flourishing all around us. In God's good time, the faithful stewards "will shine like the sun in the kingdom of their Father!"

9th Sunday After Pentecost—Matt. 13:31-33, 44-52

Good stewards in a congregation are like the yeast in today's Gospel. Their selfless gifts of time and talent help the church thrive, and their example inspires others to become good stewards, too.

10th Sunday After Pentecost—Matt. 14:13-21

In today's Gospel, Jesus feeds the five thousand with five loaves and two fish. The message of stewardship is that God's gifts, *shared,* will always be more than enough.

11th Sunday After Pentecost—Matt. 14:22-33

The beginning of today's Gospel tells of Jesus dismissing the crowds and going off alone to pray. We are stewards of the time allotted to us, as well as of our talents and material gifts; and we will be better stewards of *all* our gifts, if we follow his example and devote some share of our time to prayer.

12th Sunday After Pentecost—Matt. 15:10-28

It is the disposition of the heart that matters most, Jesus tells the Pharisees in today's Gospel, not rigid adherence to dietary laws. "What comes out of the mouth proceeds from the heart," he says. May our hearts be firmly committed to Christ, and our mouths speak only peace to our neighbors!

13th Sunday After Pentecost—Matt. 16:13-20

"Who do you say that I am?" Jesus asked Peter. He asks the same question of us. Do my living and my giving testify that I know him as Lord of my life?

14th Sunday After Pentecost—Matt. 16:21-28

When the Son of Man comes in glory to repay each of us for what has been done, will he say to me, "You have used well the gifts I entrusted to you. Well done, good and faithful servant"?

15th Sunday After Pentecost—Matt. 18:15-20

Am I my brother's keeper? Today's reading suggests that for the Christian steward, the answer is "Yes!"

16th Sunday After Pentecost—Matt. 18:21-35

In today's parable, God is the king, and we are the indebted slaves who have been forgiven so great a debt. The clear message is that, because of the great mercy and generosity God has shown to us, we must be generous and merciful with others.

17th Sunday After Pentecost—Matt. 20:1-16

In today's Gospel, the vineyard owner asks, "Am I not allowed to do what I choose with what belongs to me?" We likewise are free to choose. Among the choices we have made, is there a generous return to the Lord in thanksgiving for his many blessings?

18th Sunday After Pentecost—Matt. 21:23-32

The first son in today's Gospel said that he would do his father's bidding, but did not. The second son balked at first, but then repented and did as he was asked. What service is God calling me to do? Which son am I more like?

19th Sunday After Pentecost—Matt. 21:33-46

In the Gospel today, the owner of the vineyard sent messengers to collect his share of the harvest from the tenant farmers; but there was not a single good steward on the property! God is the owner; we are the tenants. What sort of stewards are we?

20th Sunday After Pentecost—Matt. 22:1-14

We are the wedding guests, invited to the banquet of the Lord in heaven. But if we, like those in the parable, refuse the invitation, or are too busy to care, or misuse the gifts of God, we will not be numbered among the chosen on the last day!

21st Sunday After Pentecost—Matt. 22:15-22

Each year at tax time, we conscientiously give "to the emperor the things that are the emperor's." Does my stewardship indicate that I am as faithful about giving "to God the things that are God's"?

22nd Sunday After Pentecost—Matt. 22:34-46

We fulfill the commandment to love our neighbor when we exercise good stewardship—joyfully sharing our gifts of life, abilities, and resources to meet our neighbor's need.

23rd Sunday After Pentecost—Matt. 23:1-12

"The greatest among you will be your servant," Jesus says in today's Gospel. What wonderful good news for those who give of their time in service to others!

24th After Pentecost—Matt. 25:1-13

Like the wise bridesmaids in today's parable, good stewards make sure that they, and whatever gifts are theirs to share, are ready to serve when the Master calls.

25th Sunday After Pentecost—Matt. 25:14-30

Good stewards are like the good and trustworthy servants in today's Gospel, prudently using and multiplying the gifts entrusted to them by God.

Christ the King—Matt. 25:31-46

When the Son of Man comes in his glory, may we be among those who have fed the hungry and welcomed the stranger and clothed the naked. For Jesus tells us clearly that it is those who have demonstrated good stewardship by sharing their gifts with the less fortunate that will receive God's blessing and inherit the kingdom.

NEWSLETTER

The following one-liners can be used for church newsletters, bulletin boards, or signs.

"Through charity toward God, we conceive virtues, and through charity toward our neighbors, they are brought to the birth."
CATHERINE OF SIENNA

"Have you lost the things that money cannot buy?"
WILLIAM H. DENNISON

"Giving never moves in a straight line—it always moves in circles! It goes round . . . and round . . . and round."
ROBERT H. SCHULLER

"Superfluous wealth can buy superfluities only. Money is not required to buy one necessity of the soul."
HENRY DAVID THOREAU

"It is possible to give without loving, but it is impossible to love without giving."
RICHARD BRAUNSTEIN

"Think of giving not as a duty but as a privilege."
JOHN D. ROCKEFELLER, JR.

"The be-all and end-all of life should not be to get rich, but to enrich the world."
B. C. FORBES

"In terms of downright happiness, it is my experience that the returns-per-minute from giving are far greater than the returns from getting."
DAVID DUNN

"Our greatest need and most difficult achievement is to find meaning in our lives."
BRUNO BETTELHEIM

"Unless we give part of ourselves away, unless we can live with other people and understand them and help them, we are missing the most essential part of our own human lives."
HAROLD TAYLOR

"To gain that which is worth having, it may be necessary to lose everything else."

BERNADETTE DEVLIN

"He hath made his wonderful works to be remembered: the LORD is gracious and full of compassion."

PSALM 111:4 KJV

"Kindness is a language which the deaf can hear and the blind can see."

MARK TWAIN

"Always give thanks for everything."

EPHESIANS 5:30 (TLB)

"Charity brings to life again those who are spiritually dead."

THOMAS AQUINAS

"If you haven't got any charity in your heart, you have the worst kind of heart trouble."

BOB HOPE

"In faith and hope the world will disagree, but all mankind's concern is charity."

ALEXANDER POPE

"Charity: to love human beings . . . as God does."

SIMONE WEIL

"Thanksgiving is nothing if not a glad, a reverend lifting of the heart to God, in honor and praise for his goodness."

JAMES R. MILLER

"But is it what we love, or how we love, that makes true good?"

GEORGE ELIOT

"Those who give have all things; those who withhold have nothing."

HINDU PROVERB

"What you are is God's gift to you, and what you do with what you are is your gift to God."

GEORGE FOSTER

"The sacramental use of money in the formal and gathered worship of the church is authenticated in the sacramental use of money elsewhere."

WILLIAM STRINGFELLOW

"In any congregation, there are a few people waiting to become the instruments of change."

M. D. BLACKBURN

"The least the church can do about the way people spend their time and money is to make them think a lot more seriously about it."

WILLIAM GARRETT

 SERMON HELP

Stewardship Sermon Illustrations

JOE HARDING

Priorities

Imagine a man who gets his paycheck and buys a $1,000 suit and a $200 pair of shoes. He eats dinner at one of the finest restaurants. He attends a professional ball game. Then he stops by a rummage sale and buys his wife a second-hand dress which he was able to purchase for $3.97, singing all the way, "I love my Mary Jane. I love my Mary Jane. I really do. Yes, I do. I do."

Commitment

A young man wrote his girlfriend a letter: "Darling, I love you! I love you! I love you! I would cross the burning desert to be by your side. I would climb the highest mountain. I would swim the deepest river. I would cross the dismal swamp to be with you. I will be over Saturday night, if it doesn't rain!" Deep commitment communicates a level of hard involvement, no matter what words are spoken.

Abundance

Paul commends this theology in his letter to the Corinthians: "And God is able to provide you with every blessing in abundance, so that by always having enough of everything, you may share abundantly in every good work. . . . He who supplies seed to the sower and bread for food will supply and multiply your seed for sowing and increase the harvest of your righteousness. You will be enriched in every way for your great generosity, which will produce thanksgiving to God through us; for the rendering of this ministry not only supplies the needs of the saints but also overflows with many thanksgivings to God." (2 Cor. 9:8, 10-12).

Enthusiasm

A Salvation Army trumpet player was frequently criticized for playing too loudly. One day the director really took the man to task and told him he had to play more softly.

The trumpet player looked at the director and said, "Look, when I think of what the good Lord has done for me, I could take this trumpet and just blow it out straight!" That kind of gratitude produces the enthusiasm for generosity that inspires faithful, sacrificial giving. The picture is filled with an invitation to participate in that kind of joyous praise. Hear Isaiah 44:23:

> Sing, O heavens, for the LORD has done it;
>   shout, O depths of the earth;
> break forth into singing, O mountains,
>   O forest, and every tree in it!
> For the LORD has redeemed Jacob,
>   and will be glorified in Israel.

Samaritan Stewardship

Remember the conclusion to Psalm 150:

> Praise him with clanging cymbals;
>   praise him with loud clashing cymbals!
> Let everything that breathes praise the LORD!
> Praise the LORD!

This classic outline of the stewardship theme has been used many times—the parable of the good Samaritan, with Luke 15 as the text. There are three basic attitudes toward life:

1. The attitude of the thief—What is yours is mine, and I will get it!

2. The attitude of the Levite—What is mine is mine, and I will keep it!

3. The attitude of the Samaritan—What is mine is yours, and I will share it!

That simple outline expresses the position we must choose toward our possessions, other persons, and God.

Aloof

In a display of fall coats in a large urban mall, there was one very stylish coat called a swagger coat. Beside the coat, there was this very carefully lettered motto: "This coat captures beautifully that informal air of complete unconcern." That attitude is fine for a coat. But it is an inappropriate response for a person of God who creates, sustains, saves, and gives daily hope.

Inheritance

In New England, there is the grave of an old Yankee skinflint. While he was alive, he offered his future heirs their legacy in advance, if they would give him 12½ percent interest on it. When he died, they put this epitaph on his tombstone:

> Here lies old 12½ percent
> The more he saved, the less he spent.
> The less he spent, the more he craved.
> O Lord, can Icobad be saved?

Winning Team

I was listening to a football game some time ago while trying to make pastoral calls on a Sunday afternoon. I tell you, that is a mistake. It lends itself to long drives and short calls. The Seattle Seahawks were playing in the newly completed dome stadium, King Dome, in King County. The opponents, the New Orleans Saints, were playing an outstanding game. The game was stopped for a call at a very intense moment.

The visit with the next family took far longer than I had imagined. I was anxious to get back to the game, and when I got back in my car and turned the key, I heard the announcer shouting with great enthusiasm, "The Saints are moving down the field! The Saints have got enthusiasm and spirit! The Saints seem like a great team! The Saints are winning in the King Dome!"

I thought, "WOW, it sounds like the Apostle Paul just grabbed the microphone. How wonderful to know that the Saints are winning in the King Dome." Confidence in the ultimate victory of God gives us assurance that we too can give and invest in God's causes, with great confidence that the victory has already been won in Jesus Christ.

Gratitude

In one of his sermons, Clarence Forsberg tells about a mother with five children, who became so desperate because of health and financial problems that she decided life was not worth the struggle. She took her youngest child, a preschool girl, into the bedroom of their tiny house. Carefully, she packed the windows with rags and newspapers, so that no air could enter the room. Then she turned on the gas heater without lighting it. She lay down on her bed with her arm around her little girl. She could hear the gas escaping. It would only be a matter of a few minutes now.

Then it occurred to her that she could hear another sound. Suddenly she realized that she had forgotten to turn off the radio in the other room. For some reason, it seemed important. But as she got up, she heard someone on the radio singing an old gospel hymn, "What a Friend We Have in Jesus":

> O what peace we often forfeit,
> O what needless pain we bear,
> all because we do not carry
> everything to God in prayer.

At that instant, she realized the mistake she was making. She had forgotten the resources of her own faith. She rushed to turn off the gas and open the window wide. She picked up her little girl and held her tight.

As she spoke about it later, she said, "I began to pray. I did not pray for help. I prayed a prayer of gratitude to God for his blessings. I thanked God for life. I thanked God for five wonderful children. I promised that I would never forget my faith again." She added, as if in an afterthought, "And so far I have kept that promise."

Generosity is always based on gratitude and praise. Gratitude and praise occur when there is a recognition of what God has done for us in Jesus Christ. If we take our eyes off our problems and focus upon God's generosity in Jesus, suddenly the possibility of a new day and a new way of living and giving opens before us.

Money-back Guarantee

At a board meeting at Central Church in Richland, Washington, a number of years ago, a member of the board surprised everyone present by saying, "I move we become a tithing church." The church had been in the process of trying to challenge people to increase their giving 1 percent per year.

This man said, "I think this is far too slow. God wants us to honor him with a full tithe." The motion was seconded and passed unanimously. The pastor was in absolute awe. He had not anticipated that such an action could ever be taken.

In fact, he was so excited that on Sunday morning, he preached a joyous and dynamic sermon, in which he announced: "This is a tithing church. This is a generous church. This is a church that will be blessed by God because God honors those who are faithful in the handling of God's resources. The board voted that we should be a tithing church. It was unanimous. I believe so strongly in tithing that we are offering a money-back guarantee on tithing. Try tithing this year. If you do not like what is happening in your life, we will give you your money back."

The results of the announcement were outstanding. The minister himself was shocked. The guarantee about tithing was not in his manuscript. It had just popped out of his mouth at the moment of the enthusiastic announcement. Once the announcement was made, however, there was no way to take it back.

The response of the congregation was nothing short of incredible. Suddenly, the reality of the tithe through the money-back guarantee of satisfaction communicated to people. That weekend, the congregation moved from 20 to 200 tithing families. And not one family ever expressed dissatisfaction with tithing. Not one ever complained, "The church is always talking about money."

The next year, the pastor became even bolder. He offered a money-back guarantee for any debts that might be incurred as a result of tithing, probably an overstated offer. One young man came to the pastor later in the year with a $500 debt as a result of inability to meet obligations because of tithing. The church paid the $500 debt, and never again made this challenge! (This experience happened at Central Church in Richland, Washington, with Joe Harding as pastor.)

SERMON HELP

More Sermon Illustrations

God First

Tithing is not just giving 10 percent of our income to the church. It is an outer symbol of our inner attitude, which says "God first." If we truly recognize God as our source, then our feelings that God comes first will be evident. Worthy proportionate giving is likewise the same expression of faith in God.

SECTION ON STEWARDSHIP,
GENERAL BOARD OF DISCIPLESHIP

Justice

Money is one of the important humanly created media through which the Word of God can be expressed and God's kingdom of justice and love given embodiment.

JACKSON W. CARROLL

Freedom

Are all of us to follow the Gospel teachings on money and possessions? I don't know. It probably calls us beyond where we would want to go, to a freedom from and a freedom for—but how that works out for each of us is not clear to me. What is certain is that until we can claim that inner freedom, we will be unable to claim Christian discipleship. It is also true that the by-products of this kind of living are powerful enough to set fire to the earth.

DORIS DONNELLY

Tithe

There is a widely known and much-practiced principle of life which, applied to one's tithe, quite transforms [one's] attitude toward all [one's] possessions. By the dedication of a part, the whole may be sanctified.

COSTEN J. HARRELL

Failure

The attitude toward money is fundamental to the Christian life. If we fail here, we fail everywhere. If we do not recognize that our money is loaned to us— put in our trust—then we fail in our spiritual life at every point.

G. ERNEST THOMAS,
TO WHOM MUCH IS GIVEN

Tithe

Jesus went beyond the Old Testament conception of the tithe, as he went beyond the Old Testament conception of morality and individual responsibility. He considered that all money and worldly goods are a generous manifestation of love, on the part of [God].

G. ERNEST THOMAS

Tithe

The only recorded teaching of Jesus with regard to the tithe gives the faithful Christian an understanding that the tithe is the minimum expectation of God upon those who have confessed that their lives will be his (see Matt. 23:23).

G. ERNEST THOMAS

Dough

In some oriental languages, the word *do* (pronounced dough) means "way of." For them, "do" is a system, an entire lifestyle. Christian stewardship is much like that oriental "do." It is a lifestyle. When Christians do stewardship, they do ministry and service.

EUGENE GRIMM

Idolatry

Christ offered the rich young ruler in the parable freedom from idolatry of money. Money is not inherently evil; neither is the possession of money, as such, sin. The issue is only whether a person trusts money more than Christ, and thus relies on money for assurance of moral significance, rather than upon grace.

WILLIAM STRINGFELLOW

PART THREE

THE ANNUAL CAMPAIGN

Introduction

D O N A L D   W .   J O I N E R

There is a time in every church when the financial leaders approach the membership about funding the church's ministry. In most churches, the decision of what to do and when to do it is postponed until the last minute. Somehow we don't want to think about "doing" a financial campaign. Maybe if we postpone the decision, it will take care of itself!

Designing and conducting a commitment campaign takes time—anywhere from eight to twelve weeks, at a minimum. A shorter time "short-changes" the results. A campaign is not just a time to "fund the budget," but a time to highlight the church's purpose and vision, to project the church's call for the future, and to celebrate the church's response to ministry in the world.

Tim Ek's two articles are specifically directed to the leadership responsible for designing and leading a funding campaign. His first article, "Finding a Way to Say 'Pledge,'" is not about what to *call* your program, but about how to look at it. It is not about money, but about Christians sharing in the ministry of Jesus Christ through the church. His second article focuses on the question, "What are we going to do this year?"

An annual campaign is an ideal time to lead the church in a faithful decision about commitment and how to live it out. Because the funding campaign is often led by the same leaders who design and manage the budget, the focus is most often on "money." Jim Killen's commitment program is not about money; it is about faithful commitment to God's work, through us and through the church. It provides a unique approach to the spiritual journey of faith and our commitment to respond.

Seeking Something Better is a four-week (twelve weeks to complete the entire program) personal journey of faith and commitment. Each person in your church should get a copy of the daily "Workbook for Spiritual Renewal." You may choose to photocopy these pages, or you may purchase a copy of the software edition of this *Guide,* which permits you to print the workbook file and preserve the fonts, or it will allow you to customize the workbook on a personal computer. Each day, participants are invited to study scripture, pray, and "journal" about their personal commitment. This "journal" is theirs to keep. At the end of the "journal," provision is made for a commitment about money, certainly, but also about growing, and serving, in God's community of faith.

 PLANNING TOOL

Finding a Way to Say "Pledge"

TIMOTHY C. EK

All of us have experienced times when words mean something very different, depending upon when and where they are used. Communications within the church are no exception. Over time, a church comes to use a kind of Christian "shorthand" to communicate complex ideas in simple terms to congregations. In no other area is that inclination more evident than in association with long-term commitments to giving.

A number of terms have emerged to express the concept of formalizing our financial commitments to giving—terms such as faith commitment, personal covenant, pledge, faith promise, covenant gift, and so on. While the Bible uses none of these exact phrases, there is strong biblical precedent for God's people to make vows to God. Nazarites like Samson took oaths to demonstrate publicly their sacred commitment to godliness. During the rebuilding of the Old Testament temple, God's people made pledges of gifts in support of the building program. Such pledges often took the form of tithes—demonstrations of the giver's desire to give back to God the first-fruit portion that was rightfully God's.

While Jesus does not speak specifically about pledging in the New Testament, it is virtually certain that he supported such spiritual discipline—especially since it bore witness to the kind of total-life commitment to God that he taught throughout the Gospels. If Jesus had spoken *against* disciplines like tithing or making vows, we can be sure that his enemies would have seized quickly on such revolutionary ideas and used them as further ammunition to subvert his ministry.

Today, we often hear that Christians live under grace—not under the law. Thank God that this is true. But many people use this precious truth to advocate the abandoning of concepts like the tithe or making a pledge commitment. That may sound spiritual, but we might fairly ask such advocates, "How can Christians who live under grace practice a lower giving standard than the believers who were once under the law?" For Christians who truly understand God's costly love in sending Jesus to die for us, committing a proportionate amount of income to support God's work is merely a "discipline of gratitude." It is a welcome way to praise God with our finances and ensure that the resources under our management are consistently prioritized for God's work.

Increasingly, churches are asking members to submit an estimate of their giving plans for the coming year. Such estimates are sometimes called "pledges." While not presented as a legally binding covenant, a pledge allows the member to communicate an outward evidence of an inward commitment. It also enables church leaders to more accurately estimate the income that will sustain the year's ministry. It is an exercise in strategic planning, as well as wise stewardship of God's resources.

In recent years, churches have substituted the word *commitment* for pledge, often because some members have expressed an uneasiness with the "legalistic" tone of the word *pledge.* One stewardship leader, in order to avoid misunderstandings of the word *pledge,* has used the phrase "personal giving estimate," which is, in practice, what a pledge is. His phrase does a good job of defining the function of a pledge, as well as defusing the potential for confusion. (See Volume 1 of the *Abingdon Guide to Funding Ministry,* pp. 149-50, for conditions in which a "pledge" might be interpreted as a legally binding contract between a wealthy individual and an institution.)

So what should we call the "pledge"? What we *call* our intentions to grow through giving isn't nearly as important as understanding how this discipline can

> "People think that if they were rich they would contribute to charities. My experience has been that if you don't start giving away your money when you have very little, you won't do it when you get a lot."
>
> —*ROBERT BAINUM*

provide God's people with a way to plan and follow through with ministry. Whether it's a "pledge," a "faith promise," a "personal covenant," or a "personal giving estimate," maturing disciples want to commit to disciplines that will enable them to use resources to obediently fulfill God's mission. And wise church leaders will provide avenues that allow each member of their congregations to express such Spirit-inspired devotion to Christ.

"Charity is equal to all other percepts put together."

—THE TALMUD

 ## PLANNING TOOL

Fall Stewardship Program Options for Your Church

TIMOTHY C. EK

The Personal Covenant Plan

The Personal Covenant Plan is a financial faith covenant made between church members and God for one year, and submitted to the church by the individual or family. It is a step-by-step plan for introducing and implementing a pledge or faith-promise plan to the congregation.

Ten Steps for Presenting the Personal Covenant Plan to Your Entire Church Family

1. First, members known for their faithfulness in prayer should be notified and enlisted in a prayer campaign.

2. Get the approval and commitment of the church board. In churches that have never implemented a pledge program or have not used this approach for some time, this may take a few weeks.

3. Listen to each member's "vision" of ministry for your church. This can be done through special home-visitation teams, in monitored small-group settings, or via questionnaires designed to encourage idea input. This information is a nucleus for all budget planning by various boards.

4. Return to the individual boards, in written form, all the ideas gleaned from this process, for consideration for inclusion in the budget.

5. Determine a faith-size budget for the upcoming year. Each board and commission should draw up written plans for its own area of responsibility.

6. Use worship services, all-church mailings, church school class announcements, and a churchwide dinner to present the budget. Tell everyone how congregational input has already shaped the proposed budget.

7. Plan a "Commitment Sunday" sermon and response time, so that Personal Covenant Plan pledge cards may be collected. Don't forget to follow up with letters of thanks, as well as with contacts to those who have not responded to date. Continue for three weeks.

8. Review the budget in light of the Personal Covenant Plan "giving estimate" cards received. Make a realistic but faith-sized adjustment in the budget you plan to present for final approval.

9. Vote on the budget at your annual meeting.

10. Regularly generate reports on the progress of the church budget, based on its new Personal Covenant Plan. Newsletters, bulletin inserts, quarterly financial statements, testimonies, and such should be shared, so that members can see how God is using their gifts to accomplish God's mission.

A personal covenant is not a contract. It simply affirms the spiritual principle of collective accountability in a body of believers, where each gift is needed to fully equip the whole church to fulfill

Christ's mission (I Cor. 12). It indicates a projected level of giving as God supplies the resources.

The overall goal of the Personal Covenant Plan is to build mature, tithing Christians—disciples of Christ who view whole-life stewardship as a natural extension of God's lordship and their love. The Personal Covenant Plan is not a way to raise money, but a way to raise disciples.

The "Grow One" Model

"Grow One" is a call for members of your congregation to increase their giving to the church by 1 percent of their total household income during the upcoming year. In this way, your church will have resources for new ministries, and the conferences and denomination also can fulfill their roles in helping church families move forward to reach the world for Christ.

Grow One models typically offer members "stair-step" worksheets, to determine exactly what an increase in giving of 1 percent of their income will mean in actual dollars per week, per month, and so on. For a tithing family earning $45,000 per year, it will mean a step up from a $4,500 gift last year to $4,950 in the coming year. Such a commitment accelerates the "mustard-seed" growth that Jesus calls his disciples to experience.

A commitment to giving an additional 1 percent of household or church income to Christ's work demands a significant step of faith—but it encourages growth. To estimate your congregation's giving potential, multiply the number of giving units or households in your church by $400 (the estimated 1 percent increase of the average U.S. household income, which was $41,260 in 1992).

Letter Campaign Model

This program approach is very effective, in combination with other programs or as a variation from other types of approaches. The principle tool of this program is a sequence of letters to the congregation, often from leaders of various program areas of the church, seeking to explain church programs in terms of the upcoming budget. Generally, four to six letters are needed in this type of approach.

The first letter introduces the theme and often includes a Faith Promise card. The second follow-up letter should be sent to the same households about two weeks later. The third letter should be sent just prior to your "Stewardship Sunday," with the request that pledges be presented during that special service. Persons also may be given the option of mailing their pledge to the church. The fourth letter celebrates the results of your churchwide program focus with those who have responded positively with faith-commitment forms. The fifth and final letter is to encourage those who have not yet responded.

Consecration Sunday

This program approach has been effectively used in churches of all sizes, both rural and urban. Many churches report significant increases in giving.

The program often uses Home Visitation Teams. These teams explain the proposed budget to each household in the church in terms of the vision for ministry, answer any questions, and leave commitment or pledge cards.

The program focuses on one special worship event, led by a guest speaker, in which every member is urged to participate. The highlight of the gathering is a consecration period, during which faith commitments are received. That evening, the guest speaker presides over a victory dinner, to bring together a sense of celebration and the joy of giving.

Key to the success of this approach has been good communication—early and often—promoting churchwide participation.

Follow-up letters of thanks, as well as contacts to those who have not responded with pledges, should be mailed immediately.

Whatever approach you choose, remember . . .

. . . each year, your church needs to deepen its understanding and practice of "whole-life" stewardship. Such a year-round stewardship emphasis will enable your church family to make significant strides in developing mature disciples.

But also remember—studies show that even mature Christians need to be asked to give! Of those asked to increase their giving through an organized program, 82 percent will do so! So a good stewardship program should challenge members to take a fresh look at the variety of ways open to them to respond to the blessings that all of us continue to receive—and help them affirm God's call to Spirit-led management of the resources God provides.

 COMMITMENT CAMPAIGN

SEEKING SOMETHING BETTER

**An Annual Stewardship Campaign,
Expanded into a Churchwide Quest for Spiritual Renewal**

LEADERS GUIDE

JIM KILLEN

Helpful Hint: When you photocopy the following Workbook to distribute to each participant in the campaign *Seeking Something Better,* consider using a stapled booklet of 24 pages, plus a cover, perhaps containing art work that is symbolic of your church. If necessary, the final pages of the workbook—the covenant cards—might be placed on the inside of the back cover. The cover can be made of any paper stock that fits your budget.

CONTENTS

INTRODUCTION

"Seeking Something Better" is an annual stewardship campaign, expanded to involve the whole congregation in a renewal of the members' relationship with God and with the church. It begins by addressing the yearning for a fuller life that draws people to Christ and goes on to move them toward that commitment in which fullness of life can be found.

The objectives of this program are to:

1. Recover the concept of stewardship as an aspect of the Christian's relationship with God.
2. Encourage the committed members of the church to renew and deepen their commitment.
3. Enable the committed members of the church to make a witness to the less committed members, inviting them to renew their commitment, though in a way that is winsome and not uncomfortable.
4. Increase the congregation's base of support among its members.

The major aspects of the program are:

1. Half-day retreats to deepen the commitment of the committed members.
2. Visitation to invite the total membership to participate in four weeks of spiritual renewal.
3. A four-week program of personal and family devotional activities.
4. A covenant Sunday, on which renewed commitments are made.

ORGANIZATION

The leadership team of the congregation needs to take the following steps to make this program successful:

1. The Board must adopt this program as the program to be followed in the annual stewardship campaign.
2. A proposed budget for the church should be developed.
3. Sufficient funds must be allocated to implement the program, if they have not already been budgeted.
4. The Board should elect the members of a steering committee.

5. Arrange for "Seeking Something Better" to be the primary program of emphasis for a two-month period of time.

LEADERSHIP

People selected to give leadership in this program should be: spiritually alive, faithful and generous in their stewardship, have the respect of the congregation, and have the ability and willingness to commit the necessary time and energy to accomplish the task. The following people should be on the steering committee:

1. **The General Chairperson.** This person should have the ability to envision the total program and coordinate the efforts of the whole church to make it successful.

2. **The Packet Preparation Chairperson.** This person should assemble a committee of people who are personally acquainted with as many church members as possible.

Drawing on personal knowledge and records of church attendance, they will divide the church membership into four groups: active members who will be asked to call on others to enlist their participation (about twice as many as will be needed); active members who will not be asked to visit; less active and inactive resident members; nonresident members. Lists should be prepared and duplicated for use in the retreats.

Personalized packets should be prepared for each resident family, containing: a personalized letter (Letter No. 3); a copy of the stewardship workbook (see below); a covenant folder (see below) for each adult and youth member of the family; and a copy of an annotated church budget. Family name address and phone number should be on the outside of the packet envelope. A similar packet should be prepared for each nonresident family, but these should contain a different letter (Letter No. 4), and a stamped, self-addressed envelope for returning covenant folders. These should be prepared for mailing.

3. **The Visitation Chairperson.** This should be a person who can effectively enlist and mobilize people to accomplish a task. In a large membership congregation, team captains will need to be recruited. One visitation unit (individuals or pairs) will be needed for each six resident active *and* inactive families. One team captain will be needed for each ten visitors. The visitation chairperson and the team captains will recruit visitors after the letters of invitation (Letter No. 1) go out by phoning them and asking them to attend the retreat.

4. **The Retreat Chairperson.** This person will be responsible for orchestrating one, two, or more half-day enabling retreats for committed members, who will call on other members, asking them to participate. (See the outline for an enabling retreat.)

5. **A Publicity Chairperson.** This should be someone with communication skills who will keep the program before the congregation and encourage the members to keep participating. Creativity in promotion should be employed. This person will see that all mailings get out on time. The publicity chairperson may organize one or more committees to do this work.

6. **A Food Committee Chairperson.** This should be someone who can mobilize the cooks in the congregation to prepare any breakfasts, lunches, or snacks that may be planned for the retreats.

7. **A Follow-Up Chairperson.** This person will lead a committee to be responsible for analyzing the results and planning the follow-up. Follow-up should include contacting and asking those members who do not turn in covenant folders to do so, and also seeing that the information from the folders reaches those persons and groups in the church who can enable the people to follow through on their commitments. The covenant folders are designed to be cut into three or four parts, to be sent to the agencies that will act on them: covenants to give go to the financial secretary; covenants to serve go to Nominations; covenants to grow and participate go to the Planning Council or to other groups appointed to follow up.

8. **The Pastor.** The pastor will play a key role in this program, not only in enabling the lay team but also in preparing sermons and worship experiences that will be a part of spiritual growth.

CALENDAR OF EVENTS

Four Weeks Prior to Week One, the following things should take place.

1. Plans and decisions listed above under "organization" should be accomplished. Materials should be ordered or produced. An annotated version of the proposed church budget should be prepared and duplicated.

2. Steering committee should meet, pray about the program, try to visualize what should take place in the congregation, and make plans to encourage it.

3. Each committee chairperson should recruit the help needed and begin preparing for the task.

4. The packet committee should make its study of the congregation, divide it into the four groups mentioned above, and begin preparing the personalized packets, including Letter No.3.

5. Letter No.1 should be prepared and addressed to those who will be asked to visit.

6. Preliminary publicity should make the congregation aware of what is coming and encourage the members to get excited about it.

7. The week before week one, an announcement of the program should appear in headlines in the church newsletter, and Letter No.1 should be sent out to prospective visitors.

Week One. Recruitment Week.

1. Visitation committee should contact those who are to be asked to visit, get their commitment to do so, and make reservations for enabling retreats.

2. Packet Committee, Retreat Committee, and Food Committee should finish their work.

Week Two. Preparation Week.

1. One, two, or more enabling retreats should be held. (See plans for an enabling retreat.)

2. Letter No. 2 should be sent to all resident members, except those who will be visiting.

Week Three. Visitation Week.

1. Visitors should make friendly visits to the families they have chosen, deliver packets, and encourage participation.

2. Packets should be mailed to nonresident members. Include Letter No.4.

Week Four. First Week of "Growing Days."

1. On the first Sunday, pastor preaches a kick-off sermon on the need for spiritual renewal. A lay witness will make a brief statement on a similar theme.

2. All families begin growing by using their stewardship workbooks. These can be photocopied from the workbook included below, or printed, if you are using the software edition of *The Abingdon Guide to Funding Ministry, Volume 2.*

3. Postcards are mailed to remind everyone as to where they should be in their readings. (The church can decide whether this will be repeated weekly or less often.)

Week Five. Second Week of "Growing Days."

1. Pastor and lay witness should speak on the importance of the church as an agent of God's new possibility.

2. Everyone continues personal and family devotional use of the workbook.

Week Six. Third Week of "Growing Days."

1. Pastor and lay witness talk about stewardship of time, talent, and resources, as part of our participation in God's work in the world.

2. Personal and family devotional work continue.

3. Visitors should give the families on whom they called a friendly phone call to encourage them in their participation.

Week Seven. Fourth Week of "Growing Days."

1. Pastor and lay witness talk about keeping a growing edge on our commitment to God.

2. Everyone moves into the last week of the devotional activities outlined in the stewardship workbook.

3. Letter No. 5 is sent to everyone, reminding them of covenant Sunday and urging them to participate. Additional covenant folders should be enclosed.

Week Eight. Covenant Sunday and Follow-up Time.

1. Pastor should speak on expectancy. Covenant renewal should be the theme of the service. Everyone should have an opportunity to bring their covenant folders to the altar. (Additional folders should be available in the pews.)

2. Resident members who did not turn in covenant folders should be contacted and encouraged to turn them in. Letter No. 6 should be sent to those who have not responded by the end of the week.

3. Covenant folders should be cut into parts, with the parts distributed to those agencies in the church that will act on them: Covenants to give (kept confidential) go to the financial secretary; covenants to serve go to the Committee on Nominations; covenants to grow and to participate go to the Council on Ministries, or to the people of your congregation who will organize appropriate enabling programs and enlist participation. All who make covenants should receive some invitation to act on their commitments.

4. Thank you notes (Letter No. 7) should be sent to all who assisted and\or covenanted.

PLEASE NOTE. Some who would like to streamline the program will be tempted to delete the retreats and the visitation, and send the workbooks out through the mail. This would greatly weaken the program. The workbook is just a tool. The real working parts of this program are the following, so work at maximizing the effectiveness of these aspects:

1. The deepening of the commitment of the committed;

2. The friendly witness of the committed to the less committed;

3. The dynamics of a congregation sharing a growing experience.

PROGRAM FOR AN ENABLING RETREAT

The enabling retreat should be an inspirational experience. Instructions and assignments should carry out the context of a commitment to spiritual growth. Use all the creativity at your command to make it a special experience. It should be held at a time when at least 2 hours are available for the experience. A breakfast, lunch, or refreshments may be included, either at the beginning or at the end of the retreat. The following activities are recommended:

1. Introduce the program, its purpose, and its schedule. A printed handout will be helpful. Explain the responsibilities of the workers.

2. Distribute the packets of those who are present. Invite them to take out the workbook and skim its contents, reading the lines in bold print. Allow about 10 minutes for this.

3. Distribute sheets of blank paper and ask each participant to write a single sentence on "Why I need to renew my covenant with God and the church," then fold the paper once for anonymous sharing.

4. Divide the group into share groups of ten or twelve persons. Appoint a convener for each group. The convener should collect the written statements, shuffle them, and redistribute them to be read anonymously. The convener can then lead the group in a discussion of "Why our church needs renewal of commitment."

5. Reassemble and pass out copies of the lists of active and less active members who need to be contacted. Ask each worker to review both lists and select some people they know and feel comfortable about contacting. It would be good for each worker to select three names of active members and three

names of less active or inactive members. Then let each worker or couple pick up the packets from a table where all of the packets are displayed in alphabetical order for convenience. The objective is to get each packet into the hands of the visitors who can most comfortably and most effectively enlist the family's participation.

6. When the packets have been distributed, each worker should use a form, which should be provided, to make two lists of the families selected. The worker's name should be at the bottom. One copy of this should be for the worker's record, and the other should be given to the retreat leader for control purposes.

7. The retreat leader should then instruct the workers how to call for an appointment, make a winsome explanation of the program, deliver the packet, and explain the procedures for "Growing Days" and Covenant Sunday.

8. The retreat should end in worship. Some time should be spent in prayer for the church and for those the workers hope to involve. Finally, there should be a service of communion.

Visitation should start immediately after the retreat and be completed before "Beginning Sunday."

SMALL GROUP SHARING: A SUGGESTION

In congregations where people are comfortable participating in share groups, this program could be greatly enriched by forming those members who are willing into small groups to share their growing experiences. It is best if the groups meet on Sunday evening or Monday, so that a whole unit (week) of devotional work can be dealt with at one time. A standard format might consist of: time to focus mentally, intercessory prayer, and reading of scripture lessons, followed by sharing of growing experiences. The first meeting might be held on or about Beginning Sunday. The sharing time might follow the approach suggested for the share-group time, in the plan for the enabling retreats. After that, the lead questions might be simply: "What did you find especially meaningful in last week's readings?" and "What would you like to share of your own growing experience?" It is always appropriate to end with a prayer circle.

LETTERS AND OTHER RESOURCES

The following pages contain suggested forms for letters to be sent during the program:

Four Suggestions for Letter Preparation:

1. Mail letters first class, to be received on the Friday or Saturday of each week.
2. Have all letters personally signed by the pastor, stewardship committee chairman, or other church leaders.

3. Include other material (tracts, etc.) sparingly. In the first letter, a commitment card is enclosed, with a stamped, self-addressed return envelope.
4. Continue to mail to a family until the commitment form is returned, or until you are aware of the reasons for the particular response.

Letter #1, to prospective visitors.

Dear _____,

Our church is about to enter a very special program which, we expect, will bring new life to our church and all its members. We invite you not only to participate in it, but also to help us make it successful.

We plan to expand the annual stewardship campaign into a churchwide spiritual renewal emphasis. The theme of the program will be "Seeking Something Better." We will be involving all our church members in a four-week program of daily devotional activities and special worship services, leading up to the renewal of our covenant with Christ and the church on Sunday, _____. In addition to enlisting the members' support for the church, we expect to renew our personal relationships with God.

Here is what we would like for you to do to help:

1. Attend a half-day enabling retreat for inspiration, coaching, and assignment. Retreats will be held during the week of _____.

2. Call on six persons or families, preferably some you know and can talk to comfortably, deliver a packet of materials, and encourage them to participate in the program. No, you do not need to ask them to pledge, just to participate. This should be done during the week of _____.

3. Encourage your people by phone, or by casual personal contact, to keep participating. If they fail to make it to Covenant Sunday, you may be asked to call and offer to pick up their covenant folders.

We think "Seeking Something Better" will do great things for our church. Your participation can make it even more meaningful to you. Someone will call soon to ask if we can count on you and to make your reservation for the retreat.

Sincerely,

Letter #2, to all resident church members who did not receive letter #1.

Dear _____,

Your church is about to enter into a very special program, and we would like for you to be excited about it. We hope that it will be very good for our church and for all its members.

We are expanding our annual stewardship campaign into a churchwide quest for spiritual renewal. Don't worry, you will still have a chance to pledge to support the church with your gifts and your services. But we also expect to enter into a renewed relationship with God that will make things better for you every day of your life. The theme of our program is, "Seeking Something Better."

Some time during the coming week week, one of your friends from the church will drop by to bring a packet of materials for your use and tell you more about the program. We expect to involve every member of our church in four weeks of special worship services and daily devotional activities, leading up to a special Covenant Sunday on _____, If for some reason you do not receive a packet by Sunday, _____, call the church office, and we will send you one. We want everyone to participate.

Pray for the success of this program, and plan to participate fully. We expect that God will use it to lead us all into "Something Better."

Sincerely,

Letter #3, to be included in the packets

Dear _____,

Here are the materials you will need to participate fully in your church's "Seeking Something Better" program.

Enclosed you will find a workbook for religious renewal, titled "Seeking Something Better." It is written so that you can skim it in five minutes or read through it in half an hour. But we really want you to use it daily for the next four weeks, as a guide to personal and family devotions.

Starting on Sunday, _____, pick a time every day to read the designated page. Look up the scripture references and study them. Think about what the readings say. Discuss it with your family members. Answer the questions thoughtfully. Fill in the blanks. Pray the prayers. Think about it as you go through the day. Let the book facilitate a conversation between you and God.

If you get behind, go back and catch up, for the meditations build on one another. It really won't take long. This book is intended to guide you through a really significant period of spiritual growth.

Attending church regularly also will be important. A special series of worship services is planned to lead the congregation through its growing days. The series will begin on Sunday, _____ and end with Covenant Sunday, _____.

A copy of the church budget is included, if you need to refer to it.

You also will find enclosed a covenant folder for each adult and young person in your family. After you have completed your month of religious renewal, you can use the folders to make your new covenant with Christ and the church. It will include your annual pledge to support the church with your gifts and services. It also will give you an opportunity to commit to new adventures in faith and ask the church for the help you need.

We will bring our covenant folders to the church and place them on the altar in a very special service on _____.

We anticipate that when you really put yourself into this quest for renewal, you just may get something really surprising out of it. You might experience the renewal of your life!

Sincerely,

Letter #4, to nonresident members.

Dear _____,

We know that you miss participating in the life and work of your church since you no longer live in the community. But your church is about to enter into a new and promising program in which you can participate.

We are expanding our annual stewardship campaign into a four-week quest for religious renewal. In addition to our worship services, we will be using a workbook for religious renewal to guide us through daily devotional activities. We call the program "Seeking Something Better." We expect that it will lead us all into a renewed relationship with God.

You can participate with the rest of the members of your church by using the enclosed workbook for daily spiritual-growth activities, beginning on Sunday, _____.

You also will find enclosed a covenant folder. You can use it to make your pledge to support your church financially, and also to plan the steps you intend to take to renew your relationship with Christ and the church. The members who still live in the community will bring their covenant folders to church on Sunday, _____. You can use the enclosed self-addressed envelope to return yours as well.

We regret being too far from you to involve you in the daily and weekly life of the congregation. We expect that sharing in this quest for renewal will help you experience some long-distance fellowship with us. Drop us a line to let us know how you are doing when you return your covenant folder. We would like to hear from you.

Sincerely,

Letter #5, to all members, reminding them of Covenant Sunday

Dear _____,

We expect that you have been participating daily in our church's "Seeking Something Better" program and that it has been a meaningful experience for you. Now we are approaching the climax of that program, Covenant Sunday. During morning worship on Sunday, _____, everyone will be invited to bring their covenant folders forward and lay them on the altar, as a way of renewing their covenants with Christ and the church.

If you have been using the "Seeking Something Better" workbook, you have been thinking through some significant commitments. Record those commitments in your covenant folder and bring it with you to church. We are sending an additional covenant folder, in case you have misplaced yours.

Your covenant folder will be read and taken seriously by the leaders of the church. We plan to cut your folder up into four parts. (That is why you need to sign it four times.) Your Covenant to Give will be your annual financial pledge. It will be sent to the financial secretary and kept confidential. Your Covenant to Serve will be sent to Nominations and used by people who staff the church programs. Your covenants to grow and to participate will be sent to the Planning Council and used in planning church programs and responding to your needs. If you cannot be with us on Covenant Sunday, send or bring your covenant folder to the church as soon as you can.

We hope that "Seeking Something Better" has been a really good experience for you and that it will be just the beginning of an adventure in spiritual growth.

Sincerely

Letter #6, to those who have not turned in covenant folders.

Dear _____,

Covenant Sunday has come and gone, and we have not received a covenant folder from you. We are sending you another folder and a self-addressed envelope, so that you can join the rest of the members of your church in seeking something better. Your support and participation are important to your church, and we hope that your involvement also will be important to you.

Sincerely,

Letter #7, a thank-you letter to all participants.

Dear _____,

Thank you for your participation in Seeking Something Better. Your covenants of service and financial support will enable your church to continue its work in the community and around the world. Your covenant to be a growing participant in the life of the church can help this congregation become the kind of vital, loving, serving, and growing Christian fellowship we all want it to be. Let's look forward with excitement and anticipation to the results of the renewal of our relationships with the living God.

Sincerely,

Form for use in recording names of families chosen by workers at the enabling retreat:

MY COVENANT TO VISIT

I covenant to do all I can to encourage the following to participate fully in the church's "Seeking Something Better" program.

Name	Address	Phone

1._____

2._____

3._____

4._____

5._____

6._____

My Name_____ Phone Number_____

Reminder postcard to be used as needed during "Growing Days":

Dear Friend,

Are you Seeking Something Better? We hope you are participating in your church's spiritual renewal program. By now, you should be finishing the _____ week of your daily use of the workbook for religious renewal. We hope you are having a good experience. See you in church.

Grace and Peace,
(Church name)

Covenant Folder:

MY COVENANT TO GIVE

In grateful stewardship of all that God has entrusted to me, I plan to give $_____ per _____ (week, month, year) to do the work of God through my church. (See pages 14 and 23 in Workbook.)

Check here if your pledge represents a tithe. _____

Check here if you plan to step up to tithing. _____

Name_____

....

MY COVENANT TO SERVE

Count on me to commit the following amount of time to serving God through the church. (See pages 20 and 23 in Workbook.)

I am good at:_____

I would like to try: _____

I would like to serve on the _____ committee.
Call on me to serve in one or more of the following ways:

_____   _____

_____   _____

I would like to talk with someone about how I can serve._____

Name_____

....

MY COVENANT TO GROW

I would like to do the following things to put a growing edge on my faith_____.
(See page 23 in Workbook.)
I would like for my church to enable me or support me in my ministry to the world in the following ways.
_____

_____

(See page 23 in Workbook.)

Name _____ .

....

MY COVENANT TO PARTICIPATE

I would like for my church to enlarge its ministries in the following ways:_____

_____

_____

(See page 24 in Workbook.)

Name _____

SEEKING SOMETHING BETTER

Jim Killen

Seeking Something Better

A Workbook for Spiritual Renewal

The Annual Church Stewardship Campaign usually invites you to renew your pledge to support the church with your gifts. This year, our church is inviting you to participate in a more comprehensive renewal. You are invited to participate in a quest for the renewal of your whole relationship with God and the church.

SUGGESTIONS FOR USING THIS WORKBOOK

1. First, skim through the entire book by reading only the bold print.
2. Work your way through the book by dealing with one page each day for four weeks. Look up the scriptures. Read the devotional. Think about the questions. Fill in the blanks, and pray the prayers.
3. Use your completed workbook to complete your personal covenant folder for this year.

Our Prayer: Restore to me the joy of your salvation, and sustain in me a willing spirit.　　　**PSALM 51:12**

....

SUNDAY, FIRST WEEK

Jesus said: **Blessed are those who hunger and thirst for righteousness, for they will be filled** (Matt. 5:6).

READ MATTHEW 5:1-12

Righteousness is another word for that new kind of life that results from organizing life around the reality of God. It means life lived in a right relationship with God—and it is full of exciting surprises.

> That new kind of life is a real possibility for each of us
> no matter what we have done
> no matter what has been done to us
> no matter what we have or don't have
> no matter if our lives are in a mess.
> That new life is possible because God is always there
> ready to forgive us
> ready to accept us as we are
> ready to love us
> ready to help us make a fresh start.

New life is a free gift to you from God.
It is there for you.

You can have it if you want it.
But you really have to want it. You have to hunger and thirst for it. It will make demands upon you, and if you don't really want it, you probably won't accept it.

(Still, hungering and thirsting for this new life is better than hungering and thirsting for something less valuable that you probably never can have.)

2

What are you hungry and thirsty for?

What are the strong desires that are driving you right now?

_____ [   ] _____

_____ [   ] _____

Prayer: Lord, show me how the new life you offer me can satisfy the deepest hungers of my heart. Amen.

MONDAY, FIRST WEEK

Jesus said: **No one can serve two masters . . . . You cannot serve God and wealth** (Matt. 6:24).

READ MATTHEW 6:19-24.

Most of us have a problem entering into new life because we don't want to do anything that will jeopardize the advantages we have gained—or expect to gain—through our old commitments.

Jesus once met a young man who was stuck in that kind of ambivalence. Jesus told him to go and sell all that he had and give the money to the poor, and then come and follow him. Obviously, that commandment was not for everyone. Someone has to manage the businesses and homes and funds. But that young man had a decision to make—and so do we. (Read the story in Matt. 19:13-26).

A wheel can have only one center. Either everything in our lives, including our resources, will be organized around our relationship with God, or everything in our lives, including our religion, will be organized around our pursuit of affluence—or whatever else we choose as the center of our lives.

You can't have it both ways. We have a decision to make. Our faith can't do us much good unless we allow it to really be our faith.

How would management of your business, your home, and your resources be different, if it were reorganized around a new center in God?

Business_____

_____

Home_____

_____

Resources_____

_____

Prayer: Lord, help me to catch a vision of the shape of the new life you offer, so that I can really want to choose it. Amen.

TUESDAY, FIRST WEEK

Jesus said: **Do not worry about . . . what you will eat or what you will drink, or about your body, what you will wear. . . . Strive first for the kingdom of God and his righteousness, and all these things will be given to you as well** (Matt. 6:25, 33).

READ MATTHEW 6:25-34.

3

It seems that Jesus asks us to do some very frightening things. Isn't this rather unrealistic?

There is a promise that goes with the calling of Christ that makes everything possible. It is the promise that God will be there—and that God loves you—and that God will provide for you.

This is not an invitation to stop assuming responsibility for yourself and your family. Neither is it a promise that God will miraculously give you everything you want, as if God were a great Santa Claus.

God's promise simply says that if we will let go of our anxieties, trust God, and put first things first in life, God will be with us. Only when we can trust the goodness of the One who gives life can we be free to live life fully.

> **It's like learning to swim. First you have to learn to trust the water.**
> What are the things you are trusting and depending on in life right now?

What would it mean for you to trust God to provide?
Begin listing the changes that trusting might make in your life.

_____

_____

_____

Prayer: I admit it, Lord. I am anxious and afraid. Help me to trust so that I can be free. Amen.

WEDNESDAY, FIRST WEEK

Jesus said: **You must be born from above** (John 3:7*b*).

READ JOHN 3:1-16

Did you ever wish that you could just cancel your past and start over again? Jesus invites us to do that.

The changes that God wants to make in our lives are not just changes that we have to make through our own superhuman effort and grim determination.

God is alive and at work in our lives. God can change our lives. Yes, we have to be willing, and we have to work with God. But we are not alone.

If you give God a chance, God will reorganize your life and make it new.
Being aware of the presence and reality of God can change things. It can put everything in a **new perspective.** Some things that seem overwhelming when we face them alone will seem manageable because God is bigger than they are.
　Some things that seem terribly important will seem less important and we will be free of their demands. Other things will be shown to be truly important.

Experiencing **God's love** for you can change things. It can replace anxiety with freedom; self-deprecation with healthy self-esteem; despair with hope.

Most important, in place of whatever has been the dominant force in your life, God will give you a new driving force—love. It can be exciting. Are you willing?

4

What difference could God's love make in your life?

Don't try to write down the answer to this question. Just think about it throughout this day.

Prayer: Lord, I am not sure I want a new life. I kind of like myself as I am. Even if my present life is not so good, it is familiar. I am comfortable in it. Show me the better possibility you are offering me, and help me become excited about it. Amen.

THURSDAY, FIRST WEEK

Jesus said: **The kingdom of heaven is like a merchant in search of fine pearls; on finding one pearl of great value, he went and sold all that he had and bought it** (Matt. 13:45-46).

READ MATTHEW 13:44-46

Are you satisfied with your life?
- Is the quality of life you are enjoying now what you really want? Is it full and meaningful and genuinely happy?

- Is your life making any difference for good in the lives of others or in the world?

- If you were suddenly to learn that you had only a short time to live, could you look back on your life and feel good about it?

Jesus told a story about a man who had spent his life doing nothing but accumulating wealth. Then, just as the man decided he had plenty and was about to retire and start living, he died. Jesus said that he was a very foolish man. (Read Luke 12:15-21.)

Jesus came to offer us a better life.
He came to offer us a life that is genuinely full and free and meaningful and profoundly happy. The Bible calls this life by such names as "fullness of life," "eternal life," "the abundant life," "righteousness," or "the kingdom of God."

What do you want most out of life?
Imagine that you have just learned that you have only a few months to live. Look back over your life and list the things you wish you could change.

_____   _____

_____   _____

_____   _____

Prayer: Lord, you have given me being. Help me to be fully alive.

FRIDAY, FIRST WEEK

Jesus said: **The kingdom of God has come near** (Mark 1:15*b*).

READ MARK 1:14-15

What did Jesus mean by that? He meant that God is offering an exciting new possibility to each of us and to our world.

5

Most of us believe in God.

- We believe in someone who created the world and keeps it going.
- We believe in someone who is the most important of all realities, the reality behind all other realities.
- If we believe what Jesus taught us, we believe in someone who loves us.

But too often, we act as if that God in whom we believe were somewhere else—don't we?

> If that God in whom we believe were
> standing right here among us in some form
> that we would be forced to recognize, we
> would pay attention, wouldn't we? We
> would forget everything else and reorganize
> our lives around God, wouldn't we?
> Jesus came, announcing that God is real
> and present and that we should reorganize
> our lives around God, as a kingdom is
> organized around a king.

Life that is organized around the reality of God is a new and exciting kind of life.
It is God's new possibility for us and for our world. We can have it.

What difference could God make in your life?
Close your eyes and imagine God, as you usually visualize God, standing right in front of you. Try to visualize the difference God's presence would make. Imagine that happening at home, at school, at work.

Prayer: Hello, God. Please forgive me for not recognizing you. Help me to get my life reorganized around your reality. Amen.

SATURDAY, FIRST WEEK

Jesus said: **Follow me** (Matt. 4:19).
                     Read Matthew 4:18-22
                     Also read Mark 8:34-37

Jesus invites us to go on an adventure with him.

The disciples whom Jesus called left their homes and businesses. They went with Jesus.
   They joined him in a new life, liberated by faith and shaped by love.
      They joined him in a life committed to something bigger than themselves.
         They lived in service to the purposes of God.

Jesus gives us a similar invitation.
   We may or may not need to leave anything geographical or physical, but we are called out of an old way of life.
      We are called into a new life of faith, freedom, commitment, and purpose.

Are you up for an adventure?

Are you still anxious about what you might lose in such an adventure? Then ponder what Jesus said in the second reading.

6

Those who are anxiously preoccupied with getting and saving their lives are likely to lose them.

Those who lose their lives in the service of something bigger, especially in the service of God, are likely to gain life.

Think about that.

Remember the people you have known who were anxiously striving to promote themselves.

Remember those who forgot themselves in a commitment to something bigger.

Which of them seemed most fully alive to you?

Ponder the mystery of life lost and found.

Prayer: Help me to hear you calling me to follow. Help me to be able to do it. Amen.

SUNDAY, SECOND WEEK

Jesus prayed: **That his followers might all be one.**

READ JOHN 17

On the night before he died, Jesus prayed that his followers might all be one with himself and with God. He included us in his prayers—those who were to believe because of the witness of those first followers.

The fellowship of his followers was important to Jesus.
- Jesus thanked God for his disciples.
- Jesus said that he was sending them into the world as God had sent him—to do God's work.
- Jesus prayed that God would keep us from falling.

Most of us want to be very individualistic in our faith. How often have you heard someone say, "I don't think I need to go to church to be a Christian"?

To be a Christian is to be a part of the Church.

To be a part of the Church Universal, you need to be part of some church in particular. You are called into an imperfect human institution, committed to the purpose of God.

You may need to forgive your church for many things:
- For being an institution with human failures;
- For not being the "super church" you wish it could be;
- For sometimes having let you down or hurt you. You may need to accept your church as it is, just as the church accepts you as you are.

In the church: attend it, pray for it, participate in it, support it, see yourself as part of it, just as you are part of your family.
You need to be open to your church
and let God bless you through it.

The next two weeks of our readings will be primarily about the church, because the church is important.

What is the "given name" of your local church?

_____

Prayer: Thank you, Lord, for my church. Help me to be a faithful member of it. Amen.

MONDAY, SECOND WEEK

The Bible says: **[Jesus] went to the synagogue on the sabbath day, as was his custom** (Luke 4:16*b*).

READ LUKE 4:16-21

Some remember a time when almost everyone customarily went to church every Sunday.

But now it seems that many people are out of the habit of going to church.
    Lots of things make it easy to get out of the habit;
Lots of people have come to feel like strangers to church life.
    Those who are out of the habit of going to church have lost something important in their lives.

If Jesus needed to go to church, so do we.

We need the things that happen in church to keep us living in touch with God.
    Those who were in the synagogue on the day Jesus came had a unique opportunity to encounter the Lord.
        Your church plans the things that happen on Sunday to help good things happen between you and God.
            But if you are not there, you miss it!

We also need to be in church so we can help with the good things that happen there. We are needed there. We grow through service.
In order to be a part of Christ's church, you must put yourself in it, physically as well as spiritually.

How will you work church attendance into your schedule?

_____

_____

_____

_____

Prayer: Lord, I will see you in church next Sunday. Amen.

TUESDAY, SECOND WEEK

Jesus said: **You are the light of the world. . . . You are the salt of the earth** (Matt. 5:14*a*, 13*a*).

READ MATTHEW 5:13-16

Jesus called his followers to make a difference in the world;
● Like seasoning for a dull and flavorless life,
● Like a preservative that keeps things from spoiling,
● Like light that drives away darkness.

The followers of Jesus are a people with a purpose.

Remember what you know about God.
    God created all things by bringing order out of chaos, being out of nonbeing.

God made a covenant with all the creatures, calling them to full humanity and promising to be their God.
   God loves all people and wants justice,
   well-being, and fullness of life for all of us.
"God so loved the world that he gave his only Son, so that everyone who believes in him may not perish but may have eternal life" (John 3:16).

Knowing what you know about God, and knowing what you know about the world we live in, answer these questions:

What differences do you think God wants to make in the world?

_____

_____

_____

How might God want to use the church to make those differences?

_____

_____

_____

Prayer: Lord, show me how I can be salt and light. Show me how you want to use me to make a difference. Amen.

WEDNESDAY, SECOND WEEK

Jesus said: **Consider the lilies, how they grow . . . . if God so clothes the grass of the field . . . how much more will he clothe you—you of little faith!** (Luke 12:27a, 28a, c).

READ LUKE 12:22-31

God really does provide abundantly for us, doesn't he?

Many of us have a curious habit of always talking about how poor we are, how little we have, and how hard we have had to work to survive.
   We do this, even though we are among the most richly blessed people of the earth.
Why do we do this?
* Is it because we feel guilty about our prosperity?
* Is it because we want to excuse ourselves from any responsibilities that may go with advantage?

Whatever the reason, it is a foolish practice.
* It makes us feel bad when we could feel good.
* It makes us feel weak when we could feel able.
* It makes us feel bitter when we could be joyful.

Let's get rid of our "poor me" attitudes and be grateful.

Let us be honest about our blessedness.

Count your blessings.

What has God given you?
Check and fill in the blanks below to inventory your blessings.

_____ Life

_____ Humanity

_____ God's love

_____ Love from others,

_____ The ability to love,

_____ A beautiful world,

_____ Plenty to eat,

_____ A place to live,

income to do more

_____ than meet your basic needs,

_____ A free country to live in.

Ability to make life-

_____ shaping decisions,

Some status in your

_____ community,

_____ Ability to influence others.

_____ Material possessions and property

_____

_____

_____

_____ Savings

_____ Abilities

_____

_____

_____

_____ The good news of

Jesus Christ

_____ The Church,

_____ Hope of Heaven

_____ Other Resources

_____

_____

Prayer: Thanks, Lord. Thanks a lot! Amen.

THURSDAY, SECOND WEEK

Jesus taught: **God is like an entrepreneur who entrusts his investment capital to his employees.**

READ MATTHEW 25:14-30

In the parable of the talents, Jesus tells of three people who were put in charge of certain investment funds. Two managed creatively, invested courageously, made a profit, and were rewarded. The other was afraid of his employer. He hoarded the funds, thinking it was most important to conserve them. He did not win his employer's approval.

What must Jesus have wanted us to learn from that story?

1. That all we have has been entrusted to us by God.
2. That God wants us to use all that he has entrusted to us in his service.
3. That God rewards those who invest their lives courageously in the service of the purposes of God.

Some people seem to think that Christianity means hoarding life and trying not to lose it. They are more concerned about not doing anything wrong than they are about doing something good. They tend to avoid all situations of stress and ambiguity where there might be risk.

The gospel teaches that God calls us to invest our lives courageously in doing something really good.

This sometimes requires us to move into situations of stress and ambiguity and risk. We are assured that if we make some mistakes trying to do something good, God will understand.

Those who invest in life courageously are more genuinely alive.

In what way may God be calling you to a courageous investment of life right now?

_____

_____

Prayer: I hear you calling, Lord. Give me the courage to answer. Amen.

FRIDAY, SECOND WEEK

Jesus said: **Go therefore and make disciples** (Matt. 28:19*a*).

READ MATTHEW 28:16-20

If you have found something good, you will want to share it with your friends.

We know that we should share the Christian faith with others—but many of us feel very uncomfortable about trying to do that.

It is not as hard as you think to share your faith.

If you are actively involved in your church and feel good about it, the things you say to your friends as you talk about it will make your church and your faith attractive. It will just happen.

But you can share your faith intentionally too.

The very best way to share your faith is also the easiest way.
    Simply invite your friends to come with you to church—or
    better yet, to Sunday school and worship.
        If they come, you will have put them in touch with
        Christ and the church in a comfortable way.

How do you invite someone to come to church?
    Make up a one sentence statement, saying something positive
    about your church and your faith.
        Don't be "preachy" or condescending. Make it something
        you would feel comfortable saying to your best friend.

Look for opportunities to share your statement. They will come.
    When you have given your invitation, see how your friend
    responds. Follow through appropriately.
        If your friend is not responsive the first time, watch
        for another time when he or she may be ready.

What might you say to a friend you want to invite to your church?

Write your sentence below.

_____

_____

Prayer: Lord, help me to know when and where to share my faith. Amen.

....

SATURDAY, SECOND WEEK

Jesus said: **You will be my witnesses in Jerusalem [right where you are now], Judea and Samaria [anywhere you may happen to go], and to the ends of the earth** (Acts 1:8*b*).

READ ACTS 1:6-9

How can we go into all the world to share our faith?
   That is no problem. You go into the world every day.

How can we find people who need the Christian faith?
   That is no problem. You already know some. Those you know best are most likely to be receptive.

Who will you invite to come to church with you?

List below the names of people in each of the categories suggested.
(Write small or use another sheet of paper.)

Family members:

Good Friends:

Neighbors:

People you work with:

People you play with:

People you know through clubs or organizations:

Others you know through other associations:

Now follow these steps:

1. Go back and cross off all those you know to be currently active in the life of some church.
2. Review the others and put a check by those you think might be receptive to a friendly invitation from you.
3. From among the checked names, pick two or three who may have some special need to get in touch with God right now. Circle their names.
4. Begin to intentionally prepare to invite them to church.

Prayer: Lord, prepare me and those with whom I want to share the faith. Amen.

SUNDAY, THIRD WEEK

Jesus said: **Ask, and it will be given you; search, and you will find; knock, and the door will be opened for you** (Matt. 7:7).

READ MATTHEW 7:7-11

It is important for us to learn to receive.

That may come as a surprise to you. You know that this workbook is part of a stewardship program that has to do with giving. But before you can give freely, you must be able to receive.

> Start by receiving what your church
> is trying to give to you:
>   An awareness of God,
>   The good news that God loves you;
>   Human love that embodies God's love;
>   The promise of fullness of life
>   both here and hereafter.

Once your church has taught you what to look for, look and find it all around you:
- Wherever there is beauty and genuine goodness,
- Wherever there is love,
- Wherever there is human nobility.
- Wherever there is any experience that makes you
whole and free and happy and alive—
All these are expressions of God's grace.

We need to learn how to recognize God's Grace in all the life-giving things around us,
take them into ourselves,
and let them do for us what they can.

That is part of what it means to be saved by grace.

We should intentionally seek out those experiences in life that feed and heal and liberate and enable us. God wants us to have them.

When we have received fully, we can give freely.

Where do you experience God's Grace in your life?

_____

_____

Prayer: Thank you, God, for all you are giving. Help me not to miss any of your gifts. Amen.

···

MONDAY, THIRD WEEK

Jesus said: **Where your treasure is, there your heart will be also** (Matt. 6:21).

READ MATTHEW 6:19-21

All of us are tempted to spend our time and our money and our energy in accumulating material things, or getting for ourselves all the status or pleasure or security that this world has to offer.

But these things are vulnerable and easy to lose.

The process of getting them can push us back into the practice of serving some master other than God.

Those other masters can be very cruel, unforgiving, and hard to satisfy. They can fill your life with anxiety, frustration, bitterness, and fatigue.

It is true that where we put our time, our money, and our energy, we also will put our hearts.

If we really want to give our hearts to God, we need to give our time, our money, and our energy to serving the purposes of God.

We really need to give!

We need to give so that we
can be set free from the
tyranny of getting.

We need to give so that we
can become a part of something bigger and better.

Here is good news. Laying up treasures in heaven does not mean postponing the joy of life until after you die. It means finding greater joy in a special relationship with God and with life, which starts now and never ends.

What would it mean for you to start depositing your resources in a heavenly account? Think about it.

Prayer: Lord, I really want to give my heart to you. Show me how. Amen.

....

TUESDAY, THIRD WEEK

Paul, the apostle, wrote: **Those who in the present age are rich . . . are to do good, to be rich in good works, generous, and ready to share** (I Tim. 6:17a, 18).

READ I TIMOTHY 6:6-19

Most of us don't think of ourselves as rich.
  But if we are realistic, most of us have been
  blessed with plenty.

Material prosperity is an opportunity to do good.

Money is a symbol of the ability to accomplish things.
  It can be exchanged for goods and services.
    It can be used to do good things.

If we consider ourselves stewards to whom God has entrusted all that we have, we should plan to use what has been entrusted to us to do what God wants done with it.

What might God want you to do with your material resources?

14

- Provide for the needs of your family,
- Reinvest in productive business enterprises,
- Enable you and yours to enjoy life fully,
- Help those less fortunate.

Certainly, God would want you to use part of your resources to enable your church to do God's work.

Do you really believe the church is doing the work of God?

Do you really believe that what has been entrusted to you should be used in the service of God.

Will you write the work of God's church into your budget?

Well, will you? _____

Prayer: Lord, forgive me for thinking that all I have is mine and that I can spend it just as I want to. Help me to remember that, ultimately, everything is yours. Help me to use it as you want me to. Amen.

....

WEDNESDAY, THIRD WEEK

Jesus said: **That a poor widow who put two pennies into an offering plate gave more than the wealthy people who gave large gifts.**

READ MARK 12:41-44

What did Jesus mean by saying that?
　　Obviously a gift of $100 can do more than a
　　gift of two cents in a church budget.

But Jesus was concerned about the good that giving can do in the life of the giver.
　　A small gift that represents total commitment
　　is more significant than a large gift that just represents
　　part of a surplus that won't be missed.

It is a good custom to plan our giving in terms of a percentage of our income.

The Bible recommends the custom of tithing, giving the first 10 percent of your income to serve God through the church.

If you are not tithing now, you probably think you can't afford it. But you can! You will be surprised.

If you have already committed so much of your income that you think you can't tithe right now, what percentage of your income can you give?
Can you start by giving some possible percentage of your income now, and stepping up by one percent of your income per year until you *are* tithing?

How much will you plan to give through your church?
　　Will you give 10%? _____
　　What percent will you give? _____%
　　How much does that mean you give each week? _____
　　Will you step up your giving each year? _____

How much will you probably give each week next year?_____

Prayer: Lord, set me free to give generously and gladly. Amen.

....

THURSDAY, THIRD WEEK

Jesus took a sack lunch which a young boy shared and used it to feed a great multitude.

READ JOHN 6:1-14

God can do much more with what we give than we could ever do by ourselves.

Look what God can do with what we give through our church:

1. Through our church, we have some of the most meaningful experiences that we can have: programs for people from childhood to old age; friendships; opportunities to grow in our relationship with God; opportunities to serve.

2. Through our church's influence, God works to build a better community for our families.

3. Through the benevolent outreach of our church, God meets desperate human needs of people around the world, offers the Christian faith, and works to build a better world. Do you yearn for a world without injustice, starvation, and war? The mission outreach of your church is your best chance to help make it happen.

Know what your gifts accomplish, and enjoy it.

> Yes, we really should enjoy our giving.
>
> Your church really gives you "More bang
> for your bucks." Shouldn't you be putting
> more bucks—and hours, and other resources
> into that "bang"?

Find out what your church does with the money you give, so that you can feel good about it.

Prayer: Thank you, God, for doing so much with what I give to you. Amen.

....

FRIDAY, THIRD WEEK

The apostle Paul said: **Now you are the body of Christ and individually members of it** (I Cor. 12:27).

READ I CORINTHIANS 12:12-13, 27-31

16

It is not enough merely to be a customer of the church—to go to the church for the services you want, and then pay directly for what those services cost.

It is not enough just to be a patron of the church and hire someone else to do God's work for you.

To be a follower of Jesus is to be a member of the church—a part of it, just like the parts of a person's body are members of the whole.

Just as the members of a body are interdependent, so we who are parts of the church are dependent upon it for our spiritual life—and it is dependent upon us for its health and wholeness.

The church is called the Body of Christ because it does Christ's work in the world. We answer Christ's call to service by participating in the work of the church.

We need the Church.
The Church needs us.

We must commit ourselves
to support the church by
our love, our attendance,
our witness, our gifts,
our time, and our energy.
Serve God through the Church.

How much time should we commit to serving in the Church?

Which of the following can you say to the leaders of your church?
_____ I have lots of time that needs to be invested meaningfully. Keep me busy in God's service.
_____ I will make time to spend two or three hours a week in God's service, besides my time in Sunday worship.
_____ I will be in church and Sunday school on Sunday mornings. Use me in some way on Sundays.
_____ Call on me to serve in some monthly or occasional ways.

Prayer: Lord, you must be awfully busy. Thank you for not being too busy to care about me. I won't be too busy to serve you. Amen.

SATURDAY, THIRD WEEK

The apostle Paul said: **We have gifts that differ according to the grace given to us** (Rom. 12:6).

READ ROMANS 12:1-8

Just as Jesus did great things with the sack lunch that the young boy shared, so God can do great things with the time we spend in service through the church.

God has given each of us some ability to serve.
Paul talks about the spiritual participation we can offer to the fellowship of the church, and also about the functions we can perform in the work of the church.

Find your place in the work of the church.

What are you good at? (Remember not to hide your light.)

_____

_____

What have you always wanted to try doing?
(Don't be afraid. It's O.K. to ask for help. It's O.K. to fail.)

_____

_____

Is there some aspect of the church's work in which you would
like to offer leadership by serving on a committee?

_____

Select some opportunities from this list that you would enjoy:

_____ Ushering	_____ Children's Programs
_____ Greeting	_____ Singing in the Choir
_____ Driving the Van	_____ Leading Children's Choir
_____ Office Work	_____ Instrumental Music
_____ Telephoning	_____ Handbells
_____ Kitchen Work	_____ Preparing for Communion
_____ Praying	_____ Building Repairs
_____ Scouting	_____ Grounds Maintenance
_____ Teaching Children	_____ Caring for Sick or Aged
_____ Teaching Youth	_____ Visiting Newcomers
_____ Teaching Adults	_____ Community Service Projects
_____ Youth Counselor	_____ Blood Donor

Others _____

_____ I would like someone to talk with me about service opportunities and about my talents.

Prayer: Lord, show me how you want me to serve you. Amen.

....

SUNDAY, FOURTH WEEK

Jesus said: **No one puts new wine into old wineskins** (Mark 2:22).

READ MARK 2:18-22

The new life of the kingdom of God that Jesus wants us to have is alive and dynamic and growing. It is a life that shapes interaction between a people who are spiritually alive and a living God.

Something that vital cannot adequately be contained within brittle old forms of piety or stale ways of life.

If our relationship with God is alive, it will push us to discover new and exciting ways of expressing our faith and living it out.

18

A growing faith will require a changing life.

Where is the growing edge of your faith?
How can that take shape in your life?

Where is the growing edge of your life?
What part does your faith play?

Where do you know you need
to be growing?

How will you become intentional about your growth?

_____

_____

Prayer: Lord, I know that I am a child of yours now, and I am excited about learning what I can become. Amen.

....

MONDAY, FOURTH WEEK

First John said: **Beloved, we are God's children now; what we will be has not yet been revealed** (I John 3:2).

READ I JOHN 3:1-3

Being a follower of Jesus means that we should be intentionally trying to become more and more like Jesus.

That is an adventure in faith, because we cannot know where it will lead us.

Some spiritual growth happens accidentally and spontaneously, as we live in relationship with God. We must be sensitive and responsive to what God is doing in our lives.

There are some disciplines of "spiritual formation" that we can use to keep us sensitive and responsive, and growing intentionally.

What will you do to be on a growing edge in your interaction with God?

Here are some possibilities:
_____ Attend worship weekly
_____ Join a Sunday school class
_____ Meet weekly with a prayer and sharing group
        Have daily family or personal
_____ devotional time.
        Go on a weekend spiritual-
_____ growth retreat
        Undertake an intensive
_____ Bible study course
_____ other plans _____

Prayer: Lord, I want to be like Jesus in my heart. Amen.

TUESDAY, FOURTH WEEK

Jesus said: **The kingdom of heaven is like a mustard seed . . . it is the smallest of all the seeds, but when it has grown it is the greatest of shrubs and becomes a tree, so that the birds of the air come and make nests in its branches** (Matt. 13:31a-32).

READ MATTHEW 13:31-32

Here is another parable that describes the kingdom of God as something alive and growing.

**Would you like for your
church to be alive and growing?**

Would you like for your church
to be reaching out to more people?
Would you like for your church to
be enlarging its ministries to
meet more human needs?

What is your vision for the future of your church?

Dream a while, and list some things you would like for your church to be doing that it is not doing now.

_____

_____

_____

_____

Are you willing to commit yourself to helping your church to grow in those ways? _____

Are you willing for your church to change so that this growth can happen? _____

Do you need to increase the amount of financial and personal support you promised to give your church in the Third Week, so that it can do more? _____

What will be your new plan for giving? _____

What will be your new plan for serving? _____

Prayer: Lord, is your church waiting for me to rise up and make her great? Help me to do it, Lord. Amen.

WEDNESDAY, FOURTH WEEK

Jesus said: **The kingdom of heaven is like yeast that a woman took and mixed in with three measures of flour until all of it was leavened.**

READ MATTHEW 13:33

20

It is the purpose of our faith to change our lives.

It is the purpose of the church to change the world.

Christians are called to mix with the world around them and change it, as yeast changes dough.

The work that Christians do together in the church is a very important way of serving God.

But the work Christians do as they live day by day in the world can serve God, too:
- By living a life in business and community that is shaped by the Christian faith, thus redeeming our part of the world.
- By influencing others to live by the highest standards they know.
- By witnessing through word and example to people who need a faith.

Or we may undertake to serve God's purpose in some special way beyond the program of the church.

How will you serve as leaven to change the world?

> How can you serve God in your
> everyday situation? _____
>
> _____
>
> Is there some special mission
> you will undertake beyond
> your church program? _____
>
> _____

Is there something your church could do to help you find your ministry in the world, or to support you in it?

_____

_____

Prayer: Lord, help me to serve you always and everywhere. Amen.

THURSDAY, FOURTH WEEK

Jesus said: **Just as you did it to one of the least of these . . . you did it to me** (Matt. 25:40).

READ MATTHEW 25:31-46

The new life of the kingdom of God
is a life in which we live by
trusting God and serving God.

But how can we do anything that really serves God?

What we do for any person whom God loves, we do for God.

Christ calls us to serve through the needs of our neighbors.

One of the best ways to live in growing interaction with God is to live in sensitivity and responsiveness to the human needs around us.

Our world is full of injustices and hurtful conditions
that stifle the life and well-being of some of God's
children. Christians should work to change that.
There are people you know who are poor or lonely
or hurting from the injuries of life.
You can reach out to them in love.
Some of those who need your love may not be poor
or conspicuously needy—but they may be hurting
for a caring relationship.
You will not have to look far to find them.

Being responsive is not easy.
It can disturb your sleep.
It can make demands upon you.
Besides, it is not always easy to know
how to make a loving response. It may not
always be best just to give what is asked for.

But we do not want to fail to answer Christ's call. Living in loving responsiveness can become a fulfilling adventure in faith.

To which of God's people will you reach out in love?

_____

_____

_____

_____

Prayer: Lord, help me to hear you calling through the needs of my neighbors, and guide me as I try to respond. Amen.

FRIDAY, FOURTH WEEK

Jesus said: **You shall love the Lord your God with all your heart, and with all your soul, and with all your mind. . . . You shall love your neighbor as yourself** (Matt. 22:37, 39*b*).

READ MATTHEW 22:34-40.

Trust and love are the two most important shapers of the Christian life.

If we learn to live by trusting God's love, we will be set free to live our lives in love.

Love is a basic commitment of life to life.

To love God is to love life.
To love God is to love yourself.

22

> To love God is to love your neighbors.
>   To love God is to love all the people of the earth.
>   To love God is to love the world we live in.

When we love God with our whole being, other loves do not compete with one another. They are parts of one all inclusive love.

But what is love? Our world has some funny ideas about that.

> To learn how to love, learn how God loves us.
>   God accepts us as we are.
>   God affirms our value as persons.
>   God wants what is best for·us.
>   God expects good things from us.
>   God respects our freedom to decide.
>   God forgives us when we make wrong decisions.
>   God becomes involved in our lives
>   in costly ways to help us make life good.
>   God rejoices with us in the goodness of life.

Learn more about God, and you will learn more about love.

Love keeps us moving toward new horizons in life.

Read I Corinthians 13, and think about it.

Prayer: Lord, teach me to love. Amen.

SATURDAY, FOURTH WEEK

Jesus said: **The kingdom of heaven is like treasure hidden in a field, which someone found . . . then in his joy he goes and sells all that he has and buys that field** (Matt. 13:44).

READ MATTHEW 13:44-45

We started this series of devotional exercises by saying that we were searching for something better, for a freer, happier, more meaningful life. Where will we find that better life?

We will find that better life where we least expect it.

The fellow in today's parable probably went out into the field to plow, not to look for treasure. But he found the treasure there.

In the Beatitudes (Matt. 5:1-12), Jesus said that blessedness—real happiness—is to be found in the very places where most people least expect it.

Jesus said that those who lose their life in the service of Christ and of the gospel will truly find their life and save it.

The life that is truly something better slips up on us and surprises us, while we are looking the other way.

People who are preoccupied with making their own life better may miss the better life.

But if we learn to live:
    Trusting God's love,
        Loving all that God loves,
            And serving the purposes of God,
We eventually will discover that the very best of lives has materialized around us.

Something better is there for you, right where you are.

Prayer: Thank you, God, for putting fullness of life within my reach. Amen.

MY COVENANT TO GIVE

In grateful stewardship of all that God has entrusted to me, I plan to give $_____ (per week, month, year) to do the work of God through my church.

Check here if your pledge represents a tithe: _____

Check here if you plan to step up toward tithing:_____

Name _____

_____

MY COVENANT TO SERVE

Count on me to commit the following amount of time to serving God through the church: _____

I am good at: _____

I would like to try: _____

I would like to serve on the _____Committee.

Call on me to serve in one or more of the following ways:

_____ _____ _____

_____ _____ _____

I would like to talk with someone about how I can serve._____

Name _____

_____

MY COVENANT TO GROW

I would like to do the following things to be on the growing edge of my faith:_____

_____

I would like for my church to enable me or support me in my ministry in the world in the following ways:

_____

_____

_____

Name _____

24

MY COVENANT TO PARTICIPATE
I would like for my church to enlarge its ministries in the following ways:_____

_____

_____

_____

Name _____

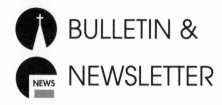

BULLETIN & NEWSLETTER

The following quotations are useful for bulletins, newsletters, and signs during an annual commitment campaign, or to reinforce year-round stewardship.

Traits of Happiness

1. Self-esteem—to like yourself
2. Personal control—in control of own lives
3. Optimism—hope-filled
4. Extroversion—outgoing
5. Social Support
   Close relationship
   Companionship
   Marriage
6. Active personal faith

"To embrace the world's needs instead of running from them ensures the best philanthropic hug you'll ever receive."

DEBBIE P. CASE

"No person was ever honored for what he received. Honor has been the reward for what he gave."

CALVIN COOLIDGE

"Love is not only something you feel. It's something you do."

DAVID WILKERSON

"Philanthropic dollars are not free. They have to be earned—with excellence and performance, with patience and long-suffering."

PAUL H. SCHNEITER

"Giving and receiving are mutual. Receiving without giving causes dependence. Giving without receiving leads to arrogance."

ROBERT E. FOGAL

"Progress begins with the belief that what is necessary is possible."

NORMAN COUSINS

"Videotaping my golf swing improved my game so much I thought I'd try it on my fund-raising skills."

The Chronicle of Philanthropy

"We don't always get what we deserve, but we often get what we ask for."

VICTOR G. DYMOWSKI

"There is not happiness in having or in getting, but only in giving."

HENRY DRUMMOND

"Giving allows me to touch the lives of people I don't even know, but whose lives I would like to help improve."

L. STANLEY CHAUVIN, JR.

"There is hardly a hobby, certainly not a habit, which does not cost us more than what we offer the church."

E. J. GALLMEYER

"Let us begin by admitting the hard fact that we are basically selfish and do not want to share our affluence with others. . . . And let's admit that most of us resist the inspiration of the Holy Spirit, which seeks to bring about a change that will make us more generous."

KENNETH PRIEBE

"The work of the stewards is not accomplished until every member and adherent of the church shall have the opportunity and desire to make a gift to God, commensurate with the blessings received and relative to their financial capacity."

DR. HAROLD VAUGHN

"To ask for little is to get it."

ANONYMOUS

"God gives so you can.
Not what we give but what we share,
For the gift without the giver is bare;
Who gives himself with alms feeds three—
Himself, his hungering neighbor, and Me."

JAMES RUSSELL LOWELL

NEWSLETTER

HANDOUT

Why I Give Money to This Church

1. Because all things are from God in the beginning (see Ps. 24:1).
2. Because the talents I utilize and develop in a paying career are gifts from the One who made me.
3. Because God made humans to be caretakers, not just consumers.
4. Because what I give back to God is a response to God's love and amazing grace toward me.
5. Because the Bible says to give to others. (If you're not up to giving 10 percent yet, try increasing your pledge by 1 percent of your income each year. Make a 5- or 10-year plan.)
6. Because giving money is not just about budgets, but rather about practicing a spiritual discipline. My personal relationship with Jesus Christ is more in tune when I give.
7. Because "practice makes perfect." Tithing is a spiritual discipline to be practiced, cultivated, and improved, just like prayer, scripture study, service, worship, fasting, and such.
8. Because giving helps me keep my priorities in order. God is our higher power. Money is a thing, and maybe a false idol, but it's not a god. Jesus Christ is Lord! Greenbacks are not god!
9. Because I said I would (and so did most of you). When we join The United Methodist Church, we give our word that we will support our local congregation with our prayers, presence, gifts, and service.
10. Because I trust the brothers and sisters who are leaders of the church, both lay and clergy. I trust their decision making about faithful uses of money. If I (or you) have questions or input to offer, I know they are welcome.
11. I give money because I have witnessed with my own eyes the transforming, resurrecting power of God's love. It affects people's lives and hearts, in part through the ministries that this church performs and provides. In the real world, ministries need supplies, leaders, staff, equipment, curriculum, paper, bread, scissors, and sheet music—worldly stuff for an out-of-this-world revelation of love!

Relevant Scriptures

Genesis 14:17-24
Psalm 24:1
Leviticus 27:30-33
Malachi 3:6-12
Matthew 25:14-30
Luke 21:1-4
II Corinthians 8:1-15

PART FOUR

MONEY MANAGEMENT IN THE CHURCH

For Pastors and Finance Teams

Introduction

D O N A L D   W .   J O I N E R

At one time, the church was the center of the community, and the major social event of the week was going to church. Those times are gone, but we still operate the church as if everything were the same as it was fifty years ago. Leonard Sweet, at a recent conference, defined "crazy" as "doing the same thing over and over again, and expecting different results."

Times are changing. People are different. That calls for a different way to think about and lead the church's funding ministry. (That's what this *Guide* is all about!) Competition in the church is not just from other denominations, but from McDonald's, MTV, the movie theater, and the way our culture has been taught to think and respond. This is a different world.

> "Money is to our generation what sex was to the Victorians—which is to say that many people are willing to read about how others handle or mismanage it, but few are ready to disclose their own involvement with it."
>
> *AN ANONYMOUS QUAKER*

If the gospel of Jesus Christ and the work of the Word is to continue, we need to look at different ways of leading in money management.

The first article in this section aims for a new direction. What is required today, as we are led into a new future, is to assist each person for whom we are in ministry to discover their gifts, their call, and their response to "being a steward," a disciple.

To lend insight for this new direction, Olan Runnels shares the "trends" in funding ministry from his perspective as a fund developer working in local congregations. The most significant trend is number 10: individualization. Treating everyone the same no longer works. How can we help each individual become what God is calling him or her to become?

The next few articles help the finance leaders do their work. It is amazing how many churches do not have a budget, or simply use last year's budget with revised figures! Two articles review ways to construct a budget for the church's financial management. Budgets are not bad: They are just ignored! We often try to make a budget do too many things. A church budget has at least two functions: a plan for how the church is going to *spend*; and a description of what the church is planning to *do*.

Do not confuse the two functions and try to accomplish both in one document. There is need for a line-item budget for the financial management of the church. There is also a need for a document to describe to the church members how that money is to be spent for ministry and mission. These are not the same documents. Most people do not care to know how each dollar is spent. They *do* want to know what

their investment through the church is going to accomplish. A narrative budget is one way to share the results of their giving.

No church receives one-twelfth of its income, nor does it spend one-twelfth of its budget each month. In most churches, anywhere from 15 to 40 percent of all giving to the church takes place in the last month of the year. Herb Mather's article points out some ways to invite members to give at the end of the year.

Trying to write a good letter is often difficult. Jim Fogle-Miller's series of letters will help you write your own letters to the congregation at different times of the year. You will want to adapt them to your church's needs. Jim shares them to spark your creative spirit.

Do you remember the story of Jesus, the disciples, and the Sea of Tiberias in John 21? Some of the disciples went fishing. They fished a long time with no results. They were throwing their nets on the same side of the boat they had always used, with no luck. Jesus instructed them to try the other side. Suddenly, their nets were full of fish! That parable alerts us that it is time to do similar things, but do them differently if we want different, positive results. This is a parable for funding ministry as we race into a new century.

 PLANNING TOOL

Developmental Stewardship

DONALD W. JOINER

Jan's initial meeting with the leaders at First Church took place more than a year ago. At that time, the pastor had told her that the church was facing a financial crisis and couldn't pay its bills.

Because Jan had worked with many churches in the area, she was not surprised by the way the meeting proceeded.

Harry began, "If our people were more committed, we wouldn't have any financial problems."

Elijah disagreed: "Our people are committed. They just don't know what's happening at the church. If we tell them, they'll give."

Ellen, the finance chair, proclaimed, "All we really need is a good finance campaign to raise the money."

There is an element of truth in each leader's statement. However, their responses will not solve the finan-

cial dilemma. Most generous givers do give out of a response to what God had done in Jesus Christ. When Christians realize what they have received, their natural reaction is to give. But *where* they give, and *how much* they give, is not guaranteed. *Where* people give depends on their understanding of, identification with, and activity in an organization. *How much* people give depends on their individual faith journeys, their economic situations, and how they feel at any given moment.

In a recent meeting, Mike commented about how fund-raising is changing. He had been asked to raise money for a new building. In the past, Mike had successfully led capital campaigns, raising significant amounts of money. His comment, following this disappointing campaign, was, "You can't do it the same way."

Mike is correct. Unfortunately, many congregations are still trying to do things "the same way." The influence of our consumer society, the availability of discretionary funds, the abundance of charitable institutions seeking funds, the tax environment, and changing demographics—all shape a different world of financial stewardship.

Typically, a congregation looks at its financial situation and organizes its fundraising programs around small, very select groups. In many cases, the finance leaders think that people in the congregation are knowledgeable about finances, willing to support the church's ministries, and able to give. With that view, the leaders attempt to "underwrite the budget." The reality is that people often do not see the larger picture, are not aware of the "results" of the budget, or have minimal contact with the church.

On the other hand, the finance leaders may decide that members of the congregation will not give unless the leaders "pry it out of them." Such attitudes will not produce results.

The church has much to learn from the discipline of marketing and from the total quality management movement. (See *Marketing for Congregations,* coauthored by Philip Kotler, Gustave Rath, Bruce Wrenn, and Norman Shawchuck, from Abingdon Press; or Ezra Earl Jones' *Quest for Quality in the Church: A New Paradigm,* available from Discipleship Resources). Marketing and the quality movement stress the importance of focusing on individuals (target audiences) rather than on the entire membership.

At present, however, local congregations tend to approach church members in three ways:

- The traditional approach is for church leaders to know what the people need and give it to them.
- The informational approach is for church leaders to give members the right information so that the members will respond.
- A third approach is for leaders to remind members of the three "Ts" (time, talent, and treasure), and of their "obligations" as members.

In truth, members do respond to all three approaches—negatively. Often, they respond by giving elsewhere!

> ## "Life is a team sport. Sometimes you give, and sometimes you get."
> —ANN PEARSON

A better approach to funding ministry in the local congregation is a *developmental stewardship approach* that takes its lead from the quality movement and from marketing. This approach has the following characteristics:

- It recognizes that individuals are unique.
- It attempts to understand the interests and needs of individuals.
- It attempts to develop and interpret ministries consistent with people's needs and interests.
- It seeks to develop an *ongoing* relationship with individuals.
- It converts interest into action.

Developmental stewardship recognizes that individuals are unique. Have you ever had a nightmare about planning an event, and no one attended? I have! Many committees identify an event that they "think" needs to occur. When the event fails because of poor attendance, the planners attribute the failure to the members' lack of commitment.

Developmental stewardship assumes that if an event, service, program, or finance campaign is for everyone, it is for no one.

Developmental stewardship attempts to understand the interests and needs of individuals. The key to developmental stewardship for the postmodern church is in building relationships with each identified audience. Understanding the audiences or target groups in your church is essential. The larger the congregation, the more audiences, and the more diverse the audiences. Leaders should understand the needs of each group and develop a stewardship approach based on those needs.

Trinity Church had planned a "Wills and Estate-Planning Workshop." Planners believed that many people would benefit from the event, but only three people attended. The next time Trinity planned an event, the leaders identified their audiences. They planned a "Wills and Estate-Planning Seminar" for persons over 55; they planned a "Retirement Seminar" for those 45 and older; and they planned a "Funding Your Child's Education Seminar" for those with children at home. Each event focused on identified needs, and each event included information about wills. More than 85 people attended the three events.

Developmental stewardship attempts to develop and interpret ministries consistent with people's needs and interests. Wayne Barrett, in *The Church Finance Idea Book* (available from Discipleship Resources), points out that "all donors are not created equal" and that approaches to financial commitment should be tailored to the donors' interests. Developmental stewardship communicates to people where they are, rather than where the church leaders are.

All Saints Church identified four audiences: (1) Those in leadership and among the top 15 percent of the givers; (2) Those involved in the Sunday church school program; (3) Those who attended church regularly; and (4) Those who showed some minimal support for the church in giving and attendance (usually at holidays). Leaders designed a specific approach for each audience.

All Saints Church provided a special dinner for the leaders and top givers to thank them for their support and invite their continuing commitment. The church scheduled a special assembly to reach those involved in church school and conducted special presentations. To reach those who attended church regularly, the leaders arranged for special presentations during the worship service each Sunday for four weeks. The pastor's messages related to issues of stewardship. Those marginally interested in the church received phone calls.

In each case, members heard a vision for ministry and stories about ministries in the church. They also had an opportunity to make a commitment. On Celebration Sunday, all four audiences came together with their commitments. Giving increased. So did the participation and commitment of the people during the following year.

*Developmental stewardship seeks to develop an **ongoing** relationship with individuals.* Attention to the audiences in the congregation should not stop after the finance campaign. Developmental stewardship encourages leaders to examine the interests of each audience and to communicate appropriately to each audience. Some communication approaches may be the same, but the majority of the communication during the year should be based upon knowledge of the audience.

Developmental stewardship converts interests into action. Just because a person has indicated interest in the ministry of your congregation does not mean that he or she has decided to *support* that ministry. Devel-

opmental stewardship identifies people, designs an approach to maximize their involvement, and invites them to move from interest into action—in their attendance, in their time, in their giving, and in their stewardship.

Developmental stewardship is basic to any congregation. It is not a new way of "doing" financial stewardship, but a new way of "thinking about" finances and faithful givers. It is not a separate function, but a part of everything the congregation does. It is the way you answer the phone; it is how you communicate; it is how you invite members to be in ministry.

Who are your audiences? What do you need to do to understand the needs of those audiences? How can you invite those audiences to join you in ministry?

> "A society is well ordered in which there is more giving than taking."
>
> —ARISTOTLE

Signposts of a Financially Healthy Congregation

- Awareness that all giving, that of ourselves as well as our financial resources, is in response to God's goodness and generosity. God gives, then we respond, and we spend our lives learning and growing in our responses.
- Discusses money in the context of worship instead of considering money a disreputable subject that should not be confused with the sacredness of worship. This distinction should not exist within Christ's church.
- Understands that the offertory is an integral part of corporate worship. Just as we bring our gifts of wine and bread to God's table, we present ourselves as an offering through our financial gifts.
- Talks about money openly and candidly in all aspects of the church's life, realizing that how we use our money says a great deal about our values and priorities.
- Engages in mission beyond its own doors and interprets this mission (both local and worldwide) through a planned year-round program. When people know how their money is used to do God's work, they are reinforced in their giving.
- Plans long-range for its program objectives and financial needs. Budget development is a long-term process.

 PLANNING TOOL

Major Trends in Fund-Raising

OLAN H. RUNNELS AND PAT CUMMINS

Churchgoers are putting a smaller portion of their incomes into the collection plates, while the number of dollars being donated to churches has risen.

A study by Empty Tomb, Inc., and The National Council of Churches reports that donations as a percentage of income have fallen from a little over 3 percent in 1968, to about 2.6 percent in 1990.

Some say this trend stems in part from disagreement with the national church bodies, while others say that people have changed from stewards to consumers. For example, they have brought attitudes to their churches where they are buying specific services—youth program, music program, and such.

Churches are also beset by rapidly rising fixed costs, which means that less of the money being dropped in the collection plates on weekends is going to governing bodies and programs outside the church walls.

Traditionally, many clergy—particularly in evangelical denominations—have urged members to give a tenth of their incomes to the church. But to a generation that resists any sense of obligation, the tithe is a symbol that is often ignored.

Many of the younger churchgoers today are more likely to choose a church based on what benefits they expect from it, such as family-oriented programs or even "a good handball court."

Generally across America, people do not mind giving to the parish as much as they mind giving money that goes downtown or to denominational headquarters. They don't trust downtown, wherever "downtown" might be.

Lilly Endowment, Inc., funded a three-year study, the "State of Church Giving Through 1991." The project was designed to analyze denominational giving data and to determine what dynamics affect church giving patterns. John and Sylvia Ronsvalle were the coauthors.

Giving patterns for eleven denominations were traced

> "What we do for ourselves dies with us—what we do for others remains and is immortal."
>
> ALBERT PIKE

for the seventy-year period of 1921–1991. Changes in U.S. per-capita income and giving data were charted on an annual basis. The study found that giving as percentage of income for these denominations was lower in 1991 than it was in either 1921 or 1933, the depth of the Great Depression.

The Ronsvalles do not anticipate that the extinction of the church is inevitable. However, they name the strong trend in giving patterns that could make that possible. They expect that the report will continue to elicit a national dialogue on how to respond to what they term a "crisis of communication and vision in the church."

On the other hand, many American church people today are seeing a strong revitalization in many quarters, with an increase in giving, church planting, and evangelism.

In the past several years, virtually all the larger Protestant denominations have been forced to make major cutbacks in national programming, in some cases forcing the termination of as much as a quarter of all staff positions. Among the denominations affected have been the Presbyterian Church USA, the Evangelical Lutheran Church in America, The Episcopal Church, the Southern Baptist Convention, and The United Methodist Church—denominations that historically have been at the pinnacle of power in American Protestantism.

Simply stated, competition for church members is forcing congregations to spend more money locally and send increasingly smaller amounts to national church headquarters. This shift may very well give a decided competitive advantage to denominations that vest authority locally.

What People Create They Will Support

1. Most growing evangelical churches in America are discovering the need to involve many parishioners in developing a vision for ministry, believing that *what persons create they will support.*

To facilitate congregations in developing a vision for ministry, some growing churches are using a visioning workshop that takes approximately six to eight weeks to complete.

111

2. Larger and more sophisticated congregations are using the services of a professional firm to assist in *feasibility studies*. Many older churches need major renovation and refurbishing; others need to build new facilities, acquire more parking, or add ministry centers. Because needs are so varied and extensive, it is almost mandatory that a feasibility study be conducted to assist in ranking the priorities of capital needs.

3. Most evangelical churches in America are quick to admit that their *per capita giving is diminishing*. There is a strong need to teach the biblical principles of Christian stewardship and develop a stronger awareness of the need for Christians to give out of their own personal need, as opposed to giving because the church needs the money. In conjunction with this discovery and realization is a strong demand that pastors and church leaders help to develop stronger awareness of stewardship in general.

4. Visioning workshops and feasibility studies reveal a need to *challenge individual Christians to be better stewards, along with the need to assist the church to be a better corporate steward*. The trends of the future will be not only to call for the discipline of developing Christians to be better participants, but to accentuate the need for local churches to raise the standard of corporate stewardship.

5. Many larger churches are discovering that the same energy and momentum being created through Capital Funding Appeals can be harnessed to *engender stronger participation when pledging to the annual budget*. Cargill Associates, after examining five years of trends, believes that churches can carry out a capital campaign and an annual ministry budget appeal at the same time, allowing each to complement the other. This trend is being well received by many congregations.

6. There is a growing trend in larger churches to think of *stewardship as a learned grace*. A dynamic tool available to each congregation is the utilization of its own constituents who have learned the joy of giving. Such people, when properly motivated and challenged, can positively articulate their own experience of Christian stewardship by sharing their stories in a variety of settings. This is a powerful source of teaching and raising giving standards in local settings.

7. There seems to be a strong trend with Development Foundations to be *more stringent in their requirements for lending churches money* to prevent burdensome debt. (The North Texas Annual Confer-

ence of The United Methodist Church uses guidelines of 25 to 30 percent of a church's annual budget as the maximum that should be allocated for debt service.) This encourages churches to engage in capital-fund appeals to raise the additional funds that cannot be acquired through borrowing. (See no. 5.)

8. Larger and growing congregations are discovering that *without more ministry funding, they are faced with the dilemma of placing clergy in congregations that do not have the resources to underwrite their salaries*.

9. There is the challenge to have *more funding appeals conference-wide, to raise the funds necessary to strengthen existing congregations and acquire properties for building new ones*.

10. *Giving will increase at the greatest rate in history between 1998 and 2002.* During this period, we will see the greatest intergenerational transfer of wealth in history. According to *Fortune Magazine,* baby boomers stand to inherit some $2.3 trillion from their parents. This transfer will occur just as baby boomers are entering their prime giving years. Considering that 81.9 percent of all charitable gifts come from individuals, this means that churches must cultivate their people *today* (if they had not already started yesterday!). Churches, more than ever before, must keep absolutely current on the most effective means of identifying individual prospective donors. Churches that utilize computerized database services will be able to identify prospects of true wealth. *However, the time-honored method of one-on-one solicitation, carried out by an individual committed steward who has a personal, peer relationship with the prospective donor will remain the best way to raise major funds!*

11. *Strong volunteers will become the most precious (and most rare) commodity a church can have.*

In the face of growing social crises such as homelessness, AIDS, unaffordable health care, crime, and failing schools, the number of institutions and organizations asking for money is on the rise. Nonprofit organizations number 1.3 million today, and more than 440,000 of those are 501(c) (3).

No longer can a pastor gather a small number of the power elite—local business leaders—who can be counted on to shake loose large gifts for major fundraising campaigns again and again.

Support from the pulpit is essential, but leadership by key business people must remain. Volunteers are absolutely essential to the well-being of the churches that do well in the future. Rather than concede defeat in the competition for volunteers, *today's churches should be making every effort to expand their volunteer bases by involving them in every aspect of the church's operation.* The more involved volunteers become, the more committed they will be. What people create, they will support!

12. One of the more discouraging trends today will be the *increasing pressure for fund-raising to become completely staff driven.* As the availability of good volunteers declines, it seems far easier to have staff cultivate and solicit donors. There is no denying that such an approach can be successful. However, such a strategy will have a damaging effect on the future of church fund-raising. In the first place, this is not the biblical way to make it happen. Second, very few staff members maintain the kind of peer rela-

> "Volunteering gives you the opportunity to exercise yourself as God's hands."
> —*JANELLE WOLFE*

tionship with prospective major donors that is so crucial to effective major-gift fund-raising. Yes, a staff member can ask for and receive a gift, but a volunteer's involvement in that task often will result in a *larger* gift.

No amount of sophisticated technology or staff solicitation will ever take the place of warm, personal, caring Christians who share their own personal commitment in asking others to do what the Lord expects.

Not all these trends are of equal weight and value. Some will generate disagreement, and even debate. That may be the *ultimate value and exercise of "Trend Identification"*—to think about and decide for yourself, as a pastor and church leader, which trends, if any, apply to your church, your conference, and your denomination—and *how your reaction to those trends can contribute to success.*

Good Communication

People who are especially good communicators use various ways to make their communication more effective. Look over this list for ideas to help you talk about the church and its mission in ways that will stir excitement in people.

1. Know what it is that you want to communicate. Know enough about your subject so that you can provide specifics, names, places, numbers.
2. Know the people with whom you want to communicate—what do they already know about the subject, what are their interests, how do they feel about the church and its mission?
3. Know the tools you can use for communicating and how to use them. Your voice—how well do you speak? Your creativity—how well do think of new and exciting ideas? Your physical skills—how well do you handle equipment and prepare displays?
4. Remember that people retain about 10 percent of what they read, 20 percent of what they hear, 30 percent of what they see, and 50 percent of what they see and hear.
5. Be brief!
6. Repeat your message—use the same picture more than once; tell the same facts over again. Repeat your message!
7. Use as wide a variety of communication techniques as possible. Don't get locked into always doing displays, or always using filmstrips, or always putting something in the newsletter or the bulletin.
8. Ask questions of people—verbally, in displays, in printed articles. It engages them in thinking about your message.
9. As much as possible, communicate one-on-one. Write articles and letters, knowing that only one person at a time will read them.
10. Use your own words, rewording material you find already printed.
11. Be bold—use bold words, bold pictures, bold sounds, bold colors.
12. Be positive!

13. Use active verbs—help, come, share, work. Avoid—is, am, was.
14. Refer to common experiences you and the people with whom you are communicating have had.
15. Ask people to do something specific, or make a particular decision, or relay a certain message.
16. Be aware of eye-level differences. Put pictures and displays at eye level for those who are to see them.
17. Use readily accepted symbols to save time and space, and make your communication more effective—green lights, arrows, thumbs up, the cross, the globe, and so on.
18. Be sure to listen to others. They will help you know what you are saying.
19. Ask congregational members to help you communicate. Others can speak to groups; children can make posters; youths can make tape recordings—audio and video.

PLANNING TOOL

5 Ways to Increase the Stewardship Level of Your Church

DONALD W. JOINER

1. Proper Every Member Commitment (E.M.C.):
There are E.M.C.s, and there are E.M.C.s

A properly run E.M.C. will involve all the members, lay a foundation for communications, increase attendance in worship and, of course, the number of giving units and the amount given through the church. A three-year plan might include:

Year 1. Every Member Visitation
Year 2. Congregational Meetings (with Home Meetings)
Year 3. A Packet Plan or Delivery Program

2. Communications:
A. A monthly mailing to all members and constituents, which would include:
Personal Financial Statement of Giving
Church Financial Status
Church Financial newsletter & testimonials
Stewardship Insert
Special Giving Opportunity

B. Lay Speakers each Sunday prior to offering: (each month)
First Sunday: Report from a program area
Second: Stewardship
Third: Report from a program area
Fourth: Missions

Fifth: Witness of one's faith
(These are to be positive, informational, and motivational.)

3. Stewardship Education: The goal of Stewardship Education is to raise the personal stewardship level of the membership (beginning with the church leaders).
A. Stewardship Education of Church Leaders—programs during the Board Meetings (three times a year), as well as special short-term stewardship studies with church leaders
B. Stewardship Preaching (at least once a quarter)
C. Winter and fall short-term stewardship study classes

4. Special Stewardship programs: (at least twice a year)
Weekend Stewardship Festival
Proportionate Giving and Tithing Emphasis
Wills Clinic
Personal Financial Management Seminar
Time and Talent (Gifts for Ministry) Emphasis

5. Estate Planning Emphasis: The intent of this emphasis is not only wills education, but to build the church's endowment fund for future financial resources.

BUDGET TOOL

Building a Budget

DAVID J. BROWN

Jesus reminded his followers to count the cost of discipleship: "For which of you, intending to build a tower, does not first sit down and estimate the cost, to see whether he has enough to complete it? Otherwise, when he has laid a foundation and is not able to finish, all who see it will begin to ridicule him, saying, 'This fellow began to build and was not able to finish'" (Luke 14:28-30).

The Apostle Paul encouraged churches to "count the cost" by gathering funds to help meet the pressing financial needs of the Christians living in Jerusalem. This attitude is replicated in the Statement of Faith of the United Church of Christ, which testifies that God calls us into the church "to accept the cost and joy of discipleship."

Part of the cost of discipleship—only a part, but an indispensable part—is financial. If your congregation is committed to mission, to doing Christ's work in the world, one of the things it needs is a plan for receiving and spending money: a budget.

More Than a Series of Numbers

A pastor once remarked that if you really want to measure a person's Christian character, look first at their checkbook stubs.

Expenditures do reveal something about a person—and about a church. So if you want to know the character of your congregation, begin by examining its budget. That budget is much more than an estimate of income and expenditure. It is much more than a guide for church officers as they undertake their administrative duties.

Your congregation's budget reveals the very character of the people who build it, support it, and act through it. It describes your congregation's understanding of mission, and it outlines your congregation's commitment to provide money for the fulfilling of ministry and mission priorities. In short, the budget is a theological statement that articulates your congregation's response to God's call to be active participants in Christ's ongoing work.

The Budget Calls for Careful and Intentional Work

Because the budget tells about the character of your congregation and describes who you are and what you intend to do, it deserves very careful and intentional development.

Adding a few percentage points to this year's budget is never an adequate way to develop next year's budget. When budgets are simply added to, there is no chance to evaluate existing programs, to study new opportunities, or to create a financial guideline that is in keeping with the congregation's mission goals.

Further, the add-on approach permits the budget to shape the congregation's ministry and mission, rather than allowing ministry and mission to determine the budget.

Your congregation needs to build its budget from the ground up to meet mission needs. That means devoting time and energy, in order to:

- Clarify the congregation's understanding of its mission;
- Study existing or emerging mission needs;
- Explore possible ministries for meeting those needs;
- Decide which ministries will receive priority attention.

Building your congregation's budget in a very careful and highly intentional way requires adequate time. The group that is responsible for budget building should have a twelve-month timeline to accomplish the various steps described in the following pages. The timeline should include the following information for each task that needs to be done: the date, time, and place; the committee or person responsible; any resources needed; and the next steps. It is a good idea to plot out a timeline.

When you take the time to be intentional and to engage many persons in various parts of the budget-building process, more members will have a greater understanding of your congregation's mission. A by-product of that greater understanding will be more enthusiastic response in support of the work covered by the budget. That support leads to an expanding and increasing ministry.

Steps in Building the Budget

STEP 1. DEVELOP A MISSION STATEMENT

What is your congregation's reason for existence? What is its purpose? What does it want to accomplish? What are its mission priorities?

These are questions that the development of a mission statement can help to answer. Through careful consideration of scripture passages, mission needs that confront the congregation, and the faith experiences of members, it is possible to produce a mission statement that will be helpful in your congregation's budget-building process.

It is important to engage a large number of members in shaping the mission statement, and then have various groups in the congregation include study and discussion of the statement in the course of their work. You may want to have the congregation take formal action to adopt the mission statement. These activities help to give broad ownership, which makes later steps in budget-building easier.

STEP 2. ASSESS MISSION NEEDS

What are the pressing needs in your congregation? In your community? What ministries that express the good news of God's love are the associations, conferences, and national agencies of your denomination pursuing? What kinds of mission work are being done by interdenominational or ecumenical groups?

These questions are typical of those that need to be explored in the assessment process. Small study groups, church-school classes, cottage meetings, all-church fellowship events, questionnaires, and such, can be employed to assess mission needs.

Another part of assessing mission needs is to ask every board or committee of the congregation to evaluate carefully its current activities and develop its program plans and budget needs for the coming year. Each group should be asked to prepare and present its proposals in light of the mission statement that was developed earlier.

It is likely that your denomination either suggests to your congregation a dollar goal for extended mission, or engages you in some process leading to your adoption of such a goal. Careful consideration of a suggested goal, or faithful participation in a goal-setting process, is a crucial part of assessing mission needs.

Each group in your congregation that assesses mission needs should be asked to prepare a brief written report that can be considered, as subsequent steps in the budget-building process are taken.

> "Budgeting is people telling their dollars where to go, instead of asking them where they went.."
>
> —*ROGERS BABSON*

STEP 3. RECOMMEND STAFF SALARIES AND OTHER BENEFITS

Very significant parts of the church's ministry and mission are accomplished by paid staff members, including the church secretary, sexton, organist, and so on. So the appropriate group in your congregation will want to consult with the pastor and other staff members to clarify goals, review job descriptions, and recommend staff salaries and supplementary benefits. Such recommendations need to be in line with the congregation's expectations of the work to be done, and with the economic realities that all your members face.

In many congregations, inadequate attention has been given to the matter of economic justice for persons employed by the church. To be sure, no one should enter the church's employ in the hope of getting rich. But that fact is no reason for a congregation to avoid dealing fairly with each member of its staff.

All staff members should be enrolled in the denominational pension plan. Also, federal law now requires that all lay employees of churches must be covered by Social Security, and the congregation must pay the employer's share of their Social Security taxes.

For Social Security purposes, a pastor is considered by the government to be self-employed. This means that a pastor must pay Social Security taxes at the much higher self-employed rate. It also means that a congregation cannot pay the Social Security directly to the government for the pastor.

Faced with these realities, an increasing number of churches are providing the pastor with additional money designated for Social Security. Frequently, these additional payments are based on the same percentage of salary as the church is required to pay for its lay employees. However, Social Security payments which the church makes to the government for its lay employees are not considered taxable as income to the pastor. Consequently, more and more congregations are providing their pastors with Social Security payments that are based on a higher percentage of salary, so as to offset the increase in the pastor's income tax caused by those Social Security payments.

All such items as housing allowance, vacation, health insurance, sabbatical leave, car allowance, and reimbursement for other church-business expenses deserve careful consideration. Your denomination office has compensation guidelines to help you.

STEP 4. PROPOSE SOME POLICIES

It is obvious that your congregation's mission must be both planned and paid for. It may not be so obvious that policy decisions concerning how to pay for mission can have an important impact on both budget building and budget fulfilling. While it is undesirable that corporate policies might become "the tail that wags the dog," it is worth looking at a few areas where policies can be crucial.

The Stewardship and Mission Committee, church council, or some other group might very well be asked to study the policy areas mentioned below, to propose either that current policies be affirmed or that new policies be adopted. Regardless of where such policy proposals originate, it is usually desirable to have them endorsed by official action of the congregation.

Guidelines for Individual Giving

What does your congregation currently hold up before its members as a guideline for giving? You may want to consider:

- Affirm intentional annual growth in all our giving for the ministry and mission of the church by individuals and families.

- Affirm an approach to giving based on a percentage of annual income.

- Challenge individuals or families to give at least 10 percent of their annual income for the ministry and mission of the church.

- Suggest that in moving toward this challenge, individuals or families determine the percentage of income represented by their present giving for the ministry and mission of the church, and then increase it by at least one percentage point each year. (For example, if individual or family giving amounts to 3 percent of income this year, it would increase to 4 percent next year, 5 percent the following year, and so on.)

- Encourage the congregation to increase its support of denominational requests by at least one percent a year. (Review carefully the congregation's current status. Have you paid the requests in full? Why? Why not?)

Would these be good guidelines to propose to your congregation? If not, what specific suggestions can you make to challenge members to grow in their financial stewardship? If you have no expectations, you expect no results.

Special Appeals

What is your congregation's policy about giving to Special Appeals?

Many congregations, feeling strongly that each person has the right to determine his or her support of each special offering promoted by the larger church family, give their members the opportunity to see the promotional materials for each special offering, and then to determine, after prayer and consideration, what their personal support will be. This practice has merit, because no person or group in the congregation is saying "No" for anybody else, in response to special appeals.

In congregations that include certain special offerings in their budget and do not ask members for special gifts on special occasions, it is very desirable that the promotional materials for these offerings be distributed to the members for educational, interpretive, and motivational values. Members need to understand what their regular weekly or monthly gifts are helping to support.

STEP 5. PUT ALL THE PIECES TOGETHER

Up to this point, your studies have identified needs, hopes, dreams, possibilities, opportunities, and policies. Now you need to put all the pieces together into a proposed budget for the coming year.

One way to do the job is to hold an all-church retreat. Many churches have found that Friday evening through Sunday afternoon allows sufficient time to consider the various program suggestions that have been made, to be intentional about long-range and short-range goals, and to develop a clear proposal for the ministry and mission of the congregation for the coming year.

Another possibility is to ask the people who have primary responsibility for budget building to invite each church committee, board, or group to designate one of its members to work with the group to develop the proposed budget. Congregations that use cottage or small-group meetings to assess needs often have a representative of each small group participate in the development of the proposed budget.

At this point of putting all the pieces together, the mission statement developed earlier in the budget-building process can be very useful. It can help to indicate which proposals seem most in keeping with the congregation's understanding of its ministry and mission.

In determining the proposed budget, it is very important to consider not only the various suggestions that have been made, but also the financial potential and present giving level of the congregation. You want the mission you propose, and the budget necessary to underwrite that mission, to challenge the members of the congregation.

If the proposed budget is too close to this year's budget, it will not challenge them. If it is too far beyond the present giving level or too close to the financial potential of the congregation, no one will take it seriously. It will be dismissed as "unrealistic."

Preparing the Budget for Presentation

When decisions have been made about the content of the proposed budget, the next step is to prepare the budget for presentation to the appropriate leaders, and eventually to the entire congregation.

If your congregation has previously used a narrative budget, you already know its considerable benefits. If not, we urge you to prepare one. It is well worth the additional effort.

Here are several ideas that will help you to prepare your proposed budget for presentation:

- Include both anticipated income and anticipated expenditures, so that the congregation knows the sources and avenues of income, as well as the ways the income will be spent.
- Organize individual budget items into several general categories, instead of one long list of expenses. It is true that financial officers need a list of the proposed expenditures in great detail, and such a list should be available to any member who wants to see it. But only a very small percentage of members are interested in a line-item budget.
- Use categories that explain what the money does, rather than who or what gets the money. Your purpose is to inform members about the ministry and mission that is proposed for the coming year. Remember: People give money to people and programs, not just to meet budgets.
- List proposed items for the wider mission before you list proposed items for the local mission. This suggestion is made because in many congregations,

wider mission is left until the end. That practice leads members to regard the wider mission as deserving only of whatever is left over after provision has been made for everything else.

When the budget has been put into a presentable form, it needs to be adopted or modified by the governing board and/or the congregation. Then it can serve as one of the resources in your annual financial enlistment.

Using the Budget

Because the budget outlines your congregation's ministry and mission, it can be used in several ways.

Certainly, the budget will serve as a control for the spending of church funds during the coming year. In this sense, it can help to ensure that the congregation's decisions about mission priorities are carried out.

"God likes help when helping people."

IRISH PROVERB

If you have done a good job of building a budget to meet mission, it is almost inevitable that the congregation will need to plan and implement a thoroughgoing financial enlistment, in order to obtain the amount of money needed to carry on the church's work.

During your financial enlistment, the budget can serve as a useful teaching aid. Because it encompasses the total mission of the church, it is very valuable in pointing to the various ministries that your congregation is providing, and helping members understand the financial costs associated with each.

One important point to remember: If you ask members to "underwrite the budget," it makes the budget an end in itself, when, in reality, it is only a means of listing and describing desirable ministries. The challenge should be to support the church's ministry and mission which the budget describes, not to support the budget.

The budget also can be a valuable part of your congregation's year-round program of stewardship and mission education. From time to time, various parts of the budget can be highlighted, to increase the awareness, understanding, and support of your church's mission:

- Presentations to boards and committees to explain mission needs and opportunities.
- Showing of audiovisuals produced locally or by the denomination, to depict various mission needs and the ministries that address them.

- Presentation by or conversation with mission visitors, who can personally tell the story of part of the church's mission.
- Discussion of the narrative budget in cluster meetings in members' homes, prior to the congregational meeting where it will be presented.
- Distribution of printed resources such as a denominational Calendar of Prayer.

Building a budget to meet mission needs and using that budget to inform, educate, and motivate the members of your congregation can be very important ingredients in increasing your congregation's faithfulness and expanding its ministry.

The Financial Potential

D A V I D   J .   B R O W N

Here are two suggested methods of estimating the financial potential of the membership of the congregation.

The Per-Member Method (Before Taxes)

Find the percapita income for your town, county, state, or standard metropolitan area. This information is available from libraries, local chambers of commerce, and such government publications as *The Survey of Current Business, Labor Statistics,* and *A Statistical Abstract of the United States.* Remember that this amount represents the average income of your members. It does not mean that every member has that amount of income. Some have more, many have less.

Multiply that amount by the number of members in your congregation to calculate the total income of your congregation. Be sure to use the official membership figure. Do not use the number of persons or family units that actually are making contributions.

The Per-Household Method (After Taxes)

Find the per-household effective buying income for your town or country. This information is available in *Sales and Marketing Management,* a periodical that is available in public libraries. Remember that this amount represents the median income of households in your congrega-

tion. It does not mean that every household has that income. Some have more, some less.

Multiply this amount by the number of households in your congregation to calculate the total income of your congregation.

When you have calculated the total income of your congregation by either the per-member method or the per-household method, multiply it by .1 (10%). This calculation will show the number of dollars that would be available for your congregation's mission, if gifts from the entire membership were to meet the guideline for giving that is recommended by the tithe. It is likely that the tithe, an ideal and long-term financial potential, is three or four times the total that members presently give. Consequently, for short-term use, such as the financial potential for developing next year's budget, it may be advisable to cut the long-term potential in half.

Another possibility is to calculate the percentage of total income of all members that is represented by present giving. Then, add one percentage point to arrive at the financial potential to be used for developing next year's budget. For example, if present giving of all members represents 3 percent of the total income of all members, the financial potential for next year might be 4 percent of total income.

The Present Giving Level

You need to consider the present giving level as evidenced by the financial contribution that members are making. Here's how to do it:

Examine the declarations of intention (pledges, commitments, and so on) that members made for the current year, the contribution actually made to date, and the history of the performance in giving recorded over the past two or three years.

On the basis of this examination, estimate the amount of money you can expect from the gifts of members during the current budget year.

The result is an estimate of the money you can actually expect, in contrast to the amount promised or the amount represented in the congregation's budget for the current year.

Deciding on a Reasonable Challenge

Your work on the costs or proposed plans, the financial potential, and the present giving level has probably produced three different estimates. Soon you will need to look at these three estimates in relationship to one another.

But first, you need to determine whether your congregation receives any income from sources other than the gifts of living members. Some of these sources may be savings accounts, stocks, bonds, other investments, bequests, rental of facilities, sales, and other income-producing activities.

Add the annual total of all such income to your estimate of the financial potential, and to your estimate of the money expected from the gifts of members during the current year.

Now consider the three estimates in relationship to one another. In a typical congregation, the money expected during the current year is the lowest of the three estimates, the money potentially available is the highest of the three, and the cost of the proposed plans is somewhere between the other two. In some congregations, the cost of the proposed plans exceeds the money potentially available.

You want to suggest a proposed budget that is a real challenge to your members. You do not want to suggest one that is only slightly beyond where the congregation is now. At the same time, you want the congregation to take the proposed budget seriously. Decide on a figure that seems to represent a reasonable challenge.

Congregations that conduct a good year-round stewardship program, including stewardship education, mission interpretation, and a challenging financial enlistment plan, can expect to increase from between 10 and 20 percent in any year.

A number of factors must be considered when establishing the goal for the proposed budget: the economic conditions of the region and the membership, the morale of the congregation, and the past financial enlistment history of the church.

If the congregation is in an economically depressed region, then money available for the work of the church may be limited. Morale also is important in determining potential giving. If there is a "can do"

"Success: the proper ratio between what one contributes and what one derives from life."

spirit because of previous successful financial projects, that is definitely a plus. However, if the congregation exhibits a timid spirit because of past failures to achieve its established financial goals, then this must be dealt with. If, year after year, the congregation has done a good job in challenging members to give, then a smaller increase may be expected in a given year. This generally means that potential increases have been met each year, and the increase in any given year will be more modest.

An increase of more than 20 percent in total giving for any year is unusual, so a goal that is between 10 and 20 percent over the previous year's giving should be in the realm of the possible. This does not mean that there won't be money available for other projects, such as capital expenses paid out over a three-year period. These comments apply only to the local current expense budget of the congregation.

Preparing a Narrative Budget

DAVID J. BROWN

Narrative portions of a proposed budget should identify the kinds of expenditures that are included in each of the categories. To prepare a narrative budget, you will need to do the following:

- Ask the pastor to estimate the percentage of his or her work that is applicable to each of the budget categories. These individual percentages must total 100 percent.
- Total the pastor's salary, housing, fringe benefits, and all professional expenses, except the reimbursement for automobile travel.
- Apply the estimated percentages to that total, and allocate the resulting amounts to the appropriate categories.
- Follow a similar procedure with other staff, such as the church secretary and custodian, in order to calculate the portion of the salaries and fringe benefits that should be allocated to various categories.

You may want your budget to reflect actual costs even more adequately. If so, you can spread the costs of "Equipping and Maintaining Our Buildings" among the other categories. To do this, estimate the percentages of the use of facilities required by the work included in the other categories, apply those percentages to the costs of "Equipping and Maintaining Our Buildings," and allocate the resulting amounts to the appropriate categories.

These are not suggestions or extensive and elaborate cost-accounting procedures. They are suggestions aimed at presenting a truer picture of how money is actually spent to fulfill your congregation's mission.

Example of a Narrative Budget

Anticipated Income: $75,000

Our income from loose offerings, church-school offerings, savings account, and other sources will amount to about $10,800 next year. Consequently, we will need pledges totaling $64,200, or $11,500 more than this year, in order to accomplish the work we are planning to do.

Total $75,000

Estimated Expenditures:

1. Supporting the Wider Mission $14,000

Our congregation's work extends far beyond our own community. Through our support of the Christian work carried on by the conference and the national agencies of the our denomination, we provide services to the congregations in our vicinity and minister to many people in our state, nation, and other countries. (Include a folder or brochure highlighting mission beyond the congregation.)

2. Reaching Out to Serve Our Community . . . $5,300

We provide a child-care center for preschool children whose parents work, a tutorial program for children and youth who need additional help to master basic educational skills, and a recreation center for teenagers that is open on weekends. We make meeting rooms available to a senior citizens group and to Alcoholics Anonymous. Our pastor visits nonmembers, provides counseling services to residents of our community, and participates as our representative in several community organizations.

3. Preparing for and Conducting Worship . . . $16,200

Worship is central to our congregation's work. Planning for Sunday morning worship, preparing sermons, conducting weddings, funerals, and other special services requires a significant part of our pastor's time. Our organist consults with the pastor, selects music, plans and conducts rehearsals for three choirs, and practices the organ. This budget category includes costs for music, bulletins, candles, communion elements, other worship aids, and guest ministers and organists who serve during vacation periods.

4. Educating Our Children, Youth, and Adults . . $8,700

Under the leadership of our pastor and the Christian Education Committee, we have developed over the years an excellent church school. Curriculum materials and other supplies, expenses for sending teachers to training sessions, costs of the annual appreciation dinner for church-school leaders, and expenses of our daily vacation church school are included here. Also included are the costs of confirmation classes for youth, church membership classes for adults, weekday Bible-study groups, and occasional forums on current issues.

5. Caring for Our Church Family $9,400

Pastoral care is a vital part of our work, especially for persons who are ill, hospitalized, bereaved, preparing for marriage, going through divorce, or facing other crises. Our church secretary provides information and other services to members, such as preparation of reports for the annual meeting of the congregation. Our monthly newsletter, occasional communications, family-night socials, and the all-church picnic are also parts of sustaining our common life.

6. Reducing Our Debt $7,680

By the end of this year, the debt incurred as a result of the major renovations we made a few years ago will be down to $14,000. Next year we plan to pay $6,000 on the principal and $1,680 in interest.

7. Equipping and Maintaining Our Buildings . . $13,720

Our custodian takes good care of our facilities. Utilities, insurance, and taxes are costs related to providing facilities to carry on our work. In addition to normal minor repairs, we plan to resurface the parking lot next year, at a cost of $4,200.

Total $75,000

121

 MONEY TALK

Coming Up Short in December

HERB MATHER

"We should make a special appeal to the congregation. Ever since the summer slump, we have been behind, and now December is here. Denominational askings are three months behind."

How often has a similar speech been made in your church? How did it feel to the person who gave it? How did it feel to the people who heard it? How effective was it?

Many churches come to the end of the year with the realization that a special effort is necessary to ensure that all the bills will be paid. Churches react in different ways to such a situation. Some reactions are healthy; some are not. Let's examine some commonly used appeals. You decide whether they will help or detract from your church's mission.

Cry-A-Lot

This popular system has worked well in many smaller membership churches. Usually, church treasurers are best at this, because they write the checks. If funds are insufficient, a conscientious treasurer feels inadequate. If you wish to use this method, make it personal. Wring your hands and shed a few tears in front of people who know you and care about you. Such a demonstration may get folks to dig a little deeper to help you.

The Harangue

Give the people who come to church a good tongue lashing about their poor giving habits. Point out that there are a lot of deadbeats and lukewarm Christians in the church; otherwise, the money would be sufficient. Quote the per-capita giving statistics of the Wesleyans and the Adventists. Make people feel really guilty. The harangue works much better orally than in writing. Some folks may get mad, but they probably were going to leave the church anyway. Although some folks will not give more, this method often brings in enough funds to meet the present crisis.

Lay-It-on-the-Line

This method is usually displayed in letters sent out about December 10. The writer quotes from the mem-

bership vows and reminds folks that when they united with the church, they promised to be loyal and uphold the church through "prayer, presence, GIFTS, and service." Sometimes this appeal is accompanied by an explanation of how much it costs "just to keep each name on the books." This method rarely brings in much money, but it makes the finance committee feel good about having done *something!*

Cry Wolf

Tell your people that the doors may be closed if more funds don't come in by December 31. You can warn them that the district superintendent may put a padlock on the church door. (Hardly anyone will believe you, but this method carries emotional value.) More believable is the word that the pastor (whom the congregation loves so much) will be punished if all the askings are not paid. This method will work only about once a generation, since people can't remember any such punishment ever happening before. (In other words, you are not likely to be believed.) However, if you have tried all the other methods, you probably will not lose anything—especially if the people like the pastor.

By this time, you must be thinking that there are better ways of making an appeal. There are. All the ones just listed give people about as much joy as bailing out a sinking ship. Such appeals do not help people see giving as a spiritual discipline. When people fail to see the church as a ministering body, they are simply keeping the organization afloat. Giving does not feel good when it is used simply for survival.

Consider how such appeals would sound to a first-time visitor. It is likely that anyone wandering into the congregation would decide, "This church is in trouble. I surely don't want to be a part of it!"

Financial problems do not wait until December to surface. They probably have been festering for a long time. The end of the year is judgment day. Although it is too late to take corrective action for the past year, you can plan a strategy for the coming year.

As a first step, examine the giving pattern of your church over the past three to five years. From the church records, list the amount received each month. Average the total receipts each January, and so on through the year. You will see that certain months are consistently high, while others are low. In many churches, the December offerings are three to four times larger than offerings in any other month of the year. If that is your pattern, why not give your "Praise" speech!

Praise

"This church has a history of giving very generously in December. Last year, our December giving amounted to $____. We anticipate that you will be equally generous this year. In fact, if you give only $____ more than last year, we will have all our bills paid; and we can go into the new year with our heads held high.

"Your generosity makes it possible for us to have a pastor who calls on the sick and homebound. Through our giving, we are helping teach children, youth, and adults about the faith. We are feeding the hungry and providing medical care to the sick. We are in ministry through our giving."

Some churches may be experiencing a shortfall for the first time. It may be the result of economic conditions in the area, or the death of several substantial givers. In situations such as these, you might want to use a "Tell It Like It Is" speech.

Tell It Like It Is

"This has been a hard year for many people in our church. I am encouraged by the dedication and generosity of many of you. You remind me of the church in Macedonia that Paul describes: 'They were extremely generous in their giving, even though they are very poor' (II Cor. 8:2b TEV). In spite of the generosity of so many, we are running short this year.

"We believe in giving in proportion to what we have. As Paul says, 'I am not trying to relieve others by putting a burden on you; but since you have plenty at this time, it is only fair that you should help those who are in need' (II Cor. 8:13-14 TEV). If you are one of those who have plenty at this time, we ask you to look upon the mission of this church as a primary place to 'invest' funds at this year's end.

"Giving is an investment in the gospel of Jesus Christ. For some of you, 'investing an investment' may be your best way of giving. Donating appreciated stock or real estate is often a sensible method of giv-

ing. We are ready to help you if one of these methods works better for you.

"Through all our giving, we are sharing the love of Christ here, and all around the world."

In all that you do concerning the financial life of the church, emphasize *giving* rather than *paying*. Help people experience the joy of giving through the church, instead of feeling they are paying the bills of the church.

Now is the time to plan a strategy, so that you will not need to make these appeals next year. Not all these ideas will be appropriate for your church. Choose the ones that will be helpful this year.

Plan a realistic, attainable budget. You want to challenge the people, but this is not the place to project the "impossible dream."

A church that chronically has a big year-end deficit should develop a different kind of budget. A core budget lists all costs that must be paid. Other costs should be listed in order of priority. "If we receive $500 more, we will ____. The next $1,200 will mean that we can ____." Every item that is met beyond the core budget becomes a victory for the congregation. And congregations need victories!

Don't focus on numbers; tell the story of what the money is doing in the world. Talk about the people who are receiving the gospel. Describe the prayer ministry of your church and the Christian education programs for children and youth. Talk about the ways you help feed the hungry and clothe those who do not have adequate clothing. Tell the stories in little bits, week by week.

Set dates for the committee on finance to meet at least once each quarter. At those meetings, evaluate the present year's giving, in relation to the giving in previous years. If you need to take corrective action, do so. Don't assume that the money will come from "somewhere" before the year's end.

If action is needed, avoid making an appeal to "help the budget." Instead, decide if one or two items in the budget have special appeal to some people. Building repair or ministry with children or youth are good choices. Highlight those budget items, and develop a campaign to raise funds as "over-and-above" giving.

Have a "Year-end Giving" emphasis that explains how people may give from new sources and—at the same time—receive help in their personal financial management.

Plan a "Memorial Giving" emphasis. Any time of the year is appropriate, but May—around Memorial Day and November 1 (All Saints Day)—are ideal times. Develop a "Wills and Bequests" emphasis for your church. Your denomination's foundation director is a good source of information to help you develop a wills program.

Finally, ask people to give, rather than asking them for money. Do you believe that the need to give is greater than the need of the church to receive money? Encourage people to give in gratitude for the One who gave us Jesus. Giving is thereby channeled through the church to minister to others in the name of Jesus Christ.

 # BUDGET TOOL

Letters

JAMES FOGLE-MILLER

Dear Members and Friends of _____.

Televangelists, with their constant appeals for money, have always made me uncomfortable. Many of them give preachers a bad name. "Well," I've said to myself, "at least we local church pastors are different."

Now, after less than a month here, I'm writing a letter for money. Is the only difference between me and the televangelists that I write rather than appeal through television? I think not. You be the judge.

God is not going to call me home if we don't raise the budget. The ministry of the church will continue, even if everyone does not give. Giving money will not guarantee you a place in heaven, or purchase a time-sharing condo at a "Christian" resort. The motivating force for giving is not guilt or fear.

What we ask is simple. In the midst of summer, when our minds are often focused on other things, remember the call to be good stewards of your resources. In your remembrance, our church will have its place. Celebrate that. Rejoice in your blessings. Give out of your spiritual abundance.

An envelope is enclosed to help us remember, and as a convenience. Throw it away if it makes you feel guilty. Use it, if your stewardship and spiritual life lead you to do so.

Whatever choices you make regarding financial giving to the church this summer, please let this letter nudge you into thinking about the wider issues of stewardship. It's more than money. It's a spiritual matter.

Your Fellow Steward,

Dear Members and Friends of _____.

Our church is going to tithe. Starting September 1, we will send to the conference treasurer 10 percent of each week's total contributions. The money will go toward our share of connectional giving.

It will not be easy. There undoubtedly will be times when we will have to choose between purchases for the church and this giving for others. Those are the risks and challenges that Christian stewards constantly face.

The Finance Committee approved this policy at its last meeting. As a congregation, we are trying to model the behavior that we pray all will follow as individuals. We believe, too, that the spiritual rewards from this effort will be great. Besides, how can we ask people to try to do what we are not doing?

There are churches that do more. Tithing 10 percent of our income to the larger church will not pay all our connectional askings. Yet we truthfully can do no less.

Pray each time you make a contribution to the church. Ask God's blessings on what we do as a congregation, and listen to the ways God would have you be in ministry.

Yours in the Lord's Work,

Dear _____ Friend,

Your stewardship makes things happen. Through your varied contributions to the church, exciting ministries take shape. Here is just a partial list. Thanks for making it possible.

- *More than 25 youngsters are participating in Children's Choir.*
- *Eighteen people are involved in the Disciple Bible Study.*
- *An exciting part-time Christian Educator has been hired.*
- *The Trustees' fund-raising project came in over the goal, permitting important building maintenance to proceed.*
- *More than 150 adults came to Fellowship Hall for our Sunday School Rally, with the Friendship Class leading the way in attendance.*

Stewardship is a corporate matter, too. You know from last month's letter that we are tithing as a church on each week's income. But there is more to stewardship than that. Here are some other ways in which your contributions are working:

- *A short-term certificate of deposit keeps funds available for use, while earning the maximum interest rate possible.*
- *Computer-controlled air-conditioning, heating, and lighting means monthly savings on our electric bills.*
- *Our maintenance custodian saves us service-call costs and keeps balky equipment running.*

Your church is being a good steward of the funds entrusted to it. Like tithing on what we receive, we can do no less.

Your contributions are valued and valuable. Thank you for entrusting them to the church.

Your Fellow Steward,

Dear _____ Friend,

The message of Christmas blares out on one channel and plays softly on another. The loud, urgent one comes from the commercial side. The softer, more gentle, but far more exciting word comes from the spiritual channel.

We know the commercial message well: "Buy! Buy! Buy!" it proclaims. And don't forget the chorus: "Party! Party! Party!" By the end of the season, we may be exhausted and spent, emotionally and monetarily.

But there is another song to sing. Remember this one?

Good Christian friends, rejoice
with heart and soul and voice;
give ye heed to what we say:

News, news!
Jesus Christ is born today!

This is a song that tends to get lost midst the strident messages of the other channel, but this is the song that makes the difference. This is the source of the magic of Christmas.

Jesus Christ is born today! What a song! The tunes vary, as do the words, but the message stays the same: "Christ the Savior is born!" Silently, softly, we come to pay homage, kneeling at the manger with others, placing our gifts at the feet of the Christ Child. And in our giving, we are reborn.

May the true miracle of Christmas again touch your life and be with you throughout the year.

Yours in the Christmas Song,

Dear _____ Members and Friends,

Thank you for your financial contributions to the church during the past year. Your generous spirit helped to make exciting things happen.

The enclosed giving statement reflects the contributions we have recorded under your name. Please check to see whether it conforms with your own records, and let us know if any changes need to be made.

The new year holds much promise. We are looking forward to growing as a church—spiritually, numerically, and in neighborliness. Your prayers, presence, gifts, and service will make the promise reality.

To be better stewards of the church's financial resources, we are sending out contribution statements quarterly, rather than monthly. This will save nearly $800 in postage alone. Should you need to check your record of giving more frequently, a simple phone call to the church office will give the information you need.

This New Year season is the time the church celebrates Epiphany, the festival commemorating the visit of the Magi to the baby Jesus. Through that visit, the light of God's love began to be made known to the Gentiles—that is, to all the world. That love touches us, nudges our neighborly impulses into action, and has us following the words of Isaiah, echoed by Jesus: "Arise, shine, for your light has come."

God bless you in this year, and enable you to let your light shine.

Yours in the Light of Christ,
Pastor _____

Dear _____ Members and Friends,

It is hard to believe that the books are closing on 1996. The year seems to have gone by so fast.

The books are closing not just on the year, but also at the church. Enclosed is your record of giving to _____ for the 1996 year. Please check carefully to ensure that we have recorded all your gifts. Contact _____ at the church office (Ph. 000-0000), if you have any questions, or if any corrections need to be made.

Your giving made so much possible during the past year. The Russian Emergency Food Lift, a second Habitat House, Hurricane Relief to Florida, new and expanding ministries here at home, the hiring of a Youth Director and a Minister of Pastoral Care, and much, much more.

We look forward to an exciting new year. We will see a new pictorial directory, the starting of a day-care center, expanding older-adult ministries, and growth in our youth program. And that's just a start!

Everything, though, is made possible because you choose to give to the church. Your presence in worship and in Sunday school, your time and talent, your financial contributions—all these gifts make things happen here at _____.

Thank you for all your gifts. God bless you and our church, as together we begin a new year of ministry.

With Gratitude,

....

Dear _____ Members and Friends,

"The Gifts of the Magi" is one of our favorite Christmas stories. It tells of a young financially struggling couple, each of whom wants to give the other a special gift at Christmas.

He has inherited a beautiful watch. She has long gorgeous hair. She sees the perfect gift, a watch chain that can display his watch. He locates a set of combs that will complement her hair perfectly. Neither has any money.

Out of their love, each makes a sacrifice. He pawns his watch to buy the combs. She cuts her hair, selling her long tresses to a wig maker to obtain the money to purchase the watch chain.

From their sacrifices, each discovers the much more valuable gift of love that they have been given. And the same discovery is available to us this Christmas.

"For unto us a child is born." God has already made a sacrifice of love for us. God sent Jesus, the very one we need to enable us to turn items of pride into gifts of love.

Our Christmas offering this year goes toward the outreach and mission programs of the Conference. With your generous gift, we can pay our asking in full for 199__. To do that, we need nearly $_____, a miracle in giving.

Long ago, when the Christ Child was born, the first Magi brought gifts to place before him. Everywhere, every year, other magi come and, like those in the story, bring their special gifts. These gifts of love change the world. They make the miracles happen. Won't you be one of this year's magi?

Bringing Gifts with You,

....

Dear Members and Friends of _____,

Rejoice! The dogwoods have bloomed. No, that's not quite it. Let me try again. Rejoice! Christ is risen! That's it!

So why are the dogwood blossoms on the Easter stationery? Legend indicates that the dogwood once was a tall, sturdy tree. It was cut down to make a cross for a carpenter from Nazareth.

The dogwood was heartbroken to find itself used for such a purpose. So Jesus promised, as he hung there on the dogwood cross, that never again would dogwoods be used for such a purpose. To this day, dogwoods are small, thin, twisted trees—and the blossom is in the form of a cross, with a crown of thorns in the center.

I do rejoice when the dogwoods bloom. They bring the promise of spring and are a beautiful symbol of Easter. In fact, many of us are "dogwoods."

As "dogwood," we may have been misused or abused. But the touch of Christ transforms us, gives us new shape, and leaves us radiant symbols of God's love.

This Easter, imagine yourself to be the instrument of Jesus' crucifixion. Pour out your heart to him as he hangs there on you. Let the Savior change you forever. Bloom like the dogwood!

Rejoice, then, for the "dogwoods" have bloomed! This new life in Christ calls us to share our gifts with others. Please make your response to God's love a generous one, through the Easter offering.

The financial blossoms that come our way through the Easter offering envelopes will be used for the World Service Fund and Conference Benevolences. That will help spread the good news of Easter. Rejoice! Christ is risen!

Changed and Giving,

....

Bonus Letter: Here's a sample stewardship letter by Yvette L. Dalton, which can be sent to children and youth.

Dear _____,

Each year, our church has a time of special emphasis on stewardship. During this time, we think about the many things that God has done in our lives and the kind of response we can make by pledging some of our money, time, and talents to the church.

Think about our church and the programs it offers for someone your age. Consider also the ways our church makes a commitment to mission by assisting and working with others in our community and in the world. We can respond to God with thanks for all the things God has done in our lives. One of the ways we can say "thank you" to God is by making a commitment to our church. Think about the ways you can make such a commitment of your money, your time, and your talents.

Enclosed you will find a pledge card that we hope you will complete and bring with you to place in the offering plate during worship on Stewardship Sunday. We believe that whatever you have to offer as your commitment to God and to God's work with our congregation is very important. YOU, as a younger member of our church, are very important to us, and we give thanks to God for your presence with us.

Peace,

 # NEWSLETTER

---

8 GIFTS THAT DON'T COST A CENT

The Gift of Listening. But you must really listen. No interrupting, no planning your response. Just listening.

The Gift of Affection. Be generous with appropriate hugs, kisses, pats on the back, and handholds. Let these small actions demonstrate your love for family and friends.

The Gift of Laughter. Clip cartoons. Share great articles and funny stories. Your gift will say, "I love to laugh with you."

The Gift of a Written Note. It can be a simple "I love You" or "Thanks for your help." A brief, handwritten note may be remembered for a lifetime, and may even change a life.

Great Job!

The Gift of a Compliment. A simple and sincere, "You look great in red," "You did a super job," or "That was a wonderful meal" can make someone's day.

The Gift of a Favor. Every day, go out of your way to do something kind.

The Gift of Solitude. There are times when we want only to be left alone. Be sensitive to those times, and give the gift of solitude to others.

The Gift of Good Cheer. The easiest way to feel good is to make others feel good.

PART FIVE

LEARNING TO GIVE THROUGH PLANNED GIFTS

Long-range Planning and Church Publicity

Introduction

DONALD W. JOINER

It is predicted that more than $10 trillion will pass through estates in the next twenty years. Most of those estate transfers will be passed on to children or grandchildren. Some of them will go to charities. Will your church be a recipient of any of those gifts?

I have worked with many people setting up estates to provide for ease of transfer, support of charitable causes, and to reduce taxes. I am now in a new role as administrator of an estate. After my friend's death, I was struck with a disturbing reality: two institutions that meant much to her (her church, and the retirement home where she lived for 14 years) were not receiving anything from her estate. Did she not care? No! I believe they were not included because no one asked! Most of her estate will go to charities. Those who asked, received!

People want to give! This is the first and most important principle of funding ministry. Some do not know that they can give to their church. Some want to give, but have restricted their thinking to giving only from earned income. The older we get, especially in retirement, the less earned income we may have.

The largest increase in giving in the future will not be from earned income, but from accumulated assets. Many older adults with whom I talk want to give to their church, but are afraid of running out of money before they die. Even those with large estates and adequate retirement income have the same fear. Estate gifts, now or at death, can be the most joy-filled gifts one can give. If they only knew they could!

Jerry Jackson, in the lead article, shows why a local congregation should be actively involved in planned giving. His three points: organization, policy, and marketing, will allow your church to be ready for growth in giving in this area.

A problem for many churches is that we organize and wait. We can have the finest organization, the most adept policy for receiving planned gifts, but if no one knows about giving through planned gifts, no gifts will be given to the church. John Tincher provides a good "marketing" outline for any church to adapt.

Involvement in planned-giving ministry is not without potential hazards. Maryle Ashley reminds us that the first step is to make a will. But everyone has a will! If *you* have not written one, the state has one for you—and no state includes charitable giving in that will.

Renard Kolasa continues his series of one-liners for use in bulletins and newsletters. (Each volume of this *Guide* will have ten more one-liners.) The key to receiving planned gifts is to continually remind people of the possibility. Often the best move is the simplest: A one-line thought, at the right time, produces results.

My favorite television program is *ER*. It is fast paced, future oriented, and works only because of the team. That will be the secret of your planned giving fund-development program. Leonard Sweet declares that the best epitaph at death is "his check bounced," because he gave it all away. What will your epitaph be? Do *you* have an up-to-date will, an estate plan? Have *you* included your church in your will?

PLANNED GIVING

Are Planned Giving Programs Appropriate for the Congregation?

JERALD JACKSON

It seems that everyone is doing it. Promoting planned gifts, that is. Hospitals, local public radio stations, community foundations, colleges, seminaries, and environmental groups—all are getting into the planned-giving act. Congregations are also discovering planned giving. That's because senior citizens, over the next decade, will bequeath more than a trillion dollars in accumulated wealth.

The planned gift is not to be confused with the Christian stewardship ideal of planning your giving. The planned gift is better described than defined: A planned gift may be a bequest, a life-income gift (such as a gift annuity, a charitable remainder trust, or a pooled life income fund), or a special insurance program. With a planned gift, the recipient (i.e., the church) does not have the use of the gift immediately. Institutions that ask people to consider making planned gifts are thinking of *future* income, rather than *current* income.

Given these definitions, is planned giving appropriate for the local church? It depends.

It depends first upon our theology of Christian stewardship. We know that for our spiritual well-being, we need to give. We know also that the church requires resources. Traditionally, resources have been understood as *current income*. Christians give a portion of their current income for the support of current ministries of the church. We can safely assume that 95 percent of a congregation's time and energy is spent in the area of current needs. The giving equation for Christian stewards is: *A Portion of My Income = This Year's Church Budget*

Usually, our practice of financial stewardship stops here. From time to time, however, we are forced to consider other levels of stewardship and need. One level has to do with capital programs, either on the local level or conference level, or even higher. That giving equation, for the Christian steward might be stated: *A Larger Portion of My Income, and Perhaps Some of My Savings = The Special Capital Needs of the Moment.*

Planned giving addresses the individual's need to consider the meaning of stewardship in relation to accumulated assets. Do our churches challenge us to extend our notion of stewardship to our accumulated assets? Largely, no—usually because the local church is not at all clear about what it would do with such resources. That giving equation for Christian stewards might read: *A Portion of My Accumulated Assets = ?*

It is not surprising that when people think of a planned gift in relation to accumulated assets, they usually think of an endowment. When the church can articulate the place of endowments in ministry, then the planned gift will make more sense to church members.

Whether planned giving is appropriate to the church also depends upon the technical capacities of the congregation. Can the church properly administer planned gifts? Gift annuities, for instance, require investment skills, reliable annuity payments to private beneficiaries, and competent handling of the IRS requirements. Charitable remainder trusts demand even more sophisticated skills.

Some larger congregations are equipped to handle such gifts, but most churches are not. Fortunately, most areas now have well-staffed denominational foundation or development offices, to which individual congregations may turn for the administration of such gifts.

If your church sees an opportunity for spiritual development in helping the congregation apply stewardship principles to accumulated assets, and if your church has access to competent fund administration, then it is ready to consider a planned-giving program.

To be successful, such a program requires the right environment. My first church (which I served in the 1960s) was situated on a former freeway route to pheasant country. The old-timers used to talk about the endless stream of traffic that had passed through the town during the pheasant season. However, the traffic had dwindled to a trickle.

What had happened? Had the hunters wiped out the pheasant population? The pheasant population was indeed down. However, the decrease was not due to *hunters* but to *farmers,* whose new plowing and cultivating practices had destroyed the pheasants' habitat.

We are much more sensitive today to environmental questions and to the needs that living things have for healthy environments. The same is true for a planned-giving program: We need to create an environment where such a program can thrive. To create that environment, we must pay attention to four fundamentals: purpose, structure, policies, and promotion.

Clearly Define the Purpose

The question mark in the third equation above must be replaced with a focus that is carefully thought out and fully integrated into an understanding of the individual's spiritual need to give, and the congregation's need to be in ministry. The ministry that planned gifts support will vary from one locale to another, but it usually will be some form of endowment. While the purpose should be clear, it also should be general enough to allow flexibility. Several congregations, when defining purposes for endowments, include one or more of the following:

- A permanent property;
- A special program endowment;
- An outreach endowment;
- A scholarship endowment.

Establish a Structure

Most churches allow for alternative structures in developing a planned-giving program. One possibility is to develop the program through the stewardship committee of the church. Another, and more effective, possibility is to form a separate endowment committee. In some churches, planned giving is an afterthought of the finance or

> "All the endowments which we possess are divine deposits entrusted to us for the very purpose of being distributed for the good of our neighbors.."
>
> —JOHN CALVIN

memorial committee. The needs of the church will determine which structure is best. Whatever structure your church uses, the purpose of the committee (in addition to the purpose of the endowment) must be clear.

Establish Policies That Create Confidence

Investment of Funds. Assuming that you have accepted the notion of endowment ministries, you will need to consider the question of investment. The temptation is to invest for income, but that may not be appropriate. An endowment fund should be invested for long-term results. While it is important to produce funds for the specific ministry for which the endowment was created, people understand and prefer to support an endowment that is invested for long-term results, rather than for high current income. Many area foundations or denominational offices of development provide investment opportunities that are not otherwise available to congregations.

What area of the congregation will be charged with the responsibility of making spending decisions? In some circumstances, this responsibility is relatively clear. For instance, the board of trustees most likely would be charged to spend any distribution from a property endowment; a program committee probably would oversee the spending of special program endowments. However, if the church is to inspire confidence, these responsibilities need to be stated and understood.

Promote, Promote, Promote

Once structure and policy have been determined, the story must be told and retold. Create and distribute a simple brochure which states the purpose of your endowment program. Wills seminars and estate-planning seminars should be offered frequently (even if few people attend). Once funds are generated for spending, the achievement should be publicly celebrated. The committee charged with promotion will need to think of ways to bring the planned-giving program to the consciousness of the congregation.

Three focuses generally command the attention of the endowment committee: investment of funds, granting of funds, and promotion of the endowment program. If the endowment committee tries to do all three, it will spend all its time on investing and spending. Assign these responsibilities to subcommittees or task groups. If no one knows about your endowment program, if no one is giving planned gifts, if no one's will includes your church, of what use is the endowment program?

 PLANNED GIVING

Ten Strategies to Market Planned Giving

JOHN M. TINCHER

For many years, the congregation has missed the opportunity to receive large legacy gifts! These gifts, often referred to as "ultimate gifts," have gone to major universities and hospitals, to the neglect of churches. Why has this happened? Congregations simply have not been asking for such gifts!

The majority of these gifts are structured as planned gifts. Although planned giving includes bequest gifts from living wills and trusts, it is also the art of utilizing charitable tax and estate-planning laws to achieve the most cost effective structuring of a donor's gift. Now is the time for the congregation to "get on board" with planned giving. While the following strategies originated in major universities and hospitals, I have adapted them for use in a congregation.

Be Sold on Your Organization and on Planned Giving

Our first strategy is to develop enthusiastic, well-informed local church bequest committees/foundations to serve as representatives for your local church! Lack of commitment breeds lack of commitment! People give to people who are committed to and represent worthwhile causes. Since planned gifts are gifts from an estate, which may not be available for twenty to twenty-five years, an added level of commitment (to the future of the organization) is necessary. Thus, your congregation's bequest committee/foundation needs a strong belief in the future of your church. Despite the high mobility of baby boomers, and a subsequent loss of loyalty to denominations, it is still possible to find persons of high commitment who are eager to affirm "my church" as the place with a vital future.

Develop Your Marketing Plan

Most local church bequest committee/foundations simply have not taken the time to determine their purpose, and thus have no marketing plan. The marketing plan outlines the reason for existence and identifies specific strategies to accomplish goals designed to move the committee/foundation in the right direction. The marketing plan needs to answer these and other questions: What is your organization's case (reason for existence)? Why do you want planned gifts? How will planned gifts be used and recognized by your local church bequest committee/foundation? What creative ways can you devise to get the word out about your desire to receive such gifts?

A section of the marketing plan should be dedicated also to goals such as: a specific number of contacts to be made during the year; a desired number of contacts, during the same period, to be made through the written word; and a bottom line number of dollars to be raised. The final section of the plan clearly identifies a budget needed to accomplish these goals.

Use of the Church Newsletter

These articles should appear more than once a year and address the need for stewardship of members' estates. Be careful to structure these articles in an informative and intriguing style, to encourage church members to consider their local church in their estate planning.

Success stories are also important to use in the church newsletter. Such stories discuss actual cases in which the church already is in the estate plan of a church member. Begin by discussing legacies that already have come to the church. Then, with the understanding and permission of leaders of the church, many of these members will be willing to share their personal plans to participate in the stewardship of their estate. Such commitment to planned giving is truly contagious!

Don't Be Afraid to Share Planned-Giving Brochures

Denominational and other brochures adorn tables and racks of most local church narthexes. Local church bequest committees/foundations miss a valuable opportunity when they fail to have planned-giving brochures prominently displayed. Such brochures are available through your denominational foundation, through planned-gift consultants, or planned-gift direct-mail companies.

Seminars Attract Attention!

Although estate planning obviously is not the main mission of the congregation, many members will find that attending an estate-planning seminar at their church provides a "safe haven" from financial and estate planners who, in some other venue, might be more interested in marketing their professional abilities rather than the church's opportunities. Within the membership of most congregations are estate-planning professionals: lawyers, accountants, financial planners, trust officers, certified life underwriters, and so on. Although most of these people are unable to address charitable gifting possibilities specifically, their general estate-planning information will be appreciated, and their remarks can be immediately followed by a member of the congregation's bequest committee/ foundation who is educated on charitable gift planning. Another valuable resource for seminars is the planned-gift consultant retained to provide the seminar. This individual, usually not a member of your church, often has the ability to attract a larger crowd, because she/he is a "visiting expert" and is knowledgeable of charitable estate planning.

I suggest that the local church bequest committee/foundation consider sponsoring two different estate planning seminars each year.

Speak Up as Often as Possible!

Church bequest committees/foundations should offer informed speakers to all adult groups in the church. Such speakers would be appropriate for men's or women's groups, large adult Sunday school classes, and other meetings. Appearances should last no longer than five minutes and should simply remind people of the importance of charitable estate planning to their local church. Variety is extremely important! In addition to using different individuals to make such cameo appearances, the material presented to the groups needs to change as well. By sharing one type of planned-gift opportunity in each appearance, the process gradually will educate all active church members on a variety of gift-planning techniques.

Develop Your Own Bequest Program

An annual stewardship campaign in a congregation is as expected as our next meal. Often viewed as less than an attractive experience, such stewardship campaigns rarely include a request for gifts from church members' estates. A bequest program is an opportunity to ask for such gifts. Before initiating such a program, it is important for the local church bequest committee/foundation to identify specific needs that can be addressed by bequests. A direct-mail planned-giving company can develop the necessary mailings and follow-up brochures needed to accomplish this task. Independent gift-planning counsel also can provide this service. Since most churches do not have members with this knowledge, it is advisable that outside help be sought to provide this program with a wills clinic as a follow-up. (A wills clinic is a program in which church members learn about the importance of wills.) After the program, it is customary to have several attorneys available to visit with attendees and assist them in the preparation of codicils to their wills that can benefit their congregation.

Establish a Separate Planned-Giving Committee

Because the local church bequest committee/foundation has many responsibilities, it should consider the creation of a planned-giving advisory committee. This committee can include members of the committee/foundation, but should be composed primarily of members who are financial and legal professionals.

> "The best use of life is to invest it in something which will outlast life."
> —WILLIAM JAMES

Most churches have a few members willing to use their ability to learn more about the various planned-gift instruments.

This committee should address the issue of planned giving and its relation to the mission of your congregation. Meetings provide the opportunity to share success stories, as well as examples of what can be done. They are also an opportunity to discuss the interrelationship of charitable and general estate planning, and how this interrelationship can benefit the local church. At first, this committee may be difficult to form, due to the lack of individuals in the local church who truly do understand charitable estate-planning vehicles. However, careful attention to these vehicles, as well as some actual experience in their funding, can result in education that can make this committee the main resource in the congregation for the cultivation of planned gifts.

Use Direct-Mail Marketing

Although marketing planned gifts is entirely different from asking for outright gifts from income, the consistent use of direct mail is very important to a successful program in planned giving. Direct-mail pieces should be fashioned tastefully and be full of generally helpful materials for the church member. Such newsletters are mailed two or three times a year, and are clearly different from the weekly or monthly church newsletter.

Direct-mail marketing consists of a newsletter with one or more articles of general interest in the estate-planning or financial-planning area. Woven into these article are ways in which charitable estate planning can benefit the donor as well as the congregation. After reading the newsletter, the reader can order a special brochure which goes into greater depth. Requests for this brochure are returned to the church office and either hand delivered or mailed to the member. Members requesting the booklet become prime prospects for tasteful and careful cultivation in the future.

Materials are available from the denominational foundation, a planned-giving consultant, or a planned-giving direct-mail company to assist in this program.

There Is No Substitution for Visitation!

Ultimate gifts are made after serious and thoughtful consideration. If the congregation is to be a participant in this process, it must supply people willing to make house calls. Visits are appropriate, as follow-up, to all individuals interested in including the church in a planned gift. Visits to people who have requested additional information from a direct-mail piece, or as a result of having attended a church-sponsored estate-planning seminar also may be appropriate.

How do you move individual church members to a decision to include your congregation in their estate plan? The most important thing to remember is that you probably won't move a donor at all. People are capable of making their own decisions. However, if your local church bequest committee/foundation does not provide them with opportunities, it is very likely that your church will be overlooked. A decision to participate in the planned giving of your local church is clearly predicated on understanding the importance of the gift to the church, as well as the varieties of ways in which it can be made.

> *Donor Needs.* Donors do not give major gifts because an organization needs money. They give them because of their own needs. The sooner you can identify the donor's needs, the sooner you will be able to close the gift. This is one reason we spend so much time cultivating the prospective donor. Keep thinking about how a gift can benefit the donor.

 PLANNED GIVING

Write Your Will and Live to Enjoy It

MARYLE ASHLEY

Why Write a Will?

Writing a Will is an experience of joy, creativity, and satisfaction. Too often, it becomes an avoided subject because of its connection to death, but writing a Will is, in fact, an important part of Christian stewardship. Perhaps we "can't take it with us," but through a Will, Christians can take responsibility for the distribution of what is left behind.

Imagine the judgment scene of a millionaire who has hoarded his wealth into a fortune, never giving away so much as a penny. Will Saint Peter be opening the pearly gates for this millionaire?

Then suppose that in the reading of the millionaire's Will, his massed fortune is designated for a congregation. Would this alter the judgment?

For most Christians, the situation is just the opposite of that of the millionaire. During our lives we faithfully tithe our income to our church, and may give even more to charity. Then in our Wills, we close our hands to freely sharing, and pass on our possessions to the next family generation—whether they need them or not.

For other Christians, the results are even more tragic. Many never make a Will at all, losing the opportunity of direction, and allow state laws to distribute their possessions, charging a fee for the service besides.

The preparation of a Will is as much a part of Christian stewardship as tithing or sharing resources or living simply. As uncomfortable as it may be for us to look at our own death, every Christian must consider the following question seriously: *If I died today, would the distribution of my possessions* **confirm** *or* **contradict** *the life of faith I have tried to live?*

A Joyful Experience

Making a Will can and should be a joyful experience. A Christian Will is a statement of caring and justice, another light of witness to the world. Some thoughts outlined below may give you a new perspective—not only on why you need a Will, but also on the fun in its preparation and the peace in its completion.

Making a Will Is Fun

Imagine yourself giving to others everything you own, picking and choosing just what to give each individual or group you want to include. Enjoy the philanthropic feeling of such generosity—how good it feels to give with abandon. Writing a Will allows you to try on that kind of giving, but without having to let go of anything you have. The feelings of compassion, creative giving, innovative selection, even reconciliation are possible in writing a Will that witnesses to your Christian lifestyle.

Making a Will Is Good Stewardship

If you do not have a Will at the time of your death, the laws of your state of residence will govern the distribution of all you own. No provisions for charity will be included. Only through a Will, can you intentionally practice stewardship.

Making a Will Is an Opportunity for Family Closeness

Deciding the distribution of your possessions for yourself puts your values into action. Sharing your Will with your family—spouse and children—mobilizes and reveals each person's values in a new way. The subject of money is often avoided because the feelings surrounding it are strong. But these feelings are also deeply held, and their expression is a way for a family to begin relating more openly than ever before.

The risk of family disagreement may be high, as between children wanting to receive as large a share as possible and parents wanting to disperse some of their assets outside the family. In other families, the children may hold different values from their parents and not want accumulated wealth handed down to them. Or spouses may disagree over the dispersal of joint assets. In every instance, the greater gift is working through conflict to a mutual understanding of one another's values. The struggle may be painful, but also can create new depths of relationship to be enjoyed for years to come.

Making a Will Is Freeing and Brings Joy

Knowing that you "ought" to write a Will but never doing it causes underlying tension that is bothersome, energy-draining, and even a source of guilt. Writing your first Will can release you from the conflict. Once you establish a Will, periodic updates are easily made. A well-written Will can be adjusted through instructions to the executor, rather than a rewriting. Having the basic structure in place brings relief; setting up creative and caring structures brings joy.

The First Steps

If you would like to prepare a Will but are still hesitant, you can take the first steps right now. The joy in imagining and planning the distribution of your assets can be experienced long before you consult an attorney. Begin now by taking these four steps: *Collection, Imagination, Distribution* and *Liberation.* In working through these steps by yourself, and then sharing your results with your family, you will become clear about your assets and your desires for their distribution. Then the application of appropriate legal options can be managed by an attorney.

Collection is a step only you can take. What are your assets? What do you own? Where is it? In gathering this information, include not only the obvious assets, such as land or bank accounts, but also all special items of sentimental value, such as a piece of jewelry or a family picture.

View the Collection step as a treasure hunt. Our relation to money and possessions is often so secretive that we ourselves are not aware of all we own. As your list of assets grows, so will your hidden image of yourself. Scripture reminds us: "For where your treasure is, there your heart will be also" (Matt. 6:21; Luke 12:34). Watch the picture of your heart that is being painted before you.

Collection is also a process not to be rushed. Forgotten assets may come into consciousness slowly, triggering other memories in turn.

Imagination, the next step, begins as the Collection process subsides. Imagination is a step of fantasy, releasing you to dream dreams and see visions. Knowing what your assets are, imagine what they could become—what you could do with this accumulated property you no longer need, how it could be

directed. Let your mind wander . . . perhaps a fantasy of giving money to a shelter for street people who roam the city sidewalks . . . or giving your car to a group that sponsors visits to the jail . . . or building a playground on that vacant lot next to the bank.

The wilder the Imagination, the better, for none of these fantasies commits you in your Will. Rather, they free your tightly controlled, businesslike mind to see new possibilities. Also, they stir your inner feelings to locate hidden urges. Imagination releases feelings about giving that you might not be in touch with— what would be fun to give, what would be helpful, what would it feel like to give this away, what feels "right," and what feels "not quite right"? Without the step of Imagination, the distribution of assets would proceed too methodically, devoid of a recognition of your inner feelings about giving. Taking time to dream brings your whole self into the process, creates a lot of fun for you, and prepares you to take the next step.

Distribution is a step of decision making. Preceded by the Collection of assets to be allocated, and the range of Imagination as to how allocations might be made, Distribution becomes a stage of making commitments. Arriving at "what is given where and when" requires a careful time of discernment.

Prayer is a strong means of discernment. Do not be bashful about asking for wisdom (James 1:5). Take regular time to become quiet before God and listen.

Gratitude is another way to discern appropriate places for giving. Reflect on those persons, or groups, or institutions that have strengthened your Christian walk and helped you become able to make your response to God's grace.

Missions to the world are other areas for discerning the places you will feel good about giving. Identify those missions that you are drawn to—whether at the level of personal involvement or through knowledge of their trusted credibility. Ask yourself what missions "turn you on."

> "The test of generosity is not how much you give, but how much you have left."

135

Family is an equal area to consider. The amount of support necessary for your dependents varies with their stages in life. If at all possible, talk to your family about their needs, their expectations from you, and your desires for allocating your possessions. Arriving at a balance of giving "to family" and "outside family" creates a stronger family stewardship. Genuine concern about giving your family too much is a deep expression of your caring.

In designating each recipient in your Will, ask a final question:

What will be the effect of the gift?

Will it help? Or will it hurt?

Too much money at the wrong time can replace a group's "growing edge" with a laxity of "having it made." Well-intentioned gifts can destroy incentive. Be especially aware of how your gift will affect the designated recipient. When giving through a Will, your presence no longer will be available to guide the impact of the gift.

Conditional giving through a trust fund can arrange for gradual or delayed distribution. Trusts are complex, and do require legal advice. If you identify areas for such giving, note them for later discussion with an attorney.

Before completing the Distribution step, ensure that you also have covered contingencies by choosing "back-up" beneficiaries. To avoid the case where a person or institution you have designated is no longer

> "There is no charity in a man's leaving money in his will; he has simply got to leave it. The time to administer your trust is while you are still living."
>
> WILLIAM GLADSTONE

in existence at the time your Will is executed, include a default designation. Decide on one or two stable organizations to which you would enjoy giving that are unlikely to disappear during your lifetime.

Liberation is the final step. Take a moment to look at the way you have allocated your assets. Are there any specific cases where doing the giving now rather than after death would be more joyful? Are there assets you no longer need to hold?

The Liberation process grows more relevant as we grow older and our need for accumulation of possessions decreases. The joy of giving through a Will may be surpassed by the joy of sharing the gift with the recipient now.

After completing these four steps of preparation, seek out an attorney who will help you prepare the Will. The attorney's place is to point out tax laws and advantages, not to revise your distribution choices. You should feel comfortable that the attorney is entering into your spirit of creative stewardship.

Once you have completed your Will, you have two remaining responsibilities. First, review your Will periodically, and update it when necessary. Second, encourage others to experience the same freedom you have found. Give them the benefit of your own "real world" experiences and enable them to complete their role as stewards of the goods they have received.

 NEWSLETTER

Planned Giving One-Liners

RENARD KOLASA

Beginning with Volume 1 of *The Abingdon Guide to Funding Ministry,* each year we will include ten "Planned Giving One-Liners."

1. Under current laws, appreciated securities and real estate can be deductible for Federal income-tax purposes at their present fair-market value. In most cases, the appreciation is not taxed to you at all. Consider using such outright gifts to pay your pledge, for special gifts, or toward an endowment.

2. Consider giving property to the church now, but keeping the annual income until your death. You might even give your home and keep the use of the property until your death. A current Federal income-tax deduction is available for the value of such gifts to the church.

3. A gift can be made to the church by selling the church an asset at less than current value. The difference between the sales price and the current value is a gift to the church when it buys the asset. This gift can qualify for a Federal income-tax deduction.

4. Consider transferring the ownership of some of your life insurance to the church. The cash value, when given, plus the annual premium, can qualify for a Federal tax deduction.

5. Consider naming the church as a beneficiary on your life insurance or retirement plan. If you have named other beneficiaries, consider naming the church as a secondary or backup beneficiary, in case the present beneficiary is deceased at the time of your death.

6. You may specify that your bank accounts are "in trust for the church." You retain total control over the account during your lifetime, but the property passes to the church at your death, without probate.

7. Stocks and bonds are an excellent means of making a gift to your church. You can be entitled to a Federal income-tax deduction, if you give these securities during your lifetime. Ask your professional advisors for assistance.

8. If you are a stockholder in a closely held corporation, consider having the corporation make a gift to the church. Like individuals, corporations can deduct charitable gifts.

9. Some corporations have programs to match gifts that are made to charities by their employees. This is a way of effectively increasing your gift to the church, if it is available. Ask your employer.

10. The church will consider gifts of jewelry, art, coin collections, antiques, mineral rights, and related items. These gifts can be made during your lifetime or at your death. Contact your tax advisor for more information about how to calculate your tax deduction.

Shipwrecked or not I never miss sending out my annual contributions!

137

PART SIX

TEACHING CHILDREN, YOUTH, ADULTS TO BE STEWARDS

For Christian Education and Stewardship Teams

Introduction

NORMA WIMBERLY

The weekly offering, long-term financial commitment, the home and family, witness, worship and workshops—all are spaces to teach and to learn. Parker Palmer has said, "To teach is to create a space in which obedience to the truth is practiced. To learn is to face transformation."

Ken Carter sets the tone for this section by inviting us to "color outside the lines." Grownups and children are transformed as they teach and learn together. Madeleine L'Engle contends that what is good for adults is also good for children—or should be. As "grownups," we are asked to witness, to teach, to guide, to learn, to stretch, and to grow. The writers of this section think we may need to go outside the lines!

Occasionally, when I work with teachers, I hear someone say, "Oh, I can't teach that!" Sometimes we are asked to teach that which we need to learn! The workshop on tithing is a personal example. God did for me what I could not do for myself. I know now, more than ever, that the way I give and use material things is a major indicator of my spiritual condition.

"Education is the controlling grace to the young, consolation to the old, wealth to the poor, and ornament to the rich."
DIOGENES LAERTIUS

John Stroman, pastor AND teacher, believes that:

Good teachers personify their message.
Good teachers are enthusiastic.
Good teachers teach people, not material.
Good teachers are used by the Holy Spirit.

"TO BE A TEACHER," 1987

If this is the last section of *The Guide* that you have read, congratulations! If this is the first, I urge you to go back to the beginning. Teachers are learners. Learners are often the best teachers. Thank you for learning with Don and me, and with others.

 TEACHING HELP

Learning to Color Outside the Lines

KENNETH H. CARTER, JR.

As a child, I remember an exercise used by an elementary schoolteacher. An outline would be given to me of a flower or a house or a fish, and I would be asked to "fill in" the outline with crayons. This exercise was intended, I am sure, to teach a sense of form and help a young child's development and discipline as a student. The exercise, to be sure, has some very positive benefits; we must learn to live with form and structure. This is especially true for a growing child.

The negative outcome of such an exercise, however, is that it teaches us to stay within the limits and boundaries that are sometimes accepted as a given. I have wondered about this exercise, as a parable for the stewardship dilemma faced by many churches. When our focus is on ministry and mission *inside* the congregation, we are limited, to a great degree, to the financial resources of church members. In contrast, if our focus is on ministry and mission *beyond* the local church, we can, in good faith, invite financial giving from individuals who are not members of our congregations. This understanding has implications not only for how we offer ministry, but also for how we carry out stewardship education.

Since this is a parable, and parables usually have the power to create mental pictures (surely this was the practice of Jesus' teaching about stewardship), consider these examples:

- A congregation seeks to minister to young people in a racially shifting context, adjacent to a city's commercial district. The church invites businesses and corporations to sponsor recreational activities and entertainment that communicate Christian values, as part of summer program for teenagers. The result is ministry that goes beyond the resources of the local church. Who benefits? The young people, the church, and the businesses.

- A congregation sends a dental-building team to a Latin American country. Two dentists appeal to colleagues and business associates for needed sup-

plies. A pharmacist who provides the medicines for the dental mission tears up the bill, in effect making a financial donation to the mission. Who benefits? The pharmacist, not a church member, has been allowed to practice stewardship and grow in faith. The church is able to extend its resources in other ways, by offering scholarships to individuals who wished to serve on the team but could not cover expenses. Additional funds are available to support community-based hunger programs in that country.

These are two brief examples of how we might learn to "color outside the lines" more often as Christian stewards. There is surely a calling to offer mission beyond our congregations. We have become so comfortable with the saying "The world is our parish" that we may have lost its radical meaning. There is an assurance that if the world is indeed our parish, we can count on a greatly expanded number of "giving units."

If we are tempted to see willing and available givers as only those who have given the year before, we might imagine that we are seated at a school desk, crayon in hand, ready to carry out the appointed task. The good news is that we can color *outside* the lines! The good news is that our mission, and the resources to fulfill that mission often lie *outside* those lines as well. We are invited to the joyful task of taking our crayons and drawing in new and adventuresome ways. The call to follow Jesus is, after all, an invitation to be his new creation.

Practical Suggestion

Draw a line down the center of a blank sheet of papers. On the left side, name one or two acts of mission that clearly could be understood as having an impact on the larger community or world. On the right side, list persons, perhaps *outside* the congregation, who might be asked to participate in the funding or fulfillment of these ministries.

TEACHING HELP

Inviting Children to Be Stewards

NORMA WIMBERLY

Christian stewardship is a response (sometimes faithful, sometimes not so faithful) to all of God's gifts. It is a spiritual understanding of the practical and economic aspects of all of life. It is a model for faithful, creative living, a way of paying attention to God, to self, to others, and all of creation. We have a responsibility to live all of life within God's world, according to the will of God as revealed in Jesus Christ. Christian stewardship opens the possibility of leaving the world a better place than we found it.

What does all this mean for teachers and leaders of children? How can we live the precepts of stewardship faithfully? How can we show that we are trying to follow Christ? How can we teach generosity?

Perhaps we should search for the simple rhythm of education that lasts—life as a process of asking questions, seeking, searching, responding. Teaching is a way of being with another. Jesus taught by being with his followers. To teach stewardship is to teach an experience of relationship. Being a faithful steward means paying attention to all the hurts, the questions, and the celebrations of the world, and exploring its possibilities, to be an educator each moment—as well as a lifelong learner.

Teachers of children must be willing to love, learn, and live with children. Faithful stewards/teachers are eager to work themselves out of a job! They realize that the reign of God depends on each of us living out God's intention for all creation. Effective teachers have no illusions, but they have vision. They concentrate on the step-by-step quality of the journey. They are willing to live with questions and leave results in God's hands. They believe in surprises. God's love, gifts, and miracles come when they are least expected.

Effective leaders/learners with children believe in the power of stories. Some story possibilities, some stewardship concepts made visible, are:
- Participation in worship
- Visiting a sick or lonely friend
- Caring for your children
- Planning a personal budget
- Giving and receiving a birthday present
- Exercising regularly
- Praying

- Consistent study of the Bible
- Talking about the life and work of Jesus
- Living with energy, enthusiasm, and joy
- Facing the issues of hunger, hurt, and want in the world, asking, "What can I do?"
- Taking time for reading and study
- Using time wisely
- Planting a garden
- Taking care of your personal property
- Practicing good nutrition
- Developing positive relationships with others
- Giving money for the mission and ministry of the church
- Taking special private time for yourself
- Remembering that there are stewardship elements in all aspects of living!

The list goes on. Teachers of children of all ages know that actions do speak more loudly than words. Each of us is called to live, to learn, and to give. Each of us needs to grow as a faithful steward. Each of us can become more willing to tell the stories, to offer our own life as a tool for teaching.

> "Real education should educate us out of self into something far finer—into a selflessness which links us with all humanity."
>
> LADY NANCY ASTOR

As Christians, one of our most vivid symbols for "showing" our stewardship is giving as a response to God. It is a challenge to teachers to show that the church is a place for offering all of who we are. Often it is necessary to undergo a time of self-examination, before we try to teach financial giving with children. How do we feel about our own giving? What invites us? What holds us back? How do we see the offering in light of the service of worship? Do we truly believe that God calls us to be givers?

With your class, or with any group of children, you may want to search for ways to show that money and other gifts are a symbol of ourselves, not a substitution.

- Create a "giving tree" for your class. Invite each one to indicate on a piece of paper a special gift to be given and shared in the coming days—anything from a hug to part of an allowance.
- Talk to your pastor about ways to include children in the offertory time during worship.
- Tell and share stories of children involved in mission and outreach.
- Create an offertory prayer to be shared with the congregation.
- Discuss the various opportunities for giving in church, at home, and in the community.
- Make a collage of people and places that are healed and made better because of our giving.

- Read Luke 19:1-10.

Teachers of children can invite them to be stewards every day, in every lesson. You can develop greater awareness of the issues of Christian stewardship, of the variety of responses. You can be a source of affirmation. You can honestly examine your own attitudes and guide children in healthier, more faithful ways. You can take action. Christian stewardship is a discipline of spirit and action—prayers, projects, practice, doing, and being. Stewardship is the most visible and accessible of the faith disciplines. Let us teach, act, and learn together.

 TEACHING HELP

15 Stewardship Activities with Children and Youth

YVETTE L. DALTON

Most stewardship programs are planned and implemented by committees. Some committees begin their work in January, while others wait until late spring or summer. Getting an early start helps a committee plan for year-round stewardship.

A program for children and youth should be planned concurrent with the adult program, so that children and youth will be included in worship, congregational meetings, special dinners, and Stewardship Dedication events. To help in this process, some committees invite the participation of youth and enlist their help in reaching their peers.

If your committee plans to produce a packet of information for each church member about the mission of the church and proposed budget, consider creating a packet of similar information especially for the younger members.

When the work of the committee is completed, it is important to conduct an evaluation, focusing on the following questions:

1. What were the responses from parents regarding the stewardship emphasis for children and youth?

2. What were the responses from the children and youth who participated?

3. What was learned from the experience?

4. Should the experience be repeated next year? If so, what additional emphasis or material will be needed for the following year?

Bright Ideas for Stewardship with Younger Members

Recognizing the importance of including youth in your church's stewardship program requires that opportunities be provided for youth participation. In this way, they are able to grow in their understanding of what it means to be a faithful steward of God's gifts, and can realize that they have good gifts to share with all members of the community of faith.

Basic Concept: Compared with elementary children, youth are more capable of abstract thinking and can understand more difficult concepts about stewardship.

Suggested Activities: *The following activities can be used in worship, church school, youth groups, or family-night suppers, and are offered to help youth answer three questions:*

1. What does it mean to be a steward?

2. What happens to the pledges of time, talents, and money that I give to the church?

3. How can I be a faithful steward?

1. What does it mean to be a steward?

ACTIVITY: STUDY BIBLE PASSAGES

I Peter 4:10-11	Genesis 1
I Corinthians 16:1-4	Mark 12:41-44
I Corinthians 12:4-7, 12-13	Mark 10:17-23
II Corinthians 8:6-15	Matthew 22:15-22
Luke 9:11-27	Luke 6:37-38
Luke 21:1-4	Luke 14:7-14

Provide opportunities for the youth to respond to the Bible passages. Some ways in which the passages might be discussed is by reading and illustrating the passage; underlining important key words; recording a reading of the passage on tape and discussing it; role playing the passage and discussing how it might be rewritten today.

ACTIVITY: HAVE A WORD STUDY

Study the following terms: time and talent, commitment, stewardship, steward, benevolent, and budget. You might design a crossword puzzle using these terms. Another way to reinforce learnings of these concepts is to ask youth to use a tape recorder to interview different people in the church about how they would define one of the terms. Plan a way the tape could be used in a planned stewardship program. Posters listing the terms and definitions could be made and placed around the church building.

ACTIVITY: INTENSIVE STUDY OF THE WORD *Steward.*

Using Genesis 1 and 2 as a biblical basis, talk about what it means to take care of the earth. Find illustrations from magazines and newspapers which illustrate ways we have taken care of all of God's creation, and ways we have failed to do this. Assist the youth in seeking ways we can be better stewards of God's great gift to us.

2. What happens to the pledges of time, talent, and money that I give to the church?

ACTIVITY: WRITE A PLAY

Enlist the help of youth in writing a short play to illustrate how the church uses the time, talents, and money that people pledge and give to the church. The play can be performed at youth group meetings or other church gatherings. It also can be videotaped and shown to small groups. The script can be adapted for a youth performance or a puppet show for younger children.

ACTIVITY: STUDY AND ILLUSTRATE THE BUDGET

Provide copies of the church's budget for the older children and youth. Allow time for them to read it and mark places where they have questions or comments. Invite a church officer or a member of the Stewardship Committee to meet with the group and answer questions. After study and discussion, the group might like to illustrate how the budget money will be used, indicating in percentages where the money goes. This illustration might be used by the Stewardship Committee in their presentation to the church family.

ACTIVITY: STUDY AND ILLUSTRATE COMMITMENTS OF TIME AND TALENTS

A similar kind of illustration could be used to show how members (of all ages) of the church share their time and talents in involving themselves in the life and work of the church, and in mission to the community and the world. Who serves on church committees? Who helps visit people who are sick or shut in? Who welcomes new people in the community? Who helps in service projects and other churches in your city?

ACTIVITY: TOUR THE CHURCH BUILDING

Take a tour of the church building, looking for ways people commit their time and talents in service to the church, community, and the world, and the ways that the money we give to the church is used. If a guide sheet is developed with questions to help them get around the building, it will be like a scavenger hunt.

ACTIVITY: INTERVIEWS

Interview any people who work in the church, whether volunteers or paid staff. The students might prepare questions ahead of time that they would like to ask the minister, organist, choir director, custodian, librarian, or clothes-closet director. Younger children might enjoy visiting the person on the job, such as the organist at the organ or the nursery attendant in the nursery, so they can actually see what the person does.

ACTIVITY: WRITE A SKIT

Write short skits to be used in worship or at church suppers. Junior- and senior-high youth particularly enjoy this kind of thing, and they do it very well.

Some suggested ideas around which skits might be written: "The Church needs you to do . . ." or "Last night I dreamed that everyone in the church made a pledge of time and talents, and I saw people doing all kinds of things, such as . . ." Following is an example of a short skit that might be used:

Lucy: Boy, this church is boring! There is nothing to do!

Sally: Well, Lucy, maybe you're just not looking very closely. There's lots to do, if you want to get involved.

Lucy: Well, I've been wanting to get involved, but I can't find the right thing.

Charlie: Well, there are a lot of things to do, like helping in the Clothes Closet, or giving them clothes you can't wear any more, or buying books and toys for children who don't have any.

Sally: Or writing articles for the church newsletter, or designing a bulletin for the worship service.

Linus: We have a lot of members who live in the nursing home. They would love to have a visit, even from "crabby old you"!

Snoopy: I'd love to visit, but they won't let me! Too bad, they don't know what they are missing.

Linus: See, Lucy, there is a lot to do!

Charlie: God wants our talents and time, as well as our tithes and offerings of money.

Lucy: Well—maybe there is something I could do! I'll . . .

ACTIVITY: MAKE SLIDES OR A VIDEOTAPE

Using write-on slides or a video camera, record the "stewardship story" of your church, illustrating how your church tries to carry out God's plan, as we care for one another and the world. This form of media allows the participants to create a visual expression of their study and learnings, and share them with other groups in the church.

ACTIVITY: WAYS TO INVOLVE YOUTH IN THE WORK OF THE STEWARDSHIP COMMITTEE

To help the stewardship season come alive, ask the youth to create posters with gentle reminders of our stewardship responsibility. Posters can be made around open-ended themes such as the following:

Stewardship is . . .

Stewardship season is a time when . . .

Give the church some time for . . .

What is your talent? Our church needs people to . . .

3. How can I be a faithful steward?

ACTIVITY: PROVIDING PLEDGE CARDS

Provide pledge cards for money, time, and talents that children and youth can understand and use. Be sure to follow up on all pledges, and find ways to use their offerings of time and talent. Alert the appropriate committees that the children and youth have made commitments.

ACTIVITY: INVITE A GUEST

Ask a member of the Stewardship Committee, a church officer, or the minister to meet with a church school class or youth group. Brainstorm around the question, "How can I be a faithful steward?" This also could be done in small groups at a church supper.

ACTIVITY: TALK ABOUT STEWARDSHIP AT HOME

Encourage parents to discuss stewardship with their children. If your church makes visits to each family, prepare a booklet to help parents talk about stewardship with their children.

ACTIVITY: COMPOSE A SONG OR WRITE A POEM

Why not try your hand at composing a song or writing a poem? Verses could tell about stewardship, with examples from the Bible and the ways we try to be stewards in today's world. Try writing verses to be sung to a familiar tune.

Using Pledge Cards with Children and Youth

We can teach children and youth that serving and sharing is a way of life for Christians by recalling the question asked of the congregation at the baptism of a child: "Do you, the members of this congregation, and in the name of the whole church of Christ, undertake the responsibility for the continued nurture of this person, promising to be an example of the new life in Christ and to pray for her or him in this new life?" (*Book of Order*, S-32.04000, Presbyterian Church [U.S.A.]). Similar questions can be found in most denominations that practice infant baptism.

We can respond faithfully to that question by taking seriously the important task of helping children and youth become better stewards and caretakers of this world. One way to do this is by using pledge cards designed for children and youth.

Some adults might ask, "Why do children need pledge cards? It just complicates our work. Do they expect to get pledge envelopes, too?" You might want to respond by acknowledging that it does require more work, but younger members learn best about stewardship by being involved in giving to the church. If this includes the use of pledge envelopes, we should encourage their use.

Please remember that when people are asked to make pledges of their time and talents, it is essential to follow up in making them aware that their gifts are an important contribution to the mission of the church. This is true for both adults and children. So if you decide to use pledge cards for children and youth, make sure that the follow-up of their pledges of time and talent is lodged with an appropriate committee.

(See Sample Stewardship Letter for Children and Youth, p. 127.)

 TEACHING HELP

Helping Children Care for God's People

DELIA HALVERSON

Scale of Giving

Draw a big scale on a large piece of paper. Give children small papers cut in the shape of weights. On each paper "weight," ask them to write reasons for giving. Then as a group, discuss the different reasons and tape them on the plus or minus side of the scale, depending upon whether you decide it is a Christian's attitude for giving. Some of the reasons could be:

- Give to church because parents tell you to.
- Give to a friend because he or she will give to you.
- Give because you desire to help others.
- Give to someone because you know it will make that person happy.

- Give to a TV ministry because the evangelist cries, and his voice "moves you," and you are sorry for him.
- Give because someone has told you that you will go to hell if you don't.
- Give so that God will love you.
- Give because you love God.
- Give because you feel privileged to give as a Christian.
- Give because you recognize that all that you have is actually God's.

Finish your discussion by reading Matthew 6:1-4.

 TEACHING HELP

Teaching Children About Money

WAYNE BARRETT

Learning to handle money responsibly was a value my wife and I wanted to pass on to our three children. Yet, where does one go to find appropriate "curriculum" for such teaching? We decided to develop our own system.

Among the values related to money management that we wanted to teach were:

1. Learning to give to God and to others.
2. Learning to save.
3. Learning to spend responsibly.

As a fundamental learning experience, we provided each of our children with three banks, as soon as they were old enough to receive money of their own. One bank was the "Spending" bank. One was the "Saving" bank. One bank was for "Giving." The kids were urged to divide whatever money they received among the banks. And this they did without complaint.

The plan worked beautifully for a number of years, until one day my oldest son came home from Sunday school.

Facing me, Chris declared, "Dad, you've been lying to me!" I couldn't imagine what he was talking about!

"You've always told me I should give away one-third of my money. Today in Sunday school, they told us to give only 10 percent!"

 PLANNING TOOL

Guiding Young Stewards

JAN COX

How children are taught to use money is a major lesson in stewardship. Parents often face dilemmas about allowances for children. They question the best age to begin, how much is appropriate, how much should be earned, how much should be saved, and how much spent. One thing seems settled, however. Parents hope to enable their children to learn to use money wisely, to view it as a valuable resource that is worked for, and as a way to give as well as receive.

One Christian family I know took the time and effort to teach their two elementary-age children some basic understandings about allowances. They used coins to help them learn how to break a dollar down into spendable amounts and learn what these amounts would buy.

Because these parents believed in the concept of tithing, they also showed the children how much one-tenth of a dollar was. One-tenth didn't look like so much when seen next to the nine-tenths.

These parents helped their children become tithers by providing a set of offering envelopes for each child. They helped them establish the habit of placing it in the offering during worship each Sunday.

How do congregations teach their children to become good financial stewards? One of the most common ways is by active involvement in support of mission projects. Some projects are in other countries, other states, or in their own towns and cities. These efforts will feel very distant to children, unless they are given an opportunity to relate personally to other persons, places, and things. Here are some ideas:

- Pictures of missionaries and the people they serve can be part of classrooms, as well as on the main church bulletin board.

- Letters can be written and answers received by classes or by individual children.

- Videos of missionary children and children of other cultures help make them believable to kids. Return videos of "us" are great fun to make and send.

- Christmas gifts and cards made especially for missionary children are good connections.

- Studies of the places our missionaries live are of great interest to children.

- Provide special times for children to meet missionaries or leaders of local outreach projects when they visit the church.

- Let children hear prayers expressed in worship for the people and projects supported by the congregation.

- Plan times for groups of children to visit and serve people in the community. For example, one congregation works with a downtown mission on a regular basis. On occasion, the preschoolers make centerpieces for each table in the dining room. Upper-elementary children make personal messages for each patron of the mission. Older children and young teens assist adults in preparing and serving the meal. It is a goal to have the children participate in this project from time to time, so that they become a contributing part.

There is an African proverb: "It takes a whole village to bring up a child." These words create the image of working together, intergenerationally, for the good of the children. It also suggests that we can do the important things in life better when we do them together. And what is more important than helping our children become their best?

TEACHING HELP

13 Stewardship Ideas for Children and Youth

NAN DUERLING

Children and youth need to be effective stewards of all of life. Our responsibility is to enable them to express their commitment to God through their relationships with God, other persons, and the earth, by a caring attitude and the sharing of their time, abilities, and possessions. Although children may have relatively little money, they can be taught to offer part of what they do have to God. Youth, especially senior-high students, often have funds from an allowance and a part-time job. They want to learn how to use their resources in ways consistent with their Christian faith.

Stewardship education needs to be scheduled regularly throughout the year, though the monetary aspect may be highlighted during the congregation's finance campaign. Here are some ways children and youth can be educated about the use of their money and led to make a commitment.

ENCOURAGE FAMILY DISCUSSION

For several weeks prior to the intensive phase of the finance campaign, use lessons on stewardship at all age levels in the church school. Denominational resources are available. Encourage families to discuss what they have learned at home, so they may begin to consider not only how much they will pledge, but why they are making a commitment.

CHILDREN'S SERMON

Ask the person responsible for the children's sermon to prepare one on a financial stewardship theme.

ILLUSTRATE BIBLE VERSES

Write out and discuss several Bible verses related to being God's good steward. Ask the children and youth to make posters or murals to illustrate these verses. If your church has selected a specific title, theme, or logo for the finance campaign, be sure to include it. Prominently display the artwork around the building.

PLAN A PUPPET SHOW

After the children have had some education about financial stewardship, plan to make puppets and enact a scene depicting good financial stewardship. The story may be ad libbed, or a script may be written by a teacher, or by the students themselves. The youth group may be willing to write a script for younger children.

"CHILDREN'S DAY" SERVICE

With advance preparation, the church school, or selected classes, can teach the entire congregation about giving by participating in the worship service. This activity can be a "children's day" type service, in which each group shares a song, or poem, puppet show, or skit on the stewardship theme. As an alternative, part of a regular worship service may be devoted to this kind of sharing. Youth classes should be encouraged to participate.

WRITE A SONG

Choose a tune that is familiar to several classes and help each group write a verse for a stewardship song. The verses can then be organized and sung at a church school opening exercise or a junior church service. Print the words in large letters on cardboard, so that every class can participate.

YOUTH GROUP DISCUSSIONS

Use one or more youth group meetings to discuss financial stewardship. A video or movie may be helpful. Cite biblical references. Your denomination may have some flyers available for use with youth. Have the group think about how they spend not only their individual resources, but their group's money as well. In what ways are they already good stewards? What changes need to be made to become better stewards?

YOUTH PLEDGE CARD

Plan an overnight or weekend youth retreat or camping experience which focuses on stewardship as a way of life for Christians. Include in your program opportunities to discuss monetary giving as one aspect of good stewardship.

CHALLENGE YOUTH-TITHING

Have the youth look at their personal budgets. Tell them that this exercise is strictly confidential—between them and God. How much money do they spend on food, recreation, school supplies, clothes, car expenses, and so on? How much do they save? How much do they return to God? After they have completed the exercise, talk with them about tithing and proportionate giving. Challenge them to prayerfully consider whether their budget truly reflects their priorities as Christian disciples.

YOUTH-TO-YOUTH VISITATION

If your church finance campaign involves visitation, recruit youth to visit other youth. Be sure to include them in any adult training and follow-up activities.

SHARE IN CONGREGATIONAL DECISIONS

If your church policy allows for youth participation on congregational committees, nominate at least one youth to serve on the finance committee. Teenagers are usually willing to support something (in this case the church budget), if they have had an opportunity to participate in decision making. A youth member will be able to interpret financial needs and opportunities to other youth and enlist their support.

"EXTRA MILE" PROJECT

Explore options for an "extra mile" financial contribution to a special project through your local church or denomination. Offer several suggestions and allow the group to select a project that excites them. Provide opportunities to learn about the project and, if feasible, communicate with persons directly involved in it.

STEWARDSHIP BOARD GAME

Create a Monopoly-type game for children or youth. Instead of using real estate, offer familiar options for spending money (e.g., ice cream cone, "in" game or toy, admission price to a local attraction, etc.), and prices that are reasonable for your area. Some of the options would relate to gifts for God (e.g., church school offering, donation for class project, money for missions, etc.). Provide opportunities on the board for obtaining money (e.g., your aunt sends $10 for your birthday, a neighbor pays you $2 for feeding his dog, etc.).

To start the game, give each player a predetermined amount of play money to spend, as in Monopoly. The game board may be a large sheet of construction paper, or if the class is large, even a piece of butcher's paper that covers an entire table. After a specified period of time (which may vary depending on your class schedule and the number of children), end the game.

This game is noncompetitive, in that players are looking at the choices they make, not the money they amass. Encourage the players to talk about the ways they received and spent the money they had. How did they feel about the decisions they made? Use this opportunity to reinforce good stewardship choices.

 **TEACHING HELP**

Children and Offerings

LESLEE ALPHANO

Near the end of a noisy, frustrating session in her church school class of nine- and ten-year-old boys, the church school teacher asked, "Why do you think I'm here?"

The children were surprised by her question. The teacher was surprised by their answer. They replied that she *had* to be there because she was being paid! More surprise came when the teacher explained that she was *not* being paid. She really wanted to be there.

This was a way she put her faith into action. It was a sharing of her love for God and her belief in God's love for others, including a noisy church-school class.

It would be great to say that this exchange led to quiet, cooperative church-school sessions. That did not happen. The class was as noisy and boisterous as ever, but something did change. By her words and actions, the teacher helped her class discover that an offering is not just something you bring to church; it is who you are and how you live in the world, in response to God's love for the world. The noise centered around a new interest—giving of oneself to express God's love for others.

Jesus invited people to be offerings in God's kingdom. When he spoke about the kingdom, it was in terms that involved action, such as a search (Matt. 13:45-46), yeast (Matt. 13:33), or a feast (Luke 14:15-24). Jesus did not exclude anyone from the kingdom because they were too old or too young, or disabled, or female. The tax-collector, Zacchaeus, became an offering as he attended to the injustices he had caused (Luke 19:1-10). The children were not pushed back, but invited into the gathering around Jesus. With their presence, they offered a symbol of entering the kingdom (Mark 10:13-16).

In the broken bread, Jesus offered himself to the world. The action that makes our celebration of Holy Communion (Eucharist) possible is the action of offering the bread. The response of each person is the giving of oneself to partake of the bread.

Too often, people come to worship looking for what they can *receive,* without discovering the gifts they *bring.* Children and youth may be treated as those who should sit back and receive the offerings of their church-school teachers or leaders. No wonder they think such persons are paid!

Excluded from the offering, how can children and youth learn the response of giving? If their offerings are not taken seriously, how can they learn to make serious responses of faith? Money stuffed into a paper cup, or a patronizing pat on the back, does not take the gifts of children and youth seriously.

The challenge is how to help children and youth discover the church as a place for offering their gifts, and for activating the offering of themselves to the needs of the world. Perhaps this is a challenge for all ages.

We need to change our attitude toward the offering. It is not a sidelight of worship and the Christian life, but the center. We also need to change our attitude toward the offerings of children and youth. They do not need to wait until they are grown to bring their gifts to share with their church and the world.

> "What greater or better gift can we offer the republic than to teach and instruct our youth."
>
> —*MARCUS TULLIUS CICERO*

The offering is central to every act of worship. Without the response of offering, worship is incomplete. Yet, in many worship programs for children and youth, the offering may be omitted, with the underlying implication that they have nothing to give. Sometimes the offering is trivialized as something to get through with embarrassment, with the same implication that their offerings don't really count for much.

Perhaps we would treat the offering differently if we saw ourselves on the offering plates. The money we bring is a symbol of ourselves, not a substitution. The offering can be a time of discovering how *we ourselves* can be gifts of time, encouragement, kindness, talents, efforts toward peace and justice. We can put more on the offering plate than money. We can put symbols of our actions and gifts for sharing with the world. This would help persons of all ages to see their actions in the context of the offering and of worship.

Look for Opportunities to Participate in Worship

Invitations to the offering can include:
- Stories of young people involved in mission and outreach.
- Stories of the local church offerings to others in the community and world.

Young people can present symbols of the offering.
- A telephone, visualizing a crisis center supported by the youth.
- Cards, made by a church-school class for persons in the hospital.

Young people can participate in the offering.
- Read mission and ministry information.
- Extend the invitation to the offering.
- Share the prayer of dedication.
- Choose or write the offertory prayer.

Use Your Imagination!

The offering is a response to the Word of God experienced in preaching, teaching, and in people's lives. Preparation for offering takes place in the sharing of stories, both biblical and contemporary, at home or in church settings. When the church-school teacher shared with her class the story of her reason for being there, she helped them discover that the offering was much more than they had thought. When she involved them in learning about the offerings of others, she also helped them learn about their own opportunities for being offerings.

By translating the church-school curriculum into actions of giving, supporting, and offering, children and youth will be brought back into the life and work of the church. Children and youth are not simply watching from the sidelines—they are the church, too!

Making room for the offerings of children and youth, and treating these gifts seriously, will communicate that their gifts do matter. Attitudes developed at home also send messages about the offering to children. Hastily given coins from the bottom of a change purse or pocket demonstrate one attitude about offerings. Sitting down as a family, discussing the offerings each can make, could involve children and youth in a more positive way. The offering of money can be seen as something in which all family members have a part. The use of envelopes and family activities, giving time, talent, and money for others, show that the offering is a way of life.

Children, youth, and adults bring to the church, and to the world, the precious gift of themselves, offered in response to God's love. The challenge is to enable and celebrate this treasure.

MONEY TALK

Witnessing to Giving

RONALD REED

For many clergy and lay people, the idea of making a presentation about one's personal giving and pledging is very difficult. The prospect of witnessing brings up in us a multitude of fears about our inadequacy, feelings of sounding like a braggart, or embarrassment about our current giving. These fears are natural inhibitors, but they can and should be overcome. They hide a deep and profound possibility for spiritual growth, for both the witnessing person and the audience. I say this because of my own personal experience in both making and hearing witnesses about giving.

One of the simplest and easiest ways to prepare people to witness is to ask them to talk about their growing-up years, sharing how money was discussed and handled in their family. The instruction is actually simple: Tell one another about growing up with money in your household. Take about five minutes each, in groups of no more than four or five. You may want to report back to a larger group.

What inevitably comes out of this group process is that people help one another understand more fully why they act as they do about money and giving. A feeling of understanding also breeds compassion and intergenerational respect for different perspectives. Finally, you can use this technique to "warm people up" for some teaching about witnessing.

My experience is that witnessing benefits the storyteller as much (or more) than it does the individual or group audience. Everyone is given a richer understanding of what the gospel really is. Three components to making a strong witness need to be taken into account: the personal story, the Bible story, and the faith tradition story. Each part of the story needs to be explored and integrated into a whole witness, which, I believe, truly brings the gospel to both the witnessing person and their audience.

The first aspect of the witness is to reflect on and know one's own story about money. That is why the small-group work on money stories can be a start-up for this process. We have learned in different self-help experiences that the more we remember and reflect on our personal stories, the more in control we feel about our lives. And so it is with money. We all have issues about money within the psychological, theological, and practical realms.

With practice, the personal story can be developed in such a way that it takes on a certain quality that helps others identify the parallels from their own life experiences. The personal and unique witness leads toward a common human identification in the story.

However, the solely personal story is not the gospel. No matter how well thought out and well presented the personal story may become, it will inevitably fall short of a witness and be only a confession, if the biblical and church traditional aspects are not integrated. How do I see my life in the Bible? How do I see myself in the events and characters of the Bible? Where do I see my pain, pleasure, joys, and sorrows in the mirror of the Bible?

What I am suggesting is not an intellectual scan of the Bible, but scrutiny from the prayerful heart. The heartfelt reflection on scripture indicates where the integration of the personal and biblical are happening at that moment. This form of reflection can be done either privately or in a small group setting. When people begin to integrate their money stories with the Bible stories, fascinating connections start to appear. The characters and events of scripture, as true economic realities, begin to open up issues such as enslavement, prodigality, Levitical and deuteronomic laws. Jesus' teachings and struggles, and other biblical issues, begin to inform the witness with rich and deep themes. Almost any part of the Bible can be used to spark a person's sense of what the scripture tells us about money, giving, and stewardship.

Finally the question is raised, "What does my denomination say about money and giving, and in general about its stewardship?" What is the history of my local congregation as related to money? What overt and secret messages have we heard, and do we hear, from the denomination and local church? What are the practical principles, like pledging and tithing, taught by the church? Where am I in all this? Do I pledge? Do I tithe? How do I arrive at my financial giving decisions?

An authentic witness opens up both the giver and the receiver to new insights and possibilities for financial stewardship, and giving in general. A sort of spiritual channel opens, in which the witness, the one who bears the gospel, lightens the burden of the hearers, who wish to find a richer depth to their spiritual lives.

This process can produce a faithful, effective, and authentic witness:

"Success is . . . a matter of adjusting one's efforts to obstacles and one's abilities to a service needed by others. . . . Most people think of it in terms of getting. Success, however, begins in terms of giving."
HENRY FORD

"The man who lives for himself is a failure. Even if he gains much wealth, position, or fortune, he is still a failure. The man who lives for others has achieved true success. A rich man who consecrates his wealth and his position to the good of humanity is a success."
NORMAN VINCENT PEALE

"Not until we can refuse to take without giving, can we create a society in which the chief activity is the common welfare."
HELEN KELLER

"It is not how much we do, but how much love we put into doing. It is not how much we give, but how much love we put into giving."
MOTHER TERESA

"Tell me, I'll forget. Show me, I may remember. But involve me, and I'll understand."
CHINESE PROVERB

1. What are the money stories from your childhood experiences?
2. How are these stories brought into the present, and how do they relate to the way you deal with money and giving today?
3. What stories, passages, and events of the Bible connect to your money/giving stories? (Don't look for rational connections as much as feeling and intuitive connections.)
4. What does your religious tradition tell you in theology, church standards, doctrines, and practice about money and giving?
5. When connecting your personal, biblical, and traditional stories, how do you practice the use of money and giving?
6. What are two or three things you wish to say regarding the gospel in making your witness?

When these six questions are answered in a process of self and group discovery and practice, new levels of faithful Christian witnessing will occur.

 SMALL GROUP STUDY

Workshop on Tithing

NORMA WIMBERLY

Leading a workshop is an opportunity for learning, for the leader as well as for the participants. Each of us can use the same guidelines and emerge with very different events. Learning experiences happen because of the topic, but are *shaped* by the persons present. Each experience can be one of encouragement and confirmation of who we are and who we are becoming.

> "Unless those who believe in Christian civilization are willing to sacrifice their good, hard-earned cash to educate Christian leaders, they will find in a few generations that their dream has vanished, that tyranny with its hard and fast ruthless rules of life will be substituted for the good life."
>
> —*WILLIAM ALLEN WHITE*

For this design, arrange the room for small table groups of no more than six per table. Each person will need to have a Bible. You, the leader, will need an easel, newsprint, markers, and tape for posting certain information, as well as for group responses. Light refreshments could be made available before the session and/or during the break. Be sure to alert the group as to the nearest available restrooms.

Time Frame—Three Hours

I. Introductions *(20 minutes)*

A. Who are you? Why are you here? What do you need?
Ask the group to state some of their reasons for being present in this particular workshop. Were they invited, recruited, fulfilling a job requirement in the church? Are they clergy or lay? Is there a particular personal need or perhaps a need in their church? Has some specific incident nudged them to learn more about teaching tithing? What are some of their expectations? These should be recorded and posted in order to refer to them as

the session progresses. This can be a way to hold one another accountable for meeting the needs of this particular group.

B. *Who am I? Relate some of your story.*
If you feel comfortable, this can be a time to relate some personal observations or experiences related to tithing and giving. When you acknowledge willingness to share of yourself, others become more open.

> "We will always learn what we have chosen to teach."
>
> —MARIANNE WILLIAMSON,
> *A RETURN TO LOVE*

II. Definitions: Toward New Understandings *(30 minutes)*

Beforehand, prepare three sheets of newsprint, headed: Definitions, Feelings, and Motivations.

A. Ask the participants to turn to a neighbor and discuss:
1. Your current definition of the tithe.
2. Your current feelings about tithing.
3. Your chief motivation to tithe or begin to tithe, or the chief stumbling block to that way of giving.

B. Record on newsprint the definitions, motivations, and stumbling blocks, for the entire group to note and respond.

C. Working definitions that may help:
1. A disciplined practice of giving to move toward and grow beyond.
2. A tool God gives us to teach us to put God first.
3. A symbol, a reminder, that all comes from God—a symbol of response and relationship.

4. A practical, visible tool that encourages us to use all resources wisely, to plan efficiently, to give joyously, to encourage faithful discipleship.

These working definitions may be put on newsprint or overhead projector, ready to post at this portion of the workshop.

BREAK FOR TEN MINUTES

III. *Guidance in the Scriptures (40 minutes)*

A. In small table groups, read and discuss the following passages:
   1. Genesis 28:10-22
   2. Leviticus 27:30-33
   3. Deuteronomy 14:22-29
   4. Malachi 3:6-12

If you had lived during the past 24 hours according to these passages, what would you have done differently? *Each table group will be assigned one passage. If there are more than four tables, you can have double reports on the passages.*

Ask one person from each table to briefly report the passage read at that table and the major points of discussion.

NOTE: *Reading the Old Testament passages related to tithing and reflecting on them in light of today's living is the foundation for New Testament spirituality and allowing tithing to be a style of life. The next experience can be a bridge between the Law and freedom in the Spirit. In your own words, talk with the group about:*

● Giving as a symbol of relationships.
● Some of what happens in conversion.
● Tithing meaning more than money, and
● The possible impact of tithing on all of life.

You may want to tell of your own experience or that of someone you know.

B. Briefly describe the concept that *the tithing life is all of life.* It is a way to reorder all aspects of living.
   1. Where do I start?
   2. How do I set goals? These could be related to finances, planning, time commitments, or relationships.
   3. How do I take a daily inventory of my plan for the day? Where is God in all of this? Does my

day look different when I put God first in all that I do? *This can be a time in the workshop when leader and participants, together, recognize that time, relationships with God and others, and money—all are affected by our perception of tithing.*

C. In small groups, read and discuss the implications for giving and your relationship with God in the following passages. As in III.A., each table will be assigned one passage.
   1. Matthew 25:14-30
   2. Luke 21:1-4
   3. II Corinthians 8:1-6
   4. I Corinthians 16:1-3

After each table-group reporter has had an opportunity to share the major points of discussion, read I Corinthians 4:1-2. Emphasize the central issue of faithfulness, or being worthy of trust. Remind the group that the faithful life is a mystery. We have Jesus as Savior, Mentor, Guide—the "Secret in Person."

IV. *A Miracle in your Congregation* *(15 minutes)*

A. As a total group, share and record what you feel/believe the job of churches to be. Where does tithing (teaching it, living it) fit? *You will need to lead this discussion, perhaps sharing some of your own ideas.*

B. In small groups, imagine the following possibilities. Each group is to discuss all three concepts.
   1. What if 50 percent of your congregation tithes? Approximately how much income would be realized?
   2. What new possibilities for ministry could you pursue?
   3. What if you began to be a tithing church? Would the church look or act differently? Try to be specific. This is a time to suspend negativity and use creative imagination!

BREAK FOR TEN MINUTES

V. *Telling the Story (one hour)*

A. Ask each person to make notes for their personal witness related to tithing. *Alert them that this is just a beginning. After the workshop, this testi-*

mony can be a part of their commitment to growth in giving. Remember that it is all right to say, "I never even thought about it before!" Allow approximately five minutes.

B. A Month of Tithing

In small groups or as a total group, depending on the number of people and your assessment of time, brainstorm possible designs for activities and emphases if a congregation decided to have tithing as a focus for one month. *This is a time for the participants to name the opportunities they see in the congregation for teaching/talking about tithing. Refer to some of the responses in IV.B. to encourage the group. Record the ideas.*
NOTE: *Use the positive energy generated in B. to introduce a suggested philosophy of planning that may be useful in putting ideas into action. This attitude about planning could be a vehicle for connecting with other leaders in the church to initiate a tithing emphasis.*

C. A Planning Model

Many groups in North American churches dread planning times. Often it is perceived as a time to analyze and review what didn't work. Encourage the group to turn the process "upside down." Suggest that planning teams can begin with a time to dream, to deal with positive visions. Once a positive goal has become clear, follow with an honest inventory of what the current situation looks like. This inventory will include strengths as well as weaknesses. *Post the following four points for discussion as a possible strategy for planning.*

1. Dream BIG!
2. Inventory: gifts, limitations, potential for action.
3. Set prioritized, celebratable goals.
4. Realize you can't do it all! *This is crucial for many planning teams and leaders in churches.*

Emphasize the importance of positive planning, balanced with reality. We can learn to program ourselves for success, rather than failure.

D. Now that a philosophy of planning has been shared, and ideas for a month-long emphasis have been discussed, divide into small groups, and:
   1. Name possible opportunities, strengths, and stumbling blocks in the congregation to teaching tithing.
   2. Choose one issue and a possible strategy for action.
   3. Share with the larger group.

VI. *Closing*

A. Review the suggested homework.
   1. Covenant with another person for one thing you will do in the next week because of this experience. *Ask the participants to share with a partner their name, address, phone number, and one thing they will do in the coming week. Each pair is to determine how they will contact each other to verify the action and hold their partner accountable. Have the group stand and mingle for a few minutes to find a partner. It may or may not be someone at their session table group. This will be noisy!*
   2. Read II Corinthians 8–9.
   3. Write a letter to your congregation.
      a. Tell them you love them.
      b. Offer a challenge related to tithing or giving.
      c. Make suggestions for ways to grow together.
      d. Tell the members again how great you think they are!

B. Read John 3:16-18.

C. Closing prayer.

PART SEVEN

BIBLIOGRAPHY AND BIOGRAPHY OF WRITERS

For the Church Library or Resource Center

Introduction

NORMA WIMBERLY

Today, worshiping communities are blessed with a wealth of books and other resources to support the funding of ministry. None of us could possibly read, reflect upon, and use all of them.

The editors asked each of the contributing writers to *The Abingdon Guide to Funding Ministry* to name one or two books they believe are "classics"—books that had a major impact on their lives and ministries. The bibliography provided here is intended for support as you continue to grow into the joy of giving. Some of the entries also appeared in first volume of the *Guide*. Good news bears repeating!

The resources listed include material for financial commitment programs to be used by local congregations. This list is provided for information and does not imply an endorsement or recommendation.

Don and I pray that your adventure is funding ministry is exciting, satisfying, and filled with spiritual wonder. The apostle Paul reminds us that stewards are required to be trustworthy (I Cor. 4:2), rather than successful. We hope you will be trustworthy, keep the faith, and believe that success is possible, in God's way, and in God's time.

Books and Resource Reviews (Vol. 2)

Dubay, Thomas. *Happy Are You Poor.* New York: William Morrow & Co., 1981. pb. ISBN 0-87193-141-9.

　Working through one's current myths and assumptions regarding money is one of the keys to learning the joy of giving. This book examines what poverty really means and dispels the assumption that destitution is required in order to be spiritually free.

Grimm, Eugene. *Generous People: How to Encourage Vital Stewardship.* Nashville: Abingdon Press, 1992. pb. 153 pp. ISBN 0-687-14045-5.

　Grimm closes his book with "A Checklist for Vital Stewardship," questions for congregations to ask about the presence and effectiveness of their financial stewardship programs. The author's narrative stresses the importance of biblical foundations, clear definitions, planning, the individual's need to give, a variety of approaches to commitment, and pastoral leadership.

Hall, Douglas John. *The Steward: A Biblical Symbol Come of Age.* rev. ed. Grand Rapids: Wm. B. Eerdmans, 1990. pb. 145 pp. ISBN 0-8028-0472-1.

　In this challenging book, Dr. Hall explores the biblical symbol of the steward through the ages and calls upon the church in North America to reappropriate this important concept.

Hall, Douglas John. *Imaging God: Dominion as Stewardship.* Grand Rapids: Wm. B. Eerdmans/ New York: Friendship Press, 1986. pb. 248 pp. ISBN (Eerdmans) 0-8028-0244-3.

　This scholarly book argues that our current ecological crisis forces us to reexamine the relationship between humanity and God. What does it mean to be created in the image of God?

Hueckel, Sharon. *The Disciple As Steward,* Kansas City: Sheed & Ward, 1994. pb. ISBN 1-55612-711-1. (Available by calling 1-800-333-7373)

　The author presents a six-week study plan for small groups, in response to the U.S. Bishops' pastoral letter, *Stewardship: A Disciple's Response.* (Also available in Spanish: *El Discipulo Como Corresponsable*)

Joiner, Donald W. *Christians and Money: A Guide to Personal Finance.* Nashville: Discipleship Resources, 1991. pb. 128 pp. ISBN 0-88177-096-5.

In a world of market pessimism on the one hand and get-rich-quick schemes on the other, we need a clear sense of Christian principles for sound financial planning and freedom. Writing in a practical and down-to-earth style, Don Joiner explores these and other questions that concern Christians and their money. Each chapter includes focus questions and exercises that bring learnings home to personal experience. An appendix provides suggestions for sharing the study in a group setting.

National Conference of Catholic Bishops. *Stewardship: A Disciple's Response.* Washington: United States Catholic Conference, 1993. pb. ISBN 1-555586-567-4. (Available by calling 1-800-235-8722).

This pastoral letter by the U.S. Catholic Bishops is printed in both English and Spanish. It is a well-written, readable statement of the interrelationship of stewardship and discipleship. The format is relaxed, with questions for reflection and discussion after each chapter.

Needleman, Jacob. *Money and the Meaning of Life.* New York: Doubleday, 1991. pb. ISBN 0-385262-41-8.

Needleman carefully investigates the meaning of money in the context of spiritual growth. The book is filled with dialogue between professor and students.

Palmer, Parker. *To Know As We Are Known.* San Francisco: Harper and Row, 1983. 130 pp. ISBN 0-06-066456-8.

Palmer presents a spirituality of education in which mind and heart work together in the quest for knowledge. He delves into the Christian contemplative tradition to help us regain the spiritual dimension that is so often lacking in contemporary education.

Patterson-Sumwalt, Susan A. *Stories for Sharing: Exploring Stewardship with Children.* Nashville: Discipleship Resources, 1993. pb. 42 pp.

Many teachers and leaders of children (of all ages) find this an excellent resource of stewardship stories, both biblical and contemporary. The follow-up process uses "I wonder" questions to encourage children into their own learning through the stories.

Roop, Eugene F. *Let The Rivers Run: Stewardship and the Biblical Story.* Grand Rapids: Wm. B. Eerdmans, 1991. pb. 108 pp. ISBN 0-8028-0609-0.

Roop offers a highly readable book that includes questions for group study. He uses stories and symbols from Genesis and Exodus to focus on biblically grounded stewardship.

Rusbuldt, Richard E. *A Workbook on Biblical Stewardship.* Grand Rapids: Wm. B Eerdmans, 1994. pb. ISBN 0-8028-0723-2.

This workbook is designed for individual or group study. The lay reader is urged to explore many facets of stewardship, including entrusting, care-managing, confronting, using money and possessions, the earth, time, talents, and gifts of the Spirit.

Senge, Peter M. *The Fifth Discipline: The Art and Practice of the Learning Organization.* New York: Doubleday/Currency, 1990. ISBN 0-385-26094-6.

The author draws on science, spiritual wisdom, psychology, the cutting edge of management, and his own work with top corporations, to name our corporate "learning disabilities." He then leads the aware student into five disciplines to assure positive learning and the recognition of new opportunities.

Wilson, Lois Miriam. *Miriam, Mary, and Me. Women in the Bible: Stories Retold for Children and Adults.* Winfield, British Columbia: Wood Lakes Books, 1992. pb. ISBN 0-929032-77-2.

This book is not directly about "stewardship." However, it includes biblical and contemporary stories of women which have excellent potential for discussions about stewardship issues.

Wimberly, Norma. *Because God Gives.* Nashville: Discipleship Resources, 1986. pb. 24 pp.

Searching the Old and New Testaments, this booklet offers a variety of passages related to giving. Included are questions for meditation and discussion.

Wimberly, Norma. *Putting God First: The Tithe.* Nashville: Discipleship Resources, 1988. pb. 56 pp. ISBN 0-88177-058-2.

Usually we give only our leftovers to God, because we forget that all creation belongs to God.

The author helps individuals and small groups learn about tithing in Old Testament times, and what Jesus has to say about giving with a joyous heart. One section offers testimonies from persons in all walks of life, concerning their adventure with the tithing principle.

Biography of Contributors

Ben R. Alford is senior pastor of First United Methodist Church in Hendersonville, Tennessee. Mr. Alford's career has involved youth ministry, higher education, human services, and the local church. While he served on the faculty of Martin Methodist College in Pulaski, Tennessee, he developed a "Lay Academy," in which he taught courses in religion and Bible.

Wayne C. Barrett is Executive Director of The United Methodist Foundation of the West Michigan Conference. He is editor of the *Clergy Finance Letter,* a personal finance journal for American clergy. The Reverend Barrett is author of *The Church Finance Idea Book* and *More Money, New Money, Big Money* (Discipleship Resources). He had previously pastored churches for thirteen years.

Hilbert J. Berger has served as a stewardship leader with the North Indiana Conference, as well as with United Methodist general agencies. He is the author of *Now Concerning the Offering* (Discipleship Resources), *Exploring the Faith with New Members,* and other articles illuminating faithful stewardship. He has pastored several growing churches in Indiana. Dr. Berger is presently retired from the pastorate but continues his work as a speaker and consultant.

Kenneth H. Carter, Jr. is organizing pastor of St. Timothy's United Methodist Church in Greensboro, North Carolina. He is the author of *The Pastor as Steward* (Discipleship Resources). He has been a contributor to *Christian Century, Quarterly Review* and to materials published by the Alban Institute.

James I. Cook is an ordained minister of the Reformed Church in America. In 1982, he was elected president of the General Synod. Since 1963, Mr. Cook has served on the faculty of Western Theological Seminary in Holland, Michigan, and is the Anton Bielmont Professor of New Testament.

Timothy C. Ek is Vice President of The Evangelical Covenant Church, which includes the position of Director of the Covenant's Department of Stewardship. He was ordained by the Covenant in 1971. Dr. Ek holds a Doctor of Ministry degree from Fuller Theological Seminary. He serves on the Ecumenical Center for Stewardship Studies Board of Directors and has also served on the World Relief Corporation Board.

James Fogle-Miller and his wife are co-pastors of Arlington United Methodist Church in Jacksonville, Florida. He has served congregations in Tennessee, North Carolina, and Florida. His experience as a researcher led him to spend some time on the staff of the General Board of Discipleship in Nashville.

Edward M. Hays is a nationally and internationally known author and speaker in the area of contemporary spirituality, prayer, and discipleship. Father Hays has been a priest of the Archdiocese of Kansas City since 1958. He serves as director of the Archdiocesan House of Prayer, Shantivanam, "The Forest of Peace."

Sharon Hueckel is Director of Stewardship and principal fund-raiser for the Roman Catholic Diocese of Lafayette-in-Indiana. A former teacher and marketing manager for a multinational corporation, she is the author of a small group study of the U. S. Catholic Bishops' pastoral on stewardship. Ms. Hueckel also writes and circulates a series of Scripture-based weekly bulletin inserts, "Stewardship by the Book."

Jerald Jackson has been Executive Director of the New Mexico United Methodist Foundation for the last ten years. Previously, he served the largest United Methodist Church in Minnesota. He has written extensively and his work is often found in church school publications.

Donald W. Joiner is director of The Planned Giving Resource Center and is with the Stewardship Unit of the General Board of Discipleship of The United Methodist Church. He previously served as Associate Council Director for the Detroit Annual Conference and as a pastor. He is the author of *Christians and Money* and coauthor of *Celebrate Giving; Cel-*

ebrate and Visit; and *Celebrate Together* (Discipleship Resources).

James Killen has served pastorates in the Texas Annual Conference of The United Methodist Church. He presently serves as pastor of the Williams Memorial United Methodist Church in Texarkana, Texas.

Renard J. Kolasa is an attorney in Farmington Hills, Michigan, specializing in tax and business law. He has worked extensively in the areas of estate and gift tax planning, retirement planning, charitable giving, employee benefits, and small business law. Mr. Kolasa is Chancellor of the Detroit Annual Conference of The United Methodist Church.

Glenna Kruger and **Roy Kruger** are members of First Baptist Church of Portland, Oregon. Glenna has worked as a human resource manager and consultant for more than twenty years, and currently is a Human Resource Development Specialist for a Fortune 500 corporation. Roy is a research and program evaluator for a nonprofit educational research organization. Previously, he was a professor of marketing and management and has worked with academic institutions, small businesses, and government agencies in research and evaluation.

Herbert Mather administers the work of the Stewardship Unit of the General Board of Discipleship of The United Methodist Church. He is an ordained minister and the author of several stewardship resources that encourage, inform, and support local churches. Mr. Mather's most recent book is *Don't Shoot the Horse Until You Learn How to Drive the Tractor* (Discipleship Resources).

Ronald Reed is an Episcopal cleric who has served in a leadership capacity in every level, from local to denominational. Although he is called on to lead in many denominational and ecumenical capacities, he also is a proficient writer in magazines for all denominations.

Olan H. Runnels is Senior Vice President of Cargill Associates. Dr. Runnels coordinates capital campaigns and related fund-raising services in the United States, Canada, and Europe. He has extensive experience in identification and enlistment of volunteers and solicitation of prospects, writing and preparing public relations materials and foundation proposals, and working with multiple staff members to implement a total campaign program.

Betsy Schwarzentraub, a clergy member from California, has been a Stewardship Associate with The United Methodist Church for ten years. Formerly a pastor for sixteen years, she is now a church consultant to denominational leaders and individual congregations.

John M. Tincher is President of Tincher Charitable Marketing Company, which offers planned-giving services to organizations that do not have a planned-giving staff, and provides guidance for strengthening endowments. Mr. Tincher is also a California licensed marriage/family/child counselor and holds a lifetime teaching credential for California Community College.

Norma Wimberly is Executive Director of the Nashville Area United Methodist Foundation, which serves the Memphis and Tennessee Conferences. For several years she served on the staff of the Stewardship Unit of the General Board of Discipleship. Ms. Wimberly is a teacher, a consultant, and the author of *Dare to Be Stewards; Earth Care; Putting God First: The Tithe,* and numerous articles for a variety of publications.